PENGUIN BOOKS

TWO SIDES OF A LIE

Elaine Chan is a journalist and writer covering Asia and Greater China. She was Shanghai bureau chief of *Bloomberg News* and had written and edited for the likes of the *South China Morning Post* and the *Associated Press*.

While growing up in her native Singapore, she also trained in Western art and painting. But realizing she'd never be a Van Gogh, she decided to pursue journalism which she believes is the society's conscience. *Two Sides of a Lie* is her first novel.

Lee Jeong-ho is a journalist and writer covering East Asia and the Korean peninsula. He has written for *Bloomberg News*, the *South China Morning Post* and *News1 Korea*. He believes that the media exists for the progression of democracy, to empower individual citizens of democratic ideals through the dissemination of information.

Jeong-ho grew up in South Korea and Australia. He had also worked as an officer for the South Korean Air Force before becoming a journalist. *Two Sides of a Lie* is his first novel.

Two Sides of a Lie

A Novel

Elaine Chan and Lee Jeong-Ho

PENGUIN BOOKS
An imprint of Penguin Random House

PENGUIN BOOKS

USA | Canada | UK | Ireland | Australia
New Zealand | India | South Africa | China | Southeast Asia

Penguin Books is part of the Penguin Random House group of companies
whose addresses can be found at global.penguinrandomhouse.com

Published by Penguin Random House SEA Pte Ltd
9, Changi South Street 3, Level 08-01,
Singapore 486361

Penguin
Random House
SEA

First published in Penguin Books by Penguin Random House SEA 2021

10 9 8 7 6 5 4 3 2 1

ISBN 9789814954075

Typeset in Adobe Garamond Pro by Manipal Technologies Limited, Manipal

www.penguin.sg

'The darkest places in hell are reserved for those who maintain their neutrality in times of moral crisis.'

Dante Alighieri

Contents

Part I

Modus Operandi

Prologue

The Assignment

The early September morning sky was overcast with rain showers as Mark Jin left his home for the airport. Jin didn't have a good vibe about his trip to Beijing. A top aide to one of China's senior party chiefs of the ruling Party had requested for a meeting today, giving him less than 24 hours' notice. No details were provided except the firm instruction that he was to come alone, not even his deputy or an assistant was allowed. The urgency of the request was unsettling and Jin, who had chucked his usual hoodie and khakis for a suit for the meeting, wasn't easily spooked despite his relatively small frame of 1.68 m. After all, as a child growing up, he witnessed first-hand the atrocities of China's Cultural Revolution and later on, knew of childhood friends turned student protesters advocating for a more open and democratic government lost their lives in the Tiananmen Square crackdown in 1989. Why this meeting was rattling him much more than those dark days, he couldn't point to immediately. He nudged his chin into his navy suit jacket as though he wanted to hide from the reality he was about to face. This was one meeting the 58-year-old entrepreneur, who founded and ran China's largest social media and e-commerce platform, feared could be his Achilles' heel, but he tried to muster as much positive energy to diffuse the unease as he boarded his flight from the eastern Chinese city of Nanjing. The residual sour aftertaste from a run-in with the Party two years ago was only beginning to peter out and Jin had been hopeful that the relationship was on the mend. Whichever way the meeting went, it won't be a walk in the park. And he braced for the worst.

* * *

It was an unusually chilly autumn evening in Hong Kong, where winter temperatures rarely dropped below 10 degrees celsius when 22-year-old Edwin Law Chi-wai was found. The waters of Yau Tong Bay on the eastern side of the city's Kowloon area were still and pitch dark until his pale body slowly surfaced. There were hardly any stars that night, perhaps hidden by the thin layer of haze perpetuated by persisting pollution from the city's larger northern neighbour China, whose rule it had come under since 1997.

Stripped naked in the cold waters, Edwin's lanky and frail frame was accompanied by remaining shreds of what would have been a black T-shirt and dark jeans, the typical attire of a young pro-democracy protester.

Five days ago, Edwin's family had reported him missing to the local police after losing contact with the young man for more than a week. Over the past four months, it wasn't unusual for the young man, fresh out of university, to stay out for a night or two where he joined thousands of young people in regular demonstrations against China's rapid encroachment of Hong Kong. The central government in Beijing had promised to let the city retain its capitalist system and for its people to enjoy the freedom of expression and rights for fifty years until 2047.

The demonstrations, set off by the Hong Kong government's intention to pass an extradition bill that would allow criminal suspects to be extradited to mainland China, had expanded to include the call for democracy and opposition towards Chinese rule. They had further polarized the society and tore families apart, where the elderly usually prioritized stability and the young generation yearned for democracy.

The city's population of seven million was predominantly made up of ethnic Chinese people who had little in common with their Chinese peers across the border in mainland China. Though many of the older generations originated from the mainland, fleeing the civil war between nationalists Kuomintang and the Communist Party of China and later on the brutality of Chinese political movements like the Great Leap Forward and the Cultural Revolution, Hongkongers built a distinctive culture based on the Cantonese dialect and an economy and government that followed the British system and the West.

In the past forty years that China had prospered economically, Hong Kong benefited as the free economy that Chinese companies and institutions count as the vital bridge to engage with the rest of the world. But politically, the two had not converged. As much as Hongkongers didn't trust the Party, they were hopeful that China would keep its promise to uphold the 'one country, two systems' principle established when the agreement was signed with the United Kingdom in 1982 to return the former British colony to China.

Over the twenty-two years of Chinese rule since 1997, Hongkongers had taken to the streets to protest against their communist rulers and called for democracy. On 4 December 2005, as many as 250,000 marched calling for the direct election of the Chief Executive, head of Hong Kong's government and the Legislative Council (LegCo), the city's lawmaking body. In 2010, protests took place in the city triggered by Beijing's introduction of electoral reforms and the arrest of Chinese activist Liu Xiaobo, who was arrested and sentenced to eleven years in prison for 'inciting subversion of state power'.

The 2010 protests were considered a precursor to the 2014 Umbrella Movement led by student leaders. Also known as the Umbrella Revolution, it was sparked off by the decision of the Standing Committee of the National People's Congress—China's lawmaking body—for the 2017 Chief Executive election, where the selection process of two to three candidates would be done by an undemocratic nominating committee. The pan-democrats saw the restrictive process as a violation of international standards for free elections as candidates unsupportive of the central government would be screened out. The process of forming the 2016 LegCo would be unchanged and following the new process for the Chief Executive election, a new system to elect the LegCo through universal suffrage would be developed with the approval of Beijing.

At first, the movement drew strong support from the public. But as time passed, the sit-ins and protests on Hong Kong's main arterial roads in core financial and commercial districts that severely disrupted business and transport, as well as economic growth fuelled public resentment. It ended after seventy-nine days in December 2014. In the course of the movement, the society became divided into the yellow and blue ribbon camps, reflecting political inclinations. Yellow ribbons represented those who supported the pro-democracy cause and protesters, while blue ribbons referred to people, generally seen as the conservatives, who were pro-business and government-backed institutions as well as the Party. Less common were the red ribbons, who were outright supporters of the Party and mainland China.

The city's evolving political landscape brought just about as much change to its media scene. The pro-Beijing media, once the minority became the majority as the economies of China and Hong Kong integrated and media companies relied more on Chinese advertising dollars. Most of Hong Kong's mainstream newspapers were now either owned or partially invested by mainland investors. Even if they weren't, a shrinking media industry at the onslaught of the Internet and China's increased global influence would have blunted the city's sharpest journalistic knives.

Beijing's proxy, the Central Liaison Office in Hong Kong controlled *Ta Kung Pao*, *Wen Wei Po* and the *Hong Kong Commercial Daily*. The erosion of Hong Kong's press freedom was buffered slightly after the 2014 Umbrella Movement by the emergence of a new breed of online media outlets such as *Stand News*, *Hong Kong Citizen News* and *Hong Kong Free Press*, attempting to carry on the torch.

The protests that began in April 2019 had been different; they had sustained longer than previous movements and they were led by no one single leader but thousands of Hong Kong youths, who felt disillusioned by a future they cannot see.

Even though tensions between Edwin and his parents mounted over their widening political differences as days turned to weeks, he had promised his family he wouldn't stay out for more than two nights and would remain out of harm's way.

Edwin's body was found by a middle-aged Yau Tong resident who was walking his dog that September evening. By the time he was pulled out of the water, a small crowd of mainly neighbourhood residents had gathered. The police asserted there was no foul play and a coroner report concluded the cause of death as accidental drowning. But his family and friends were not convinced, and fellow protesters believed it was part of a dark ploy engineered by government-backed institutions.

Edwin's death—the first that was unexplainable in the protests—was a turning point and unnerved the top echelons in the Party in Beijing, already frustrated by the Hong Kong Government's inability to quell the unrest, an overhanging cloud that was gnawing away business confidence and the legitimacy of the Party's rule. China had been drawing all the wrong international attention in the past two years: Hong Kong, a drawn-out trade war with the US that's weighing in on its economy and accusations of rights abuse in its western Xinjiang region.

The Party decided to activate its propaganda machine at full throttle, turning to the growing network of media agents it had quietly planted and acquired in Hong Kong over the last seven decades. Among them was its prized trophy, the *Han Herald*, the more than century-old English newspaper once owned by foreign establishments, now controlled by Jin and his Arcade Group.

* * *

Jin's two-hour flight landed at noon in Beijing. As he turned on his phone, alerts of all sorts flooded the screen. One, from an unknown number, caught his attention. Tapping onto it, it gave the licence plate number of a black car that would pick him up at the car park of Terminal 2. He found his ride easily at the lot. He didn't have the faintest idea of who he'd meet but for all the secrecy and discretion that was demanded of him, he thought whoever it was must be significantly important. The car drove for forty-five minutes before it reached a nondescript twelve-storey building in the northeastern part of the capital city. There was only a sprawling parking lot in front of the block, without any surrounding structures within a 5-km radius. The building foyer was dark, barely lit and empty, except for a couple of security guards who sat behind a counter by the entrance. Jin was ushered into an elevator by a young man in a navy suit who had met him at the entrance of the building. Inside, his escort pushed the number twelve button on the elevator panel. In silence, they rode to the top floor, as Jin didn't think it was wise to ask the young official for more details. While he was thirsting for information, he figured that the official's youth would put him at the lower end of the food chain. His curiosity was soon put to rest.

'Mr Jin, thank you for making the trip to meet,' a medium height man in his early 60s greeted him brightly as the elevator doors slid open. Jin recognized him as Chen Kaiming, a personal secretary of one of the top officials with responsibility for Hong Kong affairs. Although Chen was smiling, his eyes were emotionless behind the wire-rimmed glasses that framed his wrinkled face. He was large, hardly having a neck. His hair was slicked back, shoe polish black with not a streak of grey.

'Not at all, it's my pleasure,' Jin returned the pleasantry, as he shook Chen's hand, where a gold Rolex watch sat on the wrist, partially covered by the cuff of his sleeve. He followed him into a spacious meeting room two doors away from the elevator.

'I hope you had a good flight. My apologies for having you fly all the way here,' the official said.

'No trouble at all.'

'Please, please sit down and make yourself comfortable,' Chen's voice echoed in the meeting room. He gestured to the tech tycoon towards one end of the carpeted meeting room where there were two velvet-upholstered crimson-coloured armchairs with a coffee table between them. On the outer sides of the chairs, at a right angle, were two sets of two-seater sofas, one on each side. Behind the armchairs was a five by three feet large calligraphy painting of Chinese characters that read 'One Country, Two Systems, Steadfast and Unwavering', written by a former Party chief who oversaw the 1997 handover of power by Britain to China.

As Jin sat down, Chen waved his hand, nodded gently to two aides who retreated and shut the door behind them. An hour and a half later, the two men emerged, smiling. Chen wore his, grinning from ear to ear, while Jin appeared hesitant and tryingly upbeat. Whatever was discussed in the room would never be known, but it was clear a deal was struck. Jin was entrusted with a mission, one in which he can only succeed.

* * *

Nearly two weeks had passed since Edwin's body was found, accompanied by increasingly intensifying media frenzy surrounding his death. Speculation was rife and various theories that emerged all pointed towards a conspiracy by the government and the Party. Public fears were also mounting that it was only a matter of time when the Party sent in the army to quash dissent in the city, just as they did in Tiananmen Square in Beijing on 4 June 1989 to rein in protesting students fighting for political change in the Chinese government.

Two days following his meeting with Chen in Beijing, Jin flew to Hong Kong. Now at his sprawling villa, tucked away from traffic in Repulse Bay, the city's luxurious southern district, Jin had called an urgent and confidential meeting with the *Han Herald*'s Chief Executive Officer Steve Hsieh and its top editors: Editor-in-Chief Pax Yong, Deputy Editor Theresa Chu and Assistant Editor Vijay Kumar. Whilst the CEO made decisions on the business and operations of the company, the editors—whose names appear in the above order on the masthead of the newspaper—were responsible for the slant and position of the coverage.

'OK people, my instructions to you, very simple,' said Jin, hands on his hips as he paced up and down the opulently decorated study room with a wood-panelled library and a fireplace, glancing at each face of his senior team.

'The Party is disappointed. Public opinions are moving in the wrong direction and we need to fix this.

'I don't care how you do it, but make it happen.'

1

Editorial Integrity

When you were the top editor, it went without saying that guarding the newsroom's editorial independence—the holy grail of journalism—against commercial and political pressures, was your single most important responsibility. That was lost on the *Herald*'s top editors. Jin's order, on the contrary, gave each of them a shot of adrenaline and the drive to tackle the challenge, which if they succeeded, would buy them more clout with the owner, possibly the Party.

Despite the enormity on all fronts around the task, the three and Steve said little in Jin's study. The assignment without a doubt offered a pathway to further individual ambitions and for that reason, neither one of the editors thought it was wise to have them written on his or her sleeve. The stakes, conversely, were lower for Steve and he tried to kill the dead air in the room.

'Mark, do you see the business side being involved in this?' Steve wanted to test the waters—and cover his interests—with what he felt was an inconsequential question that he more or less knew the answer to.

'No, it's not about money or business. I wanted you here because you're the CEO and you oversee the company.' Jin shifted to glance at Pax, 'I would say it's more an editorial matter, one that's about swaying public opinion. This is a test of the credibility of the *Herald* . . . and the strength of our editors.'

Jin then turned momentarily to look at Theresa before returning his gaze to Pax, who looked right back at his boss with a nod of his head so slight that it was easily missed. The editor-in-chief gave little of his thoughts away but Steve heard Pax mumble lightly in Mandarin, 'I understand' under his breath. He saw that Jin seemed satisfied and for the first time during the meeting, looked more relaxed as the tension in his body eased.

Feeling assured that the responsibility was tilted towards the editors, Steve offered what he believed was the non-committal but obligatory answer.

'We'll look into it.'

Pax's almost unnoticeable responses irked Theresa, which underscored her envy of his ability to never give his cards away. She on the other hand was easily excited and as much as she hated to admit, her schemes were usually laid bare for all to see. After Jin meted out the assignment, she dropped her head to look down letting her long straight hair slide forward to cover the sides of her face and her glee.

Great! This is going to be my project, she revelled in the idea, feeling more entitled as the issue at stake fell right into Chinese politics, the area of coverage that she supervised.

She was always looking for every chance to shine. Although she was already second-in-command of the newsroom and had been at the *Herald* longer than both Pax and Vijay put together, she constantly fought a long-held battle within herself to shake off the sense of inadequacy and would habitually put the blame on everyone else. She knew deep down that the long history limited her exposure to the world beyond the *Herald*'s doors—the only company she had ever worked for. But that was only part of the reason. She overlooked the fact that while her peers invested more time and effort on frontline reporting to build journalistic experience, Theresa opted for a shorter route to elevate her career. With a mix of some hard work and luck, plenty of going by her bosses and eventually the former editor-in-chief's bidding, she rose from a summer intern to where she was now in less than eighteen years. From Theresa's perspective, Jin's order that autumn was a godsend that fell right up her alley, one she could put her skills to work once more.

I'd show Pax down, she thought, mentally immersing into the imagery of her 1.74 m frame towering over a surrendering Pax.

Theresa might have thought she masked her ambition well but everyone in the newsroom knew she aimed to replace Pax. Sitting in Pax's chair would give her both the power and respect as an international politics pundit, as well as a new degree of political influence that went beyond the Hong Kong newsroom, dreaming that she may end up being an informal adviser to the Party. To earn political credits from the above, Theresa had programmed herself, as a default, to seize every opportunity to espouse Beijing's agenda, actively executing the orders. People outside the company who met her for the first time would be baffled, sometimes amused by her enthusiasm to exert her views on world issues like US-China relations when her analyses showed she was out of her depth.

'The US has got it all wrong about China,' she once told a company of visiting American diplomats and academics to the newsroom.

As though she was a senior bureaucrat in an intense diplomatic negotiation representing her country, she started to lecture the American foreign policy experts. 'Take the case of Huawei, the Chinese technology giant,' she said jerkily. 'The US has thrown a flurry of charges at Huawei with unsubstantiated evidence. Trump thinks he's got China and the Party, but you know Trump, he's full of conflicting rhetorics himself.'

The Americans were stunned by Theresa's bluntness.

'What is China's strategy then?' one of the experts asked, intrigued.

'OK, so Beijing has lashed back at the offensive; it's really playing a long game and it has the means. The US may be the world's biggest economy where the most important part is [sic] it comes from domestic consumption or personal spending, but that is undercut by piles of consumer credit. The Chinese economy is less reliant on that type of credit. Our citizens tend to spend within their means and save,' she rambled on.

'Trump's and the US' ego is [sic] bruised because China is a real threat to its economic, military and technological supremacy. The US has always worked under the strategic premise that allowing any one nation to dominate Asia would be inimical to American and the world's interests.

'But China's rise is peaceful, its Belt and Road Initiative speaks volume of its foreign policy. You will never stop us from taking over you.'

By the time she finished, some of the American visitors had faraway gazes and a couple grimaced with slight contempt as well as awkward restlessness, reporters in the meeting later recalled.

'Theresa was totally resistant to any other interpretations of US-China relations other than her own—or Beijing's,' said one of them. 'I wanted the floor to open up and swallow me up. What she was saying was like a bad joke.'

Theresa's paradoxical personality to her profession was on full display in a meeting with the newly-arrived French consul-general to Hong Kong in May 2019. The consul-general's lunch invitation was a routine and typical outreach by diplomats to engage local journalists to expand their scope of influence and gather insights into the current landscape. Theresa accepted the invitation and said she would bring along another editor and a reporter from the China desk.

At the appointed time of the meeting, she and the editor were nowhere to be seen. The reporter James Lai, sitting across the table from the consul-general, a deputy consul-general and a consul, was left profusely apologizing on behalf of his superiors and trying to rack up a conversation for thirty minutes until Theresa showed up. She was late because of a scheduling conflict in her calendar that she didn't bother to resolve.

'Oh my God,' Theresa shrieked as she dashed into the sleek private dining room at the French restaurant the consulate had picked, which was a stone's throw from the *Herald*'s office. The sharp click-clacking sound of her loud high heels as she rushed in had irritated every diner in the restaurant.

'I am so sorry! What can I do?' she continued, breathless, hair out of place, giving every sign to impress that she tried her utmost to be on time.

'It's fine. We understand,' the consul-general said, gently smiling, as he and his colleagues rose to their feet to greet her.

'And also, I must add, our editor is sick,' Theresa said before she gave a fake sigh. 'So it's just me and James here, our principal reporter at China Desk.'

'Things happen all the time. Don't worry about it,' said the diplomat, a tall silver-haired man with a slight hunch, delicately. His professional gestures spoke of an experienced and competent diplomat.

'It's my pleasure to meet you, Ms Chu,' the consul-general said as he passed his business card to her. 'I am the new consul-general here.'

'Thank you. Here is mine,' Theresa said, rummaging the pockets of her suit for her cards before finally taking out an entire plastic box filled with them from a side pocket of her white skinny trousers. 'It's Theresa here and I am the deputy editor of the *Herald*.'

The eyes of the diplomat momentarily lost their focus from confusion. He stopped dead, before lowering his silver reading glasses to the tip of his nose, as though he was trying to study what was written on the card.

'The card says you're a different person,' the consul-general chuckled. 'Vijay?'

'Oh my God! I am so sorry,' Theresa screamed, covering her mouth with her hands. 'I took the wrong business cards,' she gasped, her face turning bright red. 'Sorry, I was in a rush. I will e-mail you my contact details once I get back to my office later today.'

James was silent, his eyes downcast throughout the entire exchange, ashamed by his boss' unprofessionalism. His shoulders slouched and he had curled his 1.8 m frame into a ball as much as possible to reduce his presence in the room. A good-natured reporter who liked meeting new people, he would have enjoyed the engagement with the French diplomats better if Theresa wasn't around. Lately, James had felt less tolerant and increasingly contemptuous of what he saw as Theresa's rationalization of factual distortion of the news and current affair issues to curry political favour. The chaotic greeting was just the beginning of the afternoon's embarrassments.

'I am a big fan of your paper,' the consul-general said. 'One of our jobs here is to read your paper and find out where Hong Kong's public opinion is heading to.'

'Thanks for your kind words,' answered Theresa, delighted. The euphony in his speech made her blush. 'Please allow me to introduce our paper,' a cue where she launched into an extended introduction about the company, its detailed history and the aggressive expansion after Arcade's takeover for the next ten minutes.

Oh God, not again, James thought. He had heard the same line coming out of her mouth about a hundred times. It was a boring, propaganda-like introduction of how great the company was and would be in the future. Subtly scanning the diplomats across the table as Theresa's ramble turned into background noise for him, he wondered whether the men were interested in the story, as no one from his memory was in the past. The diplomats smiled and nodded politely, but they seemed distant.

It was when she moved on to her next topic that the diplomats pricked up their attention.

'You see, the Chinese government is using us as test-water for their policies,' Theresa said solemnly. 'Chinese government knows that if they release some information through its state media, then it becomes too obvious that the government has a specific agenda,' she said proudly, presenting herself as an international politics expert.

'Also, if you want to know about where the international opinions are heading, it would be better off for them to use us, as we are seen as relatively more objective, which already has a large number of loyal international audience.'

'Wouldn't the *Herald* be walking a tightrope then? Why take the risk?' asked the consul-general. The deputy consul's lips twitched, silently frowning, and he shifted in his seat.

'Not at all, balanced reporting is what we uphold,' Theresa defended. 'As a global platform, we want to allow for multiple voices, for our readers to see China from different angles.'

At the time, the *Herald* was publishing a myriad of speculating and 'exclusive' stories quoting unnamed Chinese foreign ministry sources that the US-China trade negotiations were progressing positively with the Chinese president due to meet his US counterpart to sign a truce deal in Washington DC. It had been nearly a year into the trade war and the fallout, reflected in worsening economic numbers, was denting China's growth. The narrative of the articles tilted towards stretching the truth, but they served Beijing's interest as reports of easing tensions would prevent the collapse of Chinese stock markets.

'And we are happy to play the role,' Theresa stressed, as she bit into her crisped sauteed foie gras with buttered golden apples and melfor vinegar. James' stomach lurched from serious discomfort.

'What about Hong Kong? What is your assessment on the political controversy of the extradition bill, would it pass a second reading debate on 12 June at LegCo?' asked the deputy consul-general.

'Where is the city likely heading if it became law?'

Theresa took a sip of water from her glass.

'Well . . . I think the bill's a great thing for the city,' she said, evading the deputy consul-general's real question. 'At least you could be transparent of what's happening in Hong Kong.

'Because we currently don't have one, it threw the society into unnecessary disorder and created political innuendo when five employees of Causeway Bay Books in Hong Kong went missing in 2015,' she rationalized to the French men.

'Four years later, we still cannot be sure of what happened. The common belief is that at least two of them disappeared in China and one in Thailand. They were believed to be detained in China for writing a book that contained inappropriate contents. If we had the law then, we'd know exactly what happened. So whatever people speculate about, the Party's dark side will no longer remain dark.'

James closed his eyes and clutched his mouth tight, wishing he could do the same with his ears.

'China is going to continue its secret operations in Hong Kong anyway,' Theresa continued. 'The city is part of China. And if the bill is passed, we don't have to see another author being kidnapped to China any more.'

'But would the Hong Kong Government have the power to reject China's request?' the deputy consul couldn't help asking, putting his cutlery down as he had lost his appetite.

'No. You're right. Absolutely not. But China would have to at least go through an official channel. Isn't that a good thing? Yes, the results would be still the same, but people will at least know who's been taken to the mainland.'

James, who had been listening quietly throughout the conversation, was once again astounded by Theresa's argument. *Is she intoxicated? She might have just as well told them she's not about to uphold free speech and the Herald would accommodate the demand of the Chinese government over human rights or freedom to publish.*

James had been at the *Herald* for seven years now, after eight with a local Chinese media company he joined upon graduating from the Chinese University of Hong Kong. He had watched Theresa's rise in the newsroom and how her hunger for power 'justified' the way some of the China stories were written, mostly in favour of the Party. Increasingly, those stories had skirted on the realm of what he considered twisted perspectives, like her spiel on the extradition bill. He lifted his eyelids and stole a quick look at the diplomats. The consul-general's forehead creased with thoughts and looked intently at the editor but not to the point of scrutiny as it would have appeared rude. Theresa, who had progressed to her main course, continued to devour on her Le Boeuf Wagyu. The deputy consul-general's eyes narrowed behind his round-rimmed glasses, perplexed by what she stood for. James felt ten times more embarrassed than before Theresa showed up late. The consul, the youngest of the three men, bit his lips and his tongue, to restrain himself from commenting aloud. The reporter was sure the three men were underwhelmed, but being consummate diplomats, their facial expressions betrayed little of what they truly thought of her. They had, however, stopped eating altogether.

Shortly after the lunch meeting, Theresa who steadfastly pledged her support of the legislation disappeared from the newsroom for a month-long holiday before the second reading of the controversial bill.

Pathetic, James thought. As Theresa left Jin's villa that autumn evening, she already had in mind how she was going to take charge and ownership of the assignment. And of course, in due course, the credit as well.

* * *

The editors met at eight o'clock the next morning at a pocket-sized cafe around the corner from the *Herald*'s office in Hong Kong's central business district. Theresa had suggested the venue for the meeting she initiated the previous night. It was a joint she frequented. She liked to project herself as a connoisseur of coffee among other things. At the office each morning, she ground her coffee beans and hand dripped her brew. 'Why do you grind the coffee beans yourself? Can't give up the texture of a hand-drip brew?' James once asked.

'No. If I don't grind coffee beans, I might end up grinding the faces of editors,' she snorted in derision.

Theresa had arrived twenty minutes earlier, ordered her coffee and was seated at a discrete corner table by the window with a plan she prepared overnight when Pax and Vijay stepped in. Seeing that she already had a coffee, the two men headed towards the counter to make their orders. Cafe Nobody was strangely quiet, with no early morning rush common among cafes in the business district. The editors got their orders in minutes and walked towards Theresa. Before the two men could settle down onto their seats, she began firing off her proposal.

'To be fair, the Party has a very valid reason to be angry with these wild and unfounded speculations,' she began, putting down her notes next to her coffee which looked untouched. 'On what grounds are these protesters pinning Beijing and the Party to this? It's one thing for them to oppose China, but another to call Beijing a murderer.

'The Party would not be so stupid to screw up this way. Yes, they are angry with the protesters and their mobster-like violent acts, but Beijing has higher-level issues to tackle. If it wants to quash the protesters, it can easily do so.'

'So how do you want us to do this?' Vijay asked gingerly.

Unlike Theresa, the assistant editor was less decipherable on the surface. He said little in the meeting with Jin, erring on the side of caution. He was always collegial towards Theresa and would appear to be on the same page, but he wished for her failure. Just as Theresa intended to oust Pax, Vijay's ultimate goal was to replace Theresa and the best way to realize that was to distance himself from the frontline of the narrative war she had already started in the newsroom, cautiously waiting for her to fall.

'I say we go on the basis that while we dig into how Edwin Law died, our underlying objective of this exercise is the *Herald* will tell China's story, be its voice, as the Western media is biased and trying to shut down that voice. This should be our purpose whatever the inside story may turn out to be,' she said. Drawing her eyebrows closer together, she continued, 'To emphasize that we are objective, let's set up a Hong Kong protests task force team to investigate the circumstances behind the death.'

Under Theresa's plan, the task force would be made up of six people: a photographer and five reporters from the China and Hong Kong desks. The team would focus on three areas: interviewing Law's family and friends, Hong Kong and Chinese government officials and the local police.

'We need to have stories detailing what kind of a person he was, his background and family upbringing, which are very important. What was his role in the protests, his final hours leading to his death, so on and forth. Talk to as many people as we can. It's not about just this one student, but this profile could represent those radicals out in the streets.' Theresa leaned forward from her seat, pressing one hand on the edge of the small wooden table and looked from Vijay to Pax.

'I think these kids need to know the price of creating havoc in the society and the price they have to pay.'

'In other words, we find out stuff that may demonize the protesters,' Vijay contributed, half-mockingly.

'Don't use that word, please,' Theresa snapped, frowning at Vijay. 'The authorities—whether it is the Chinese central government or at the local level—will also have a voice, as will the Hong Kong police.' Straightening her back, she reclined backwards slightly, her face relaxing a little. 'We can also use this series to rein in what's not correct out there, put some perspective to the coverage, areas overhyped or ignored by the Western media, additional themes related to the protests.'

Theresa went on to stress that the newsroom needed to see the task force as an investigative piece of journalism characterized by balanced and fair reporting, using air quotes to amplify investigative journalism, balanced and fair. 'It is to say "the *Herald* is being proactive, we take ownership of the story, drive the narrative",' she told her colleagues.

With his hands tucked under his crossed arms, Pax looked somewhat indifferent to what he had heard so far. His gaze shifted upwards a couple of times—he could be thinking while mindlessly watching shadows of the leaves from a tree outside the cafe flicker on the low ceiling, or simply stretching the front of his neck. He observed Theresa's delivery without revealing any kinds of emotion in silence but was disdained by the irritation that was plain in Vijay's eyes, his flared nostrils and tightened jaw. Pax had a knack for picking up nonverbal cues, however subtle they were and it cannot be any clearer now that Vijay was eager to search for any hidden agenda in her speech and the chance to interject.

'Ermm . . . I think . . . ' he began.

Whether Theresa sensed it didn't matter, as she wouldn't have allowed that to happen. She evaded Vijay's eyes and raised her voice a little to drown off his as if to overlook his presence. The assignment had a dual track, she said, her face looking purposeful, where the second path of the work rested on the three of them to regularly 'seek advice from our sources' to guide the reporting team in framing their narrative.

'Let's expand our thinking. Being balanced can come from multiple perspectives and we shouldn't limit ourselves,' she emphasized, looking hard at Pax as if they had a mutual understanding. 'I'm sure we're on the same page as far as our agendas go.'

She recommended for the task force to meet regularly with her to report on its findings and plan on the stories to write and publish. She also pulled out a list of team members, which she explained came from varied backgrounds for a wider representation to reflect objectivity. It comprised James Lai, the *Herald*'s principal China reporter and widely liked among the reporters, Heather Hua, who came from a state media in China, Daniel Liu, a Taiwanese who covered China politics, Victor Trezise from the Hong Kong political desk, an Australian who grew up in Hong Kong and spoke fluent Cantonese and Mary Wong, a senior Hong Kong reporter, as well as Alan Choi, a photographer and video producer.

* * *

By the time she finished, Theresa had talked non-stop for twenty minutes, successfully preventing her colleagues from interjecting. Pax wasn't impressed with the plan but he kept that to himself. A medium-built and soft-spoken man of fifty-five years, he was usually very closed off, despite the constant smile he wore on his face to present an approachable no-airs Editor-in-Chief image. He dressed modestly, a plain shirt whose long sleeves were rolled up to just below the elbows, tucked into dark tailored pants and lace-up black leather shoes, compared to Theresa's power suits and Vijay's designer garb and chokingly strong cologne. While many may pass him off as hard to read, perceptive colleagues believed Pax was less complicated than most thought. His agenda and action simply stemmed from his loyalty to the Party. He was also risk-averse.

He didn't intend to refute Theresa's proposal, partly because he had none to counter as an alternative. What's more, he knew his priority laid elsewhere to stay at the top. Nonetheless, he felt ambivalent about Theresa. She wasn't an imminent threat to his position, but she was the protégé of his predecessor whose shoes the industry doubted he could ever fill, a sting to his ego that he had yet to shake off after five years in the top seat.

Pax's wariness was inevitable. Like Theresa and her mentor, who was also his former boss, he was born and grew up under the communist regime in the mainland. He arrived in Hong Kong at a university-going age while Theresa came when she was a secondary school student. And like many from the system, Pax learnt not to trust others easily.

He also knew how to survive in the most treacherous sea; he was one of the senior editors at a now-defunct television station that misreported the death of a former Chinese president in 2011. Although his role in the misstep was never clear, he would always be associated with the bogus report. His close ties with the State Council's Hong Kong and Macau office and the information ministry, as well as the Central Liaison Office developed over the decades of spinning positive China stories incited dubious assumptions, including being a party member, among journalists in the newsroom.

'Every time Pax lunches with these Chinese officials, we'd end up writing a what-China-wants-to-say analysis, paired with an editorial. Without fail,' pointed out Samuel Lee, one of the *Herald*'s few senior writers responsible for daily editorials, which represented the publication's position on important issues.

To reporters, Pax constantly stressed the importance of fair and objective reporting. 'We must seek the truth in our reporting, based on facts, be balanced.' Yet he was apathetic of the double standards he displayed or the insidious effect on the morale of staff.

Pax was not considered the brightest of journalistic minds of his generation. His resume was unimpressive and bland; twenty-something years in the Hong Kong Chinese-language newspapers and local TV stations covering Hong Kong-China relations. But his strengths were knowing his weaknesses and how to manage upwards.

Ever since Arcade took over the *Herald*, he had tirelessly strengthened his internal network, making numerous trips to the parent company's headquarters in Nanjing to engage with senior executives. He published articles that praised the acquisition and gave Arcade a platform to refute allegations that the purchase was engineered by the Party. He stood behind Jin on the stage at industry forums when the owner defended criticisms the takeover would cost the *Herald*'s editorial independence. 'Trust us,' Jin said, 'People underestimated us. Just wait and see.' The audience would see Pax, with thinning hair and semi-rimless eyeglasses, nodding his head in agreement.

In the first eighteen months into the new ownership, Jin installed one of his top aides Patrick Chao as a special assistant to Pax in the newsroom for 'better coordination'. No explanation was given on what the coordination meant and no one quite knew what Patrick's job was. 'Probably a spy to figure out how we work, to use the newspaper for Arcade's commercial benefits,' said a senior business reporter Charlie Tanner, who's been at the *Herald* for more than thirty years and witnessed its different ownerships.

Patrick, a Taiwanese-American in his early 40s, tried to be discrete, except for the bright-coloured Hermès silk ties he had a soft spot for. He sat in on all the daily news conferences, as well as the budget meetings and management offsites to strategize development plans. He played mostly the silent observer and kept pretty much to himself, including his views. Every now and then, he held lengthy closed-door meetings with Pax. By the end of Patrick's secondment at the Herald, Pax felt he had successfully built a relationship with Jin based on trust as long it served both sides' interests. Pax's other strength was patience. Waiting out was his best strategy and he had excelled at that.

Vijay was the opposite; he lacked patience and self-awareness. Since he joined the *Herald* from one of India's media groups in 2013, he had been all but anxious to show off his credentials. He talked excessively. Something that could be said in ten words usually ended up with a hundred. Stockily built and with an obsession for designer clothing, he felt short-changed for his talent as a journalist and considered Pax and Theresa, who weren't fluent in English to begin with, unqualified for their jobs. He constantly rivalled with Theresa and privately disregarded her as ranking above him because he reported directly to Pax.

The reporting structure was odd, but it was how Pax purposely intended to keep Theresa in check despite the organisational hierarchy. It added to Vijay's frustrations because with Theresa in the way, it meant he'd need to hop over an additional barrier to reach the top job when the time came for Pax to leave. What he conveniently forgot was, with or without her, a promotion to the top wasn't a given. Vijay was passed over for the chief editor's role although he was number two at the Indian newspaper when the management decided to recruit an outsider for the top job. He had blamed office politics, but his former employer thought Vijay wasn't Editor-in-Chief material and had spared him the truth.

Vijay came from a family of doctors and lawyers, which fostered his sense of entitlement. The Indian elitist background was of no value in the Hong Kong and broader China contexts. He didn't speak or write Chinese to be able to accumulate the depth or breadth in understanding China, in which the *Herald* had built and staked its reputation. His bigger disadvantage that he appeared oblivious to was he would always be viewed as a foreigner at the *Herald*, now a property of Arcade. His goal was to be a chief editor before he turned forty-five and he had three years to succeed.

In the six years at the *Herald*, he had painstakingly carved out a portfolio overseeing the Hong Kong, Asia and foreign desks of the newspaper, playing the supportive and submissive deputy to Pax, while struggling to strengthen his network with senior executives of Arcade.

The Hong Kong desk was one of the busiest sections in the newsroom and the second biggest after the China desk. For Vijay, running the desk without the Chinese language and the local Cantonese dialect fluency was an endless battle, compounded by his innate politicking personality where he viewed all his senior journalists and anyone that he didn't personally hire with distrust.

'However small the news issue, you need to give me full updates at every hour,' he ordered the deputies whose responsibilities were to mete out and coordinate assignments to reporters and keep a tab of the news flow of the day. 'I don't care if that means taking the extra time to translate the materials from Cantonese to English. I'm the boss, just do it!'

There were fewer clashes with his deputies on the Asia and foreign desks as the news feeds and articles were from English-language international news agencies. The bulk of the Hong Kong coverage, however, came from staff copies based on information and reporting in Cantonese. The speed at which news broke and developed meant his deputies had little spare time to translate matters and issues of the moment for Vijay. Being reminded of his Chinese language shortcoming constantly infuriated him and he was a man who kept grudges. The simmering undercurrents between him and his Hong Kong desk deputies who ignored his order to report on every single piece of news on a regular news day were barely tolerable. The tension multiplied many more times during the months of the Hong Kong protests. Since they broke out in April 2019 and evolved into a Hong Kong–China political crisis, the tensions had spilt over to include those with the China desk. The fights were over seemingly mundane operational issues such as whether a China or Hong Kong desk reporter would write a particular story, how the article would be angled, or which desk would take the readership traffic for a published piece. Inconsequential as they might have looked, they reflected judgement calls by desk editors, which in turn could end up as personal slights for Vijay and Theresa, deepening the discord between the two.

The *Herald*'s newsroom was an open plan office, spread out over two floors of some 5,000 sq ft in a prime commercial building. Desks were arranged in clusters centred on a hot-desk system in which staff were encouraged to sit at any workstation they pleased, intended to raise workplace transparency, build trust and prompt interaction and collaboration among reporters. Only a handful of senior managers including Pax and Steve had their rooms, which meant conversations were in earshot of colleagues. The open office also meant the rivalry between Theresa and Vijay was often visible for all to see.

The inter-desk rivalry had intensified after Arcade took over the *Herald*. The new owner's pledge to pump in infinite resources to expand subscriber numbers and viewership for the paper's online platform, in a 'digital first' strategy, fostered an unhealthy internal competition to secure resources. Arcade's five-year commitment to spend in a globally shrinking media industry had raised eyebrows, but the tech company's goal was to amass invaluable big data to create analytics that would be used to bolster the group's overall businesses that spanned from e-commerce to cloud computing and online payment.

Arcade's infinite investment unleashed a slew of mindless hiring spearheaded by Theresa and Vijay, lashing on the opportunity to expand their respective turfs in the newsroom.

Vijay began hiring more hands for the Asia desk, falling back on his limited network of regional journalists. With few connections in the city, he had to rely on Pax's recommendations in recruiting reporters for the Hong Kong desk. One of them was Mary Wong, who had worked with Pax at the shuttered television station. After three years onboard, Vijay promoted her to a senior reporter and saw her connection with Pax as an asset that could help him rise the ranks. Between late 2016 and 2019, the Asia desk doubled its headcount to ten people and the Hong Kong team grew from fifteen reporters and editors to twenty-five.

Vijay's enlarged base paled in comparison to Theresa's territory. The China desk was already the biggest division before Arcade's entry. The *Herald*'s newfound mission gave Theresa reasons to expand without hesitation. She opened two news bureaux in the US—New York and Washington DC—as well as hired numerous correspondents, editors and stringers in Europe and Australia, which she stressed was necessary for covering 'China's increasingly prominent global role'.

At the Hong Kong headquarters, she expanded the digital team of editors and approved a huge budget to build a video section that grew to a team of twenty editors, producers and videographers, areas that Steve emphasized to be the next hotspots that will lift subscriber numbers. Nothing pleased Theresa more than lording over an 'empire'. In the last three years that she had travelled to cover China's annual National People's Congress, she made sure an entourage of no fewer than ten reporters flew to Beijing with her, very much like how a Chinese communist leader surrounded himself with scores of officials at official events.

While Vijay and Theresa built their troops, Pax laid his focus on bringing in a few 'strategic' deputies to be placed on the China desk, video and digital teams. Then he invested in himself—spending the money and time to speak in forums and conferences around the world and hobnobbing with Chinese officials and international think-tanks and businesses, anyone important who supported China's global ambition.

Until the *Herald* came into its fold, Arcade was a technology company whose knowledge and experience with the media world was as much as how they worked in China—government-controlled and propaganda machines. The chief executive officer it handpicked, 36-year-old Steve Hsieh, came from a small start-up that streamed videos in the US but he was the nephew of one of Arcade's early cornerstone investors. As Arcade's brief to him was to digitalize the more-than-century-old *Herald*, increasing the clicks on the online platform was the most important performance measurement for him. Two things now mattered for the *Herald* under Jin and Arcade: traffic volume and the Party.

Steve's hurried efforts to reorganize the newsroom and change the *Herald*'s culture and operations left many, who only understood traditional media, grappling with the transition to a digital environment dominated by mobile and social channels. Editorially, Arcade's official mission was to transform the newspaper into a global platform in the coverage of China affairs, providing an alternative voice in the English-speaking world and influencing opinions, especially in the US.

'We will lead the China conversation,' stressed Jin in his first address to *Herald* employees after the takeover. 'With a voice that is credible,' he added, without elaborating.

As an American, Steve portrayed himself as a believer in free speech, which he made clear to all staff in his first town hall with them.

'While the *Herald* needs to transform from a legacy Hong Kong newspaper to a global media company, we must all remember—there is one underlying and most important principle that will not change. Our responsibility to guard against any form of pressure to do what journalism sets out to achieve and protect—editorial independence and the freedom of speech. The journey we're about to embark on, though exciting, won't be easy and we will encounter distractions and pressures of all sorts, but I promise you, as your team leader, I'd have your back. Your job in the newsroom is to deliver the stories most professionally and credibly.'

When Steve first arrived at the *Herald*, staff morale was its lowest point, dampened by a near decade of cost-cutting and eroding editorial independence that Pax, Theresa and Vijay contributed to. A third of the newsroom were journalists who had been there for nearly twenty years or more, who neither understood digital media nor knew how to transition to one. Many were waiting out for retirement, disinterested in changes that forced them out of their comfort zone. Another third were novices who were inexperienced and didn't know better. The remainder split into a small fraction in administrative and non-journalistic work, a group that regarded reporting as simply a job and those who continued to fight the editors' constant caving into political and commercial pressures.

Ironically, the biggest hiccup in the progression to a digitally-savvy global media came from the masthead editors, who were from traditional print and broadcast media and had never worked for any international organizations. Pax's experience stretched only as far as a Beijing-based correspondent for Hong Kong media outlets two decades ago. Theresa's first and only job had been in the *Herald* and Vijay came from a local government-controlled newspaper that the world cared little about.

With their collective local, at best regional experience, the editors sometimes fell short in front of Steve, a millennial from Boston, who had no qualms about taking advantage of their sense of inadequacy to use the newsroom to further business objectives. Dismayed reporters assigned to write sponsored features for clients of the company's newly-created in-house native advertising firm—where publishers use their skills to create ads that resemble traditional editorial work—risk incurring the wrath of their bosses if they declined the work.

An economics reporter covering China's auto industry, Lily Chan found herself in that predicament when she declined to write a sponsored feature for a Chinese automaker.

'Julius, the carmaker is allegedly covering up fraud and cooking its books and you want me to write a glowing article which it will pay for? It's also a distortion of the reality,' she told her editor Julius Hamster who reported to Theresa.

'I understand where you're coming from, but we don't have a choice. You don't have a choice, you'd have to write the piece; Theresa said so. This came directly from Steve.'

Still, the masthead editors' accommodating approach won them little respect from Steve. He was everything that the mastheads were not, from the physical appearance to how he operated. His standard dress code at work were khakis or jeans, a polo T-shirt or checkered shirt and sneakers. While Steve was articulate and could hold his own before any audience, Pax struggled to string his words coherently when addressing the newsroom.

'Good afternoon, the management has decided to restructure the newsroom's operations and I want to take this opportunity to tell you more about how this will work and how it will affect you,' Pax told staff in a joint townhall he hosted with Steve on the landing of the staircase that connected the two floors of the newsroom in the office's open area.

'From now on, all reporters will write stories for online publication, that is the website. There will be no reporters writing for print products. Our new print team will be a small one of mainly backend production editors—designers and sub-editors—who lay out the pages for the newspaper.' Pax's delivery incited a flurry of gasps and buzz among the journalists. *What does he mean? No print reporters? Will I be fired?*

That was when Steve felt compelled to step in. 'Guys, let me elaborate on the restructuring plan. In addition to what Pax said, this means every one of us will be focusing on creating content on our online products, which aligns with our 'digital first' strategy to build a truly global platform. This restructuring will strategically strengthen our resources to generate world-class content that builds both our online and print products efficiently.'

He paused to look up and down at the faces gathered on the two floors around the staircase, encouraged to see expressions of relief and calm returned. He continued.

'There will be no divide between online and print reporters, journalists from next week. If you were previously under the quote print section and unquote, that's no longer the case. The print team of sub-editors and production editors will, under the editorial direction of Pax and Theresa and Vijay, decide which stories to go into the print edition daily.

'We want to assure everyone that the restructuring entails no cuts. In fact, we'd continue to expand and increase new roles as we build our platform,' he added.

After the town hall ended, Steve groaned privately to his assistant. 'Holy cow, I'm surrounded by imbeciles. How am I ever gonna make this a global company?'

The relationship between the CEO and the editors was a curious one. Each side thought little of the other though both knew they needed the other to succeed. Their common ground became spending and the relentless drive to raise the website's online traffic volume.

What was new for the CEO were the inner workings of the media industry and running a company of more than 800 people. But Steve was a fast learner; he knew at the outset that he needed to be in the thick of editorial operations to cement his authority even if the editors were less than welcoming. An easier way, he decided, was to create new products beyond the newspaper that he could directly supervise. Thus he launched two 'awesome' app-based China newsletters which targeted young readers in the US, the *Herald*'s top target market. For the remaining and bulk of his time, he went on global roadshows to 'promote the *Herald*'s brand for tomorrow'.

Steve also removed the paywall, which coupled with the endless resources poured into creating content, the number of users surged, albeit without returns. The bigger consequence was an erosion in the quality of the stories, but no one cared.

The most widely read stories, reporters found, were bizarre tales like the one of a Chinese woman throwing a coin into an airplane engine for luck before she boarded.

'Kudos to Nancy Chang for her story today, which was read by 500,000 users in just one morning. Keep up the good work team,' Theresa wrote in an e-mail to the newsroom. 'To celebrate, we'll be popping champagne at the common area at 6 p.m. Please join the party.'

Quirky stories, as nonsensical as they were, began to flood the website as desk editors commissioned them to drive up the traffic numbers.

James remembered he was drilled in journalism school that a media company was more than a business by all measures; it had the power to sway public opinions and influence society at large. Which made it a business that counted social responsibility as a measurement, but that's only qualifiable when the management and journalists within the outlet placed integrity at the core of their work.

Steve might have argued when he first landed at the *Herald* with the credibility of his support for freedom of expression because of his American background. He was, however, no journalist but a native of Silicon Valley where the ethical dilemma was now the biggest challenge. And he was also ambitious. The *Herald* was the Stanford graduate's biggest job to date, but he saw it as a stepping stone—with invaluable Asian business experience—to something bigger back in the US. With the Internet disrupting the media industry and the current editorial leadership, the *Herald* had seen better days.

* * *

Like Pax, Vijay felt he had little ground to object to Theresa's plan. Theresa had shrewdly included his top lieutenant Mary Wong and Victor Trezise, the Hong Kong political reporter. He blamed himself for letting Theresa get ahead of him. *How could I not have seen it coming?* he agonized, momentarily muting out Theresa's ongoing ramble about the task force. *But no, even if I asked to lead the project, it's a China issue involving the Party, Pax wouldn't agree. The stakes are too high, better she takes the fall if anything went wrong,* he consoled himself. Vijay took a large sip of dandelion root tea to ease the monster of his internal anger. As ambitious as he was, he knew he needed to play safe and bide his time. He would play along, but he wasn't going to give Theresa an easy time.

As he gargled the warm tea in his mouth to soothe his burning irritation, he desperately tried to come up with reasons to reject or at least alter Theresa's plan. He came up with none to dismiss the idea. In fact, it would be a losing battle to go against Theresa, whose plan fell in line with the Party's stance. But he would find a way to insert his influence via engaging his army of sub-editors and graphics artists in the plan.

'Theresa, thanks for such a well-thought-out plan,' Vijay said with a wide smile. 'I think it's great and we really have the potential to do some good work here, even submit the series for awards next year. I know you've already drawn up the core team, but I also think we need to bring the production people on board as well: sub-editors to clean the copies, artists for graphics.

'Let me know how I can support and I'd also be happy to sit in on those regular team meetings so that we can be sure that you will get all the resources you need from my teams.'

'Thanks Vijay, we should talk more about the extended team later,' Theresa replied tersely. 'Right now, it sounds like we have an agreement here, so let's get the task force members together today and brief them, they need to get to work straight away. Time is of the essence,' she said looking at Pax.

'That's right,' her boss answered. 'Also, most importantly, Theresa and Vijay, the three of us must absolutely keep in close contact, keep this team really tight because this is sensitive work, but I'm sure we'll do a good job.

'Theresa, especially keep me looped in at all times as I need to update Mark and Steve, which is a priority,' added Pax.

The three made small talk after that. They finished their drinks and left the cafe fifteen minutes before the 9.30 a.m. morning conference. The conference, the first of the two sessions daily, was where editors from all sections, including sports, features and video, met to discuss and deliberate which were the day's top news items and how to cover them, as well as coordinate any cross-desk collaboration to avoid overlapping.

They walked across the street towards the office building in silence, but without any air of awkwardness as there was an unspoken understanding that no rudeness was intended. They shared no common interests except the goal to advance their positions. This morning, each was lost in his or her thoughts, building individual agendas.

* * *

Theresa sprang into action after the morning conference. She felt like the woman of the moment since the meeting with Pax and Vijay. She would speak to James now, ahead of the afternoon's first meeting with the task force.

Theresa walked across half of the newsroom from her workspace to where the China desk was. Reporters were now accustomed to the annoying click-clack sound of her heels when they hit the concrete parts of the flooring that was uncarpeted. She signalled to James to follow her into a small meeting room, an act that usually rekindled her displeasure for not getting her own office, which she believed was Pax's way of degrading her to Vijay's level.

'James, we are going to set up a task force to investigate an issue related to the Hong Kong protests and I want you to be leading it in the reporting work,' Theresa said, motioning for him to sit down, while she closed the door of the room. A desk and two chairs were placed next to the windowed wall that looked out into the Victoria Harbour. She then sat on the corner of the desk furthest away from James' seat, with a leg dangling over the edge and the other standing lightly on the floor.

'The stories will be packaged into a special series, the coverage, looking at how Edwin Law died, to separate fiction from fact. The protesters are adamant that there's a conspiracy but it may just be in fact a suicide as some quarters think,' she continued, tapping her index finger on the desk and looking down at James. 'There's a very good story here, it's just that we need to find the right way to tell it, with the right context.

'We are going to brief the team later this afternoon. In addition to whatever they say, I need you to know that I'm your first go-to person, foremost, in case issues become complicated, which they could. Byron, your immediate supervisor will be a coordinator of the team,' Theresa looked at James for a split second, as though expecting a response.

'I think you've done great work in the years you have been here and I think you should take a bigger role,' she added and began shifting her gaze around the room to avoid eye contact with James. 'I can't promise you anything at this moment, but this assignment is your chance to show how you can rise up to that bigger role.'

Before James had a chance to respond, Theresa slid off the desk, mumbling under her breath that she was late for her next meeting.

'Let's catch up later if you have any questions,' she told him, with one foot already out of the small room. James found her abrupt closure of the meeting to be particularly annoying on this occasion when she had dangled a carrot in front of him and left it hanging.

Her evasiveness was nothing new. Editors and reporters who worked with her all knew it was her way to dodge hard-hitting questions or issues she didn't want or know how to address. On the other hand, she always had time for those who cosied up to her and sang praises of the China coverage. Those who held different perspectives on news issues were by default regarded as challenging her authority. For two years, Wu Xianwen, a loud and self-centred deputy editor whom she didn't hire, was a thorn in her side until Wu changed tact. Preying on Theresa's vanity, Wu showered her with excessive compliments for her 'insightful' analysis and story angles on US-China relations. She became a favoured subordinate.

The deputies hired by her to co-ordinate and issue assignments to reporters bore common traits that eased Theresa's insecurity. They were submissive, loyal, did not hold clear political stances and on the surface seemed to worship the ground she walked on. Her biggest hiring requirement for a China editor to oversee the desk's operations was the candidate needed to be just moderately knowledgeable about China, but 'doesn't know it too well' that would show her down. The China desk was divided into four teams covering diplomacy, politics, economy and social news, led by eight deputies with no real autonomy. Reporters called them 'Theresa's harem' and knew better to take their word seriously, because Theresa was rarely satisfied with their performance, openly reprimanding that they lacked 'leadership' and story ideas. Not that the deputies didn't try but after a while, they gave up because anything that wasn't from the editor herself was relegated to 'rubbish'. Her meetings with the team always turned out to consist of top-down directives and one-way conversations. Another group of sub-editors whose job was simply to clean up copies for accuracy and consistency also reported to her.

To maintain an upper hand, Theresa adopted the 'divide and rule' policy which pitted the deputies against one another, so that no one person had the complete picture. She told herself that it fostered healthy competition that encouraged the teams to come up with better stories. The environment bred a culture of distrust, where the deputies wormed themselves into Theresa's good books. They would never counter her views even if they were suggestions for discussion and with some going further.

'I've never met someone as smart as Theresa, with such a deep understanding of the Party psyche, the US-China relations space, totally mind-blowing,' one of the deputy editors Julius Hamster told two other peers a few weeks after he joined the *Herald*.

Her deputies rarely spoke to reporters about story assignments without the pre-fix: 'Theresa says . . . ' It arose more from fear than respect for the editor.

The reporting troopers were a mixed bunch. Out of the fifty reporters in the Hong Kong newsroom and China offices—Shenzhen, Shanghai, Beijing, Chengdu and Guangzhou—fewer than ten were experienced journalists, with the remaining mostly young novices. From Theresa's point of view, the old hands were players on the bench, to pick up any slack and support the younger reporters on a need-to basis. 'The future of the *Herald* is with our young reporters and we only do well if they do, which means we must do all that we can to nurture these talents,' was her mantra.

James was an exceptional case among Theresa's small group of experienced China reporters. His fate in the newsroom was the opposite of his peers. He was also one of the few from the China division who dared to challenge his desk editors, even to the extent of disagreeing on news issues with Theresa. Theresa had not been pleased but she had accommodated for the time being because a) she hired him, so there was some trust involved and b) she needed him to execute on the big stories.

But James had found himself struggling harder to come to terms with the *Herald*'s coverage of China, particularly on the narratives of the Hong Kong protests and the US-China trade war, skewed towards favouring the mainland, on many occasions transcending from being pro-China to distortions. He had confronted Theresa a few times but the latter had always concocted various rationales to defend the compromised publication decisions and deflected the concerns. The scale and frequency of distortions widened recently. Theresa assured reporters that the *Herald* was merely embarking on narratives to offer readers fresh perspectives in leading the 'China conversation'. But James couldn't fathom how articles on the Hong Kong Government and police's use of excessive force to quell demonstrations without the protesters' side of the account, or stories on the US-China trade war seen only from Beijing's perspective, constituted credible journalism and meaningful discussions.

What he saw was an established loose relationship with the truth that was reflected in the attitude towards reporting, the stories published, internal engagements and communications. The top editors didn't stop this but were in fact the biggest proponents. They awarded cash prizes to journalists for stories that favoured the government and the Party or exemplified the achievements of China in the newsroom's 'Monthly Best' programme.

James remained in the small meeting room for a while. He leaned back against the chair, removed his horn-rimmed round glasses, looked up towards the low ceiling and replayed in his head the one-way conversation he just had with Theresa. The task force proposition was out of the ordinary under the current circumstances where the *Herald* had been gradually moving towards a narrative that sided with the institutions. The shift had sparked dissent among his colleagues, which Theresa and editors turned a blind eye to.

That the newspaper even initiated an investigative piece of journalism is incredulous, he thought. *Maybe there is more that meets the eye? Or am I just overthinking this?* He hoped to get some answers at the briefing in the afternoon. *But I shouldn't hold my breath,* he reminded himself as he walked back to his desk.

2

Blurring the Line

Ping, the *Herald*'s intranet messenger buzzed, distracting James from writing a story.

To Sichuan meeting room now, Theresa's secretary texted, as a new pop-up window blocked the word document that he was working on.

What's this about? he typed back, frustrated, glancing at the clock on his computer, realizing that he only had an hour to meet his deadline.

Theresa wants to talk to you. I don't really know anything further.

Annoyed, James got up from his seat and walked towards the meeting room. He guessed that it would have to be about the task force. He was expecting the meeting but not at the hour when he was rushing to file his article—although it was just another mundane China diplomacy analysis piece—before wrapping up for the day.

God, she does this all the time, he grumbled to himself.

Theresa had a penchant for calling meetings at times when the journalists were busiest—writing their articles to desperately meet their deadlines—not that it mattered to her. Mentally giving up on making his deadline, James slowly walked to the room.

The *Herald*'s brand-new office was sleek and lustrous. Scattered across the two floors was a myriad of common areas with snooker tables, chess boards and video game consoles to encourage activities that enhanced communication among employees, 'casual collision' as Steve put it. Different shaped tables, colourful chairs and sofas were put in place to stimulate staff's creativity. Vending machines selling chips, crackers and soft drinks at a discount and the latest fancy models of coffee machines, Java and Nespresso, were placed throughout these areas. The only problem though was the areas were usually empty. Few people had the time or interest to use the facilities. Over time, the common areas became pieces of ornamental displays for visitors—outsiders—of the *Herald*'s purported openness and the open platform it aspired to stand for, in keeping with international media standards. Reporters joked that they were utilized more by touring visitors than employees. Part of the 'skin-deep' strategy of the Arcade-era management team, they said.

The biggest interests to tour the newsroom came from Chinese and Hong Kong government officials, as well as corporate executives and institutions, with motivations to keep the media on their side of the room. They arrived continuously in groups of between two to twenty in the first year the *Herald* moved into its new home. An editor or a marketing executive usually acted as the tour guide and could host anything from two to seven groups on a given day. The visitors would move across the newsroom floors, peering at reporters at work, at times nodding their heads or even clapping in agreement with what their guide was saying, not missing a step of what staff described as the 'safari tours'.

'We are the exotic breeds they came to look at,' editors often joked with reporters.

James walked past one of the empty common areas—The Hub—and reached a long corridor. Steve called the walls along that corridor leading to the Sichuan meeting room, the *Herald*'s 'Hall of Fame'. The strong chemical odour from the newly laid-out grey carpet on the corridor was burning through his nostrils. James held his breath for as long as he could. The illustrations on the ivory-coloured walls by a *Herald* artist depicted a timeline of the newspaper's history: how the company had strived and flourished since its foundation in the 1900s. They captured the milestones over more than 100 years, including every relocation of the Hong Kong headquarters, opening bureaux in Beijing, Shanghai, Shenzhen and Washington DC, alongside the city's major historical events when the *Herald* won some of its historic exclusives. The front pages of the paper's major stories over the years were framed individually and displayed next to the timeline, boasting the company's glowing achievements since Hong Kong was under British colonial rule. The timeline ended in 2017, a year after Arcade bought the company and when the *Herald* moved to its current office.

* * *

James stepped into the meeting room, a medium-sized space large enough to fit a long table that could sit a group of ten around it. The biggest wall in the room was a mural of the city's Wan Chai district, now a battlefield between protesters and the police over the city's fight for democracy. James was gripped by a rush of anguish as he came face to face with the wall painting of the district during happier times. Heather, Alan, Daniel, Mary and Victor were seated around one end of the table. The room was quiet as the journalists were busy swiping the screens of their phones. They looked up and James made brief eye contact, nodded, before planting himself on a chair behind the group. He didn't bother to find out if they knew what the meeting was about, as from experience and his brief conversation with Theresa earlier, any information shared would have been incohesive. The problem of ineffectiveness and lack of communication was so chronic that the only way the masthead editors knew how to tackle the issues was to not deal with them and prayed that all hell didn't break loose.

A few minutes later, Theresa entered the meeting room with a strange vehemence, an air of greater intensity from a few hours ago, James thought. With one sharp push, she elbowed the door shut behind her and walked towards the empty end of the table, laid down a folder with her notes and a bottle of Evian water and sat on the edge of it, her twisted body facing the reporters on the other end. She removed her black-framed reading glasses, pushed up her jacket sleeves and leaned forward as if to narrow the distance between herself and the reporters. She was wearing a brand new power suit; a double-breasted blazer piped-trim top and bottom waist pants. Her face wore no emotions. *Here she goes again,* James complained to himself, as he watched her warmed herself to deliver her prepared speech. She looked firm, excited and strangely more determined than usual.

'Across the world, free speech is atrophying,' began Theresa, projecting herself more forcefully than usual for a strong start as a champion for freedom of speech. The acuteness of her shrill voice pierced the cold air in the room.

'But I have to say it's absolutely disgraceful to publish something unverified, especially without an approval.' There was no elaboration on whose approval she was referring to.

'So I am going to launch a task force to stop the spreading of fake news. There is a spreading of fake news on social media in Hong Kong that a young guy . . . what was his name . . . Edwin, yes that's it, Edwin Law, was abused, tortured and murdered by the police backed by Beijing,' the editor continued. 'That's fake news.'

From where he was, James noticed that Victor, who had his back towards him, shifted uncomfortably in his seat before his shoulders dropped into a slouch with a soft sigh under his breath.

Was he feeling exasperated with this whole freedom of speech nonsense? James thought as Theresa went on.

'This task force aims to find out who's behind this rumour. Is it America? Taiwan? The Fujian gang? Or the Hong Kong protesters? You must bring me some evidence of who they are and what they want to achieve by demonizing the police and the government. The last thing we want and need in our society is demonizing others,' she said, her voice unwittingly raised.

'Now, go and find out what happened. Why are they targeting the Party? What is America's endgame?' Theresa said commandingly, like a field commander on a battlefield.

'What the hell?' Daniel leaned backwards scratching his ear and whispered to James, rolling his eyes skywards.

James shrugged but thought, *Ha, I can finally relate to those who work in Chinese state media.*

The room was filled with dead silence like it usually did after Theresa spoke. No one offered any feedback or asked a question, not that they didn't have any, but because everyone knew better.

'With Theresa, it was like a police state,' Daniel once summarized, with his usual dosage of cynicism. 'The dictator had given the order and that was final. There's no other way, only Theresa's way.'

A long time resident of Hong Kong, Daniel had been keeping close tabs on the city's political evolvement, drawing parallels to what might occur in Taiwan, which China considered a renegade province. James also knew from his time at the *Herald* that Theresa didn't take lightly to questions at meetings. Those who asked them were viewed as challenging her authority publicly. He decided that the only way he wouldn't compromise journalistic standards was to engage in the task force project and use hard facts to counter Theresa's hypothetical assumptions. What amused him was how Theresa's carefully thought out 'freedom of speech' card had actually backfired; everything she said was all but free speech.

Why would she have argued for freedom of speech when she knew she would be scoffed at? Was she attempting to deflect, conscious of the worries among journalists towards the self-censorship measures in the Herald, predominantly led by her?

He knew that she often used a fear tactic to exert control over the newsroom, to the point of hollering at journalists when she believed she wasn't heard. The few brave ones who questioned her editorial instructions were quietly moved to less important desks, or even different cities—ultimately silenced. Many senior and experienced reporters left the company because of her coercion. Those who chose to remain learned to avoid her wrath by diluting the narrative in their stories to what they thought would satisfy her demands. Whatever her intention was today, it irked James that she had used the free speech principle to get them onboard whatever plot she was scheming.

While he was turning these issues over in his head, he caught sight of an awe-stricken Heather from the corner of his eye, visibly moved by the editor's press freedom speech. Heather's eyes were shining and she felt inspired.

Finally, a piece of real investigative journalism to set the record straight! she thought, her face glowing with excitement. She took detailed notes, the only one in the room to do so, as Theresa spoke.

James counted Heather as a friend even though their values were as different as night and day, especially when it came to how each defined journalism. They agreed to disagree and wouldn't confront or challenge each other's values to avoid unnecessary conflicts. But Heather's attitude in the meeting room instantly built a wall between them, as it reminded him of the few recent encounters he had with her—they had disturbed him.

The Hong Kong protests reached a turning point on the weekend of 21 July which changed the course of the widening political crisis and the *Herald*'s approach to its coverage. Tens of thousands of protesters descended on China's Liaison Office on Hong Kong island's Western district, directly challenging Beijing on its turf. The activists, wearing black masks and shirts to cover up their faces, pelted the Liaison Office building with eggs and sprayed black graffiti on its walls, as well as defaced the Chinese emblem that hung at the entrance as they demanded an independent inquiry into alleged police brutality. That night, hundreds of riot police fired off a record amount of tear gas and rubber bullets in an ugly face-off with protesters that stretched into the early morning, ending only after an unknown number were arrested and injured, amid the fading echoes of police and ambulance sirens.

The *Herald*'s reports focused on China's fury towards the *radical* protesters rather than the cause of the protests, claiming the vandalism had offended *all Chinese people* and *divided Hongkongers from the mainland Chinese*. It wasn't the angle of the articles that caught James' attention on Monday morning, but Heather's reaction to the weekend's demonstrations.

'Are you all right?' James asked Heather, who had buried her head at her desk, her shoulder-length straight black hair covering the sides of her face and her body shaking with anger. 'What's wrong?'

'Nothing, I'm just a little tired,' she answered, lifting her head sideways to look at him, revealing a pair of swollen, inflamed eyes. James didn't ask any further questions.

'Actually, I couldn't sleep last night,' she said, a minute later.

'What happened?'

'I just couldn't . . . these lapdogs of America are attacking my country.'

'You mean the protesters?'

'Yes . . . I mean no. You should call them terrorists,' she said with indignation. An awkward silence followed before she added, 'I'll find out who's behind this terrorism.'

James was taken aback by Heather's outburst, seeing another side of her for the first time. 'Well . . . good luck with that,' he muttered as he hurriedly walked past her to his seat. He didn't know how else to respond.

The second incident took place ten days later when China's military—the People's Liberation Army (PLA)—in Hong Kong released a three-minute video on anti-riot drills on its official Weibo social media account. The PLA troops were filmed firing guns and even rockets. Tanks, helicopters and missile launchers were shown in the video. 'To preserve the stability of the society,' said the subtitles, as a thinly-veiled warning that Beijing could use force on its people in the name of 'stability'. The footage also covered troops marching with shields and truncheons towards people, firing rifles into the air, as tear gas and water cannons rained down on protesters. Scenes of armoured personnel carriers with battering rams racing forward and troops laying barbed wire coils on the ground were featured, as a soldier voiced over in Cantonese.

'All consequences are at your own risk!'

The video disturbed James.

Aren't people the state itself? How can you sacrifice your people to secure a state's interest? What is state and what is people to Beijing?

The extent of his distraught, he later found, was no match for Heather's immeasurable pride. She played the video over and over again, more energized and beaming with unfettered pride at each replay. James found the scene so surreal that he wondered if she was all that naïve or even delusional.

To him, it was clear that they defined what was a state differently, which meant they protected different values as journalists. For her, the state came before its people—thus anyone who could harm the state would be framed as radicals causing instability or an act of treason. The difference between Heather and him, James reasoned, was the issue of whether to protect national interest by restricting an individual's freedom or the individual's right to voice (even if the voice is only a minority) through limiting the power of a state: it was a matter of whether to work for state or people.

Still, nothing was as telling of Heather's politics and view of the world than her response to an article from the American think-tank Cookton Foundation. The commentary penned by its editor Timothy Heathrow argued for why American social media companies Twitter, Facebook and Google—risking the backlash of restricting freedom of expression—removed and suspended thousands of accounts on their platforms believed to be held by the Chinese government too, in his words, 'deliberately and specifically attempting' sow political discord in Hong Kong, including undermining the legitimacy and political positions of the protest movement. Twitter highlighted in a statement that it found a 'significant state-backed information operation' originating from within the Chinese government targeting Hong Kong protesters.

'How ridiculous!' Heather bellowed to James. Her big eyes flashed with anger and she banged her fists on the desk.

'It's fuelling hatred towards China,' she said, shivering. 'There's no proof!' she continued. 'This guy is a racist!'

'I think it's a fair commentary,' James said.

'Well . . . I can't just sit here and do nothing about America's dirty propaganda!'

Ignoring James, she returned to her seat and started to compose a lengthy letter of protest to Heathrow. She worked on it for the whole day, before finishing her masterpiece that was punctuated with typos and grammatical mistakes and sending it off in the early hours of the morning using the *Herald*'s e-mail account.

From: heather.hua@hanherald.com
Tuesday, September 17, 2019, at 4:20 am
To: timothy.heathrow@cookton.org
Subject: My thoughts on your propaganda piece

Hi there. This is Heather from the Herald. I noticed your latest propaganda piece about terrorism in Hong Kong. I am currently following the issue too and just wanted to share a few thoughts.

We are angry that Western social media shut down some accounts from China. It's a fallacy to believe that these accounts are controlled by the Chinese government.

Also, China has a Great Fire Wall that blocks people from using such a platform. But actually, Chinese common people still can access some of the blocked websites via using VPNs, as our government values free speech. Our government has the full capacity to detect and monitor those common people who visit the blocked websites, but the government doesn't take any actions against such behaviours, as it still allows people to explore Western materials as long as it doesn't hurt our national sovereignty.

Since you are in the US and you are not depicting the full picture here. Terrorism that's taking place here is becoming really ugly and I can tell you as someone living in this city. These separatists are using violence and that is wrong. A typical example is the beating up of a reporter from my country's state media at the Hong Kong international airport. This made many of my fellow countrymen express their anger in the Western social media using VPNs as they want the outsiders—people outside China's Great Fire Wall—to know the true picture of what's actually happening here, something that Western media chooses not to report.

A friend of mine, who supported Hong Kong police in Western social media, got her account closed. The social media said that her post was a hatred remark. But, if this line is a hatred remark, why the Western social media platform never shut down any accounts that support protesters' violent actions? This is purely a double standard, don't you think?

In my eyes, these so-called protesters are too violent, they are now more like a group of terrorists. Hope you can write a more balanced view on Hong Kong in the future.

Best wishes,
Heather

It took about a week before her e-mail got captured and circulated among American journalists, and subsequently found its way back to the *Herald*'s reporters. Victor showed James the screenshot of the e-mail.

'We all have different politics, but she shouldn't be abusing her journalist position to propagate political views,' he moaned to James. 'I feel so ashamed.'

'James!' a voice yelled, bringing him back into the meeting. It was Theresa. She was scribbling something on the glass writing board and had caught him drifting away. 'Are you with us or not?' She was always annoyed if she wasn't given full attention in meetings.

'I'm listening,' James grunted.

'This is the division of labour,' Theresa said, as she synchronized her Xiaomi Pad 4 Plus with a TV screen in the meeting room.

James: victim's family, Chinese and Hong Kong officials
Heather: Hong Kong and Chinese police
Daniel & Alan: checking surveillance camera
Mary & Victor: victim's friends

'These are the targets you need to reach out to in the next few days,' she said composedly. 'Make sure you find something so that we can lead the global conversations on China towards the right direction using accurate and politically correct narratives.

'Before we end this, do you have any questions or objections?' she asked. Nobody responded, as though they weren't hearing her. 'No? Good. Then I'll wrap up today's meeting.' She hastily concluded the meeting and was already halfway out of the room.

With Theresa gone, a buzz began to emerge, mostly of confused grunts and murmurs. Daniel and Alan looked at each other trying to figure out why they had become part of this and how they were going to carry out their assignments. Mary was lost in thoughts as she wondered where her boss Vijay fitted in this and how she needed to wriggle through the politicking between the Hong Kong and China desks, while Victor sighed again.

As Daniel and Alan made their way out of the meeting room, a few curious colleagues seated nearby gathered around them to suss out what the assignment was about. In the room, James exchanged knowing looks with Mary and Victor. Having worked on stories and travelled together on assignments, the three had bonded as colleagues and friends. They were waiting impatiently for Heather to leave the room so that they could have a private conversation. But before they could do that, Mary and Victor were summoned by Vijay, who was anxiously waiting for a download from the reporters.

At that moment, James heard a low humming murmur from Heather's vibrating mobile phone on the table. Curious, he discretely leaned forward to steal a peek over her shoulder at the text reply that popped up.

Come to my office upstairs and see me for a while, it read. It was right above Heather's previous text: *The meeting just finished.*

There was only one office upstairs—Pax's.

* * *

The editor-in-chief was sitting on a brown leather armchair drinking Earl Grey tea and reading the *Herald*'s print version. It was his daily moment when he patted himself on the back and swooned at how he had again set the agenda adequately to lead the China conversations. His long day was nearly over, not that Pax did much in the newsroom and he began to unwind after the 4 p.m. afternoon news conference where the stories for overnight and print publications were decided. His routine was pretty set. He woke up going through the 'news' on the Chinese state media on his tablet for cues of shifts in the narrative from the Party in the morning and ended his day admiring his contribution to the Party.

Pax was scanning the Twitter account of a famous Chinese state media editor on his phone. He dreamed of becoming someone as influential as the editor one day, garnering more than 460,000 followers. To achieve that, he would need to make the *Herald* as good as the state media. His own follower numbers, a fraction of the Chinese editor's, frustrated him and he shuffled his feet, slowly at first but rubbing harder on the large expensive-looking Persian carpet placed under the brown tea table. The carpet which he bought during a 2014 Chinese government-sponsored media tour of China's western

Xinjiang region was one of the two trophies in his office. The other was his collection of books about China. Pax shot up from his chair and marched towards the antique wooden bookshelves that lined two walls of the room. There was an urgent need for him to know more about Chinese leadership, which would one day help make him an editor like the one he so admired. He carefully chose a book and placed it on the tea table. The book entitled *The China Thoughts* and a gift from the Chinese Liaison Office would offer insights he needed to reach his goal, he thought.

The self-indulgence was cut short by the sight of Heather. He quickly recomposed himself as he watched her walk towards the room through the glass wall that was joined to a glass door to symbolize transparency at the *Herald*. But as Heather stepped in, Pax clicked on a button of his remote control to draw down the roller blinds. Pax had a clear and simple agenda for meeting Heather. He wanted to publish a few stories to score political credit from the above, whilst keeping check of Theresa's influence in the newsroom. The two editors held the same editorial stance, but he didn't feel secure leaving the assignment solely in her hands, which she might use as leverage to outmanoeuvre him to grow her clout with Jin and the Party. It was a complex task at the same time because he couldn't afford for Theresa to fail with the task force as that would anger the higher-ups, ultimately undermining his leadership. That left him, he thought, with only one option—to appear supportive in giving Theresa a free hand but to take credit for the stories published before she did. And Heather, who used to report to him at the shuttered TV station, making them an ally to each other, was the perfect reporter to carry out his plan. They had a mutual understanding and shared the same politics.

'We need to be preemptive and make our move first,' Pax said, skipping the greetings.

'Do you have any suggestions?' he asked, as he placed his right hand on *The China Thoughts*, as though he was taking an oath on the Bible.

'What we need is a story from a human interest perspective,' Pax continued without waiting for Heather to reply. 'To make our global audience empathize with the Hong Kong Government, police and the Chinese people.'

'I have an idea,' Heather answered vivaciously. 'I always thought it is absolutely unfair for Chinese mainlanders to be discriminated against in this city.'

'You have a point.'

'Hongkongers are terrible. They smear us and scorn at us. I feel extremely unsafe, you know. How about we do a story on that? In fact, it can be a few stories on this theme. There's lots to say.'

'Not a bad idea, Heather. Work on it now. But as I said we have to move before *them*. I trust you to file it by next week,' Pax said. 'You may leave now.'

* * *

Heather returned to her desk, her heart skipping as she wrote an e-mail with the story pitch to Theresa. Needless to say, the idea struck a chord with Theresa's own agenda to demonize the protesters and she immediately approved of the pitch, oblivious of Pax's involvement.

For the next five days, Heather worked tirelessly on the story; she conducted face-to-face and phone interviews with various sources, who were predominantly her friends and stayed beyond her usual eight hours in the office to write. The story was published the following week with a special push by the marketing team to promote it across online platforms and social media.

I am being hated in my home: mainland Chinese fear speaking their own language in Hong Kong, the headline screamed. *Chinese people under emotional attack, as a protest mutates into a violent terror against all Chinese, hurting national sovereignty,* read the sub-headline.

Heather's story was heavily one-sided, uncannily in line with the Chinese government's stance. The voices of three anonymous mainland Chinese formed the narrative of the article which centred on how these people didn't want to be identified for fear of being targeted by Hongkongers. The story explained at length how the Chinese felt unsafe speaking Mandarin in the city.

'Since when has it become a sin to be a mainland Chinese?' asked 64-year-old Shirley, whose real name has not been mentioned as she feared becoming a victim of brutality if her identity was revealed.

Her story also quoted by name a few sociologists and experts who were well-known Chinese government mouthpieces. Their views focused on the threat that Hongkongers felt from mainland immigrants who were threatening their jobs, obscuring the reasons behind the protests. Without the context and voice from protesters, the story portrayed them as violent mobsters and implied that the police's use of excessive violence as self-defence was justifiable.

Frustrated and put off by the biased report, James turned off his monitor and stood up from his seat. Then he walked away to The Hub—which was unsurprisingly empty—wanting to think a little more about Heather's value of journalism.

What is journalism to her? James wondered again. *Shouldn't journalism, a watchdog that protects the individual's rights and freedom from overbearing government and institutions, contribute to the progression of democracy?*

Such a concept was clearly lost on Heather. Coming from China where the system had indoctrinated her as a child, she would never see why Hongkongers were fighting for their rights and political freedom. Neither did she want to understand, despite having lived in the city for a decade and held a Hong Kong Special Administrative Region passport. She single-mindedly condemned the demonstrations as acts of *radicals* who attempted to destabilize her country. Publishing and giving the story excessive prominence made her and the *Herald* tools for party propaganda that served the needs of the state.

As soon as Heather's story was published, Pax pushed it out on his Weibo and WeChat social media accounts. The accounts were soon flooded with complimentary comments.

The story went on to win the Monthly Best award for October in the *Herald*'s internal award programme for best stories. The editors commended her for 'adequately reflecting' the company's values in an e-mail to the newsroom that explained why and how they rated her story.

* * *

Real China hands would tell you that reading the Party and Chinese politics well came with experience. On the China desk, such skill sets were a rarity as Theresa's draconian management style drove talent away from, more than retained them. She wasn't bothered that inexperienced reporters, therefore, accounted for the majority of the team. It was a setup she preferred as young minds were easy to impress and manage. Her strategy was to fill vacancies with fresh graduates, often mainland Chinese or Asians holding foreign passports, who were anxious to break into the China reporting scene. The young reporters dared not question Theresa's authority and didn't have critical thinking: a perfect tool for propaganda spin. They were also not trained to contribute to the progression of democracy and fight for individual freedoms against a state. Her agenda therefore often produced confused young reporters, whose youthful idealism spurred them to strive for journalistic integrity, but their ambitions made them yearn for Theresa's endorsement.

Nancy was one such jumbled mess. She often slammed Theresa behind her back for endorsing self-censorship in the newsroom but was notorious for being one of the most avid agents of Theresa's editorial instructions to appease Beijing. She initiated an online group chat rallying reporters to take up the case with Theresa when the *Herald* repeatedly labelled the Hong Kong protesters *radicals*. But offline, she didn't once object or apply any critical thinking—as she was afraid of going against Theresa's almighty instructions—to the agenda-loaded stories she was assigned, which often centred on Beijing's views on international affairs including its condemnations of individuals, groups or countries who acted against China's interests. She simply wrote quietly at her desk and delivered those China-appeasing stories she was tasked with.

James experienced Nancy's brand of hysteria first-hand during a work trip to Beijing. The two of them had arranged to meet a US-

China relation expert for dinner one evening. Before the dinner appointment, James had a meeting with the Beijing bureau chief. But when he emerged from the meeting, Nancy had deliberately left for the restaurant without him. She wanted to get even with him for helping an editor correct a mistake in a story she wrote, which she saw as a personal attack.

James stepped onto the street to hail a taxi. It was pitch black and light from the street lamps was dimmed by the rain that had been pelting down hard the entire day. His leather shoes were soaked and his pants wet to around his shins by the time he finally hopped onto a taxi and arrived twenty minutes late for the appointment. Nancy was engrossed in chatting with the US-China relations professor. James could feel himself glowering at her back with disgust as he walked towards their table to join the party.

After they finished dinner and the professor had left the restaurant, James tried to clear the air with Nancy regarding the correction matter.

'I just wanted to talk to you about the story correction a few days ago . . . ' he began.

'Calm the hell down!' Nancy roared, cutting him off mid-sentence. 'Yes, it was a mistake but I have no shame about that because our standard is really low anyway.'

Her outburst threw James off briefly and drew curious glances from the few remaining diners at nearby tables. Before he could find the right words to respond, she burst into tears.

'Work is so stressful . . . Theresa keeps breathing down my neck . . . and I don't wanna be her puppet. And also, I think many people know that I am dating three men in the newsroom. Should I quit?' Her tears had smeared her mascara and were streaming down her face, with strands of her hair starting to stick on the sides of her damp cheeks.

'What are you talking about?' James felt confused but quickly came to his sense that it was a bastard case to try to clarify anything with Nancy. 'You know what, it's not my business. You need to fix your own problems.'

He grabbed his bag and coat, picked up the bill on the table and headed towards the cashier to pay. Outside, the rain was still pouring hard.

Why did we hire someone like her? James thought as he dragged his tired body towards the nearest subway station.

That answer could be traced back to Theresa's acute insecurity and her unquenchable thirst for power. Young reporters were easier to control. Experienced and more knowledgeable journalists often did not agree with her politically-driven news angles and would not take things lying down. Many of them had left the *Herald* as a result and those who remained were silenced in the newsroom. Even a few of the young reporters had realized that they needed to leave if they were committed to the profession. But it wasn't easy for most, as their coverage in the *Herald* was heavily biased and other media outlets were hesitant to hire someone from a pseudo-media.

The *Herald's* strategy for keeping experienced reporters with critical thinking in line was best illustrated in Jeffery Chen's case. On the same night that thousands of protesters descended on China's Liaison Office, dozens of masked, stick-carrying men wearing white shirts made brazen assaults on pro-democracy protesters at the Yuen Long subway station in the New Territories, the city's northern area that was closest to China. The Hong Kong police were nowhere to be seen as the bloody attacks raged on and assaulters hit commuters at the station too. The police later confirmed that some of the attackers arrested were gangsters connected to the city's notorious organized crime syndicates, known as the triads. Most of the Chinese triads came from Fujian—a Chinese southern coastal province—and were based in the North Point district on Hong Kong island.

The next day, Theresa came over to Jeffery's desk. Jeffery was originally from Fujian and moved south to Hong Kong with his parents when he was five.

'Please go to Fujian tomorrow and track down these gangsters. I want to know everything about them,' she instructed the reporter. 'I want to know whether they exist and if they do, whether they are acting on their own or following instructions from the top.'

Jeffery's brows furrowed a little. He knew better than to say 'no' straight away and contemplated for a while before replying.

'Sure. Will do that,' he said. 'But I would need more time to plan some groundwork here.'

'What groundwork?' Theresa asked, her voice slightly rising, a sign that she was about to explode into one of her tantrums.

'I would need to figure out which groups to target, where to go in Fujian and who I should contact to achieve your agenda.'

'We don't have much time. You can figure that out in Fujian. Just go there.'

'The earliest I can go would be next week.'

Theresa's face gradually turned red. She took the rejection of her order as a personal humiliation. What bothered her more was Jeffrey had made a valid point.

'Fine, I will get someone else to go then,' she cut him off and walked back to her seat. Theresa sent two young reporters to the region the following day.

3

The Build-up and Compromising

As protests in Hong Kong heated up, the *Herald*'s attempt to demonize protesters became increasingly blunt and incriminating. From editorials, news stories, to columns, it began to mimic China's state media. They focused on the violence committed by a few extremist protesters, but failed to report on what caused the violent backlash. James' agony had built up over the weeks and months and was nearing a point of implosion by late August. The intensifying clash between the Hong Kong Government and its people was snowballing; it was a vicious cycle. As the police fired more rubber bullets, projectiles, water cannons, tear gas and pepper sprays on citizens, protesters hurled back with molotov cocktails and bricks, setting public facilities such as trash cans and entrances of subway stations on fire.

On the reporting frontline, he witnessed with agony the abuse of police power—excessive use of force on unarmed protesters—that undermined the force's own accountability and turned it into the people's main antagonist in the protests. Footage and videos of the police's misuse of crowd control weapons—including tear gas, bean bag guns and batons—filmed by reporters, first aiders, lawyers and non-government organizations circulated widely on social media, inciting local and international outrage. The Hong Kong Government, caught between its people and its political masters in Beijing, not only failed to deescalate the tensions, but its refusal to inquire into the abuse and its unwavering support for the police fanned the flames further. Increased groups of armed officers patrolling the streets and riot police scouring the subway platforms became a common sight; authorities were tightening their surveillance of citizens and hunting down protesters.

Pro-Beijing citizens—predominantly those who came from the mainland and the conservatives—maintained it was the *rioting* protesters that forced the police to take strong measures. The pro-democracy camp countered that it was police misconduct which provoked some protesters to respond violently and called for the force to stop abusing its power against the people.

James watched tensions flare to new levels with each passing day, bitterly ripping the city that he grew up in. The Fragrant Harbour, as its name translated in Cantonese, was enveloped in shrouds of tear gas that greyed its people's pride and future. The biggest showdowns occurred over the weekends, where violence escalated to the highest point as the night fell. Weekdays were also laced with smaller-scale protests. For a city known to never sleep, businesses in the densest commercial districts now closed their stores by 8 p.m. with no sign of a semblance of normality.

In theory, Hong Kong's political turmoil would have been one of the biggest and most exciting stories for a China reporter. That was far from the case if you were a *Herald* journalist, James came to realize.

When he saw for the first time police officers using pepper spray on people who posed no obvious threat, James had taken a photo with his phone and filed a short report with the picture to Byron Mo, his immediate supervisor who reported to Theresa. Theresa killed the story.

Similar story's already been written by the Hong Kong desk, Byron delivered Theresa's message in a text. *No need for an overlap*.

The Hong Kong desk in fact did not run that story, James found out later.

A second and similar report he filed met with the same fate and Byron didn't respond to his e-mail. By the third time, he concluded it was useless to broach the matter. The *Herald*'s coverage of the police's use of force constructed a narrative that was the opposite of what he and thousands of others saw on the streets.

When the firing of bean bag rounds ruptured a female protester's right eye on 11 August, the paper omitted the wide-spread public call for an investigation into excessive use of force. The *Herald* took a similar stance when the police fired pepperball rounds at point-blank range at protesters inside the Taikoo subway station. It replicated the approach in its report of a mysterious white shirt-clad mob that attacked protesters with bamboo sticks in the North Point district, home to many mainland immigrants from Fujian. The mysterious gangsters later retreated into Ming Yuen, the Fujian Clan's premises, but the police didn't investigate the link between the two. In Hong Kong, individuals, business groups, associations and clans linked to Chinese provinces were part of the United Front—a covert network the Party used to expand its influence and control in the city.

Orderly chaos was James' first impression out on the field. The Hong Kong streets in the Admiralty district seemed like a place of total disorder and confusion from the outside, but it was the opposite. There was order and discipline, but most of all it was humanity that formed the backbone of the protests. When James walked towards a standoff zone between the demonstrators and the police, hundreds of protesters were already forming a frontline against the officers. Dozens of reporters stood in between the frontline with their cameras. The protesters towards the back were gearing up to help the physically wounded from the standoff zones.

'Here, take this,' one female teenage protester stopped James as he edged towards the standoff zone.

'Is this your first time?' she asked, grinning. 'You need to cover up your face.' She handed him a blue surgical mask fished out from her duffle bag and was pointing at the line of riot police that had formed; the faces of the officers were hidden under visored helmets behind acrylic shields.

'They'll record you and use it against you,' she said, raising her voice slightly, unconsciously venting her frustration. 'These guys will do anything to put you behind bars. Don't forget,' she added before she scurried off.

'Thank you,' James yelled after her. It was then that he picked up on the young protester's warning. Between every ten to twenty riot police, there was a uniformed policeman carrying a monopod attached to a camera. They were responsible for capturing each and every face at the demonstration. It reminded James of a conversation he had with a South Korean diplomat a week ago.

'A few years ago, when the Umbrella Movement took place in Hong Kong, the police arrested hundreds of people,' said the diplomat. 'But they couldn't charge them as the protesters were all wearing masks, failing to prove that they were protesting,' she said. 'So this time the police are trying to identify as many faces as possible.'

As the riot police urged the protesters to disperse, the uniformed policemen began to raise their monopods and cameras higher for a wider shot of the action. James took a quick scan of the frontline. Every face was well covered up. He then started to retreat from the standoff zone, walking towards the back of the group. The majority of the protesters also wore masks. But what intrigued him more was how it wasn't just youngsters in the mix. Young people, mostly students, were forming a barricade with railings dismantled from pedestrian sidewalks, trash cans, whatever large objects they could gather as the first line of defence when the riot police charged. Others who looked slightly older were responsible for giving first aid to the wounded; the middle-aged and elders were handing out food and water. It was a mixed bunch, but they were united by a common cause.

James pulled out his yellow press vest from his backpack. After putting it on hastily, he approached a middle-aged woman who was handing out water bottles to others.

'Hello ma'am,' James began. 'I'm James from the *Herald.* May I ask you a few questions on the record?'

'Sure,' the woman said. 'I'm not afraid. Got nothing to hide too!'

'Your name and age please.'

'I'm Grace Cheung, fifty-six years old.'

'Why are you handing out these water bottles?'

'Well . . . I had to do something to help out the young people . . . I can't fight with them on the frontline! So I've decided to supply water to them.'

'Did you buy all that yourself?' James asked, pointing to three dozen-sized boxes of bottled water behind her.

'Yes, I did.'

'Why are you doing this?'

'It's damn bloody simple,' Grace said, raising her pitch. 'I don't want my two sons to live in a world without freedom. This battle is for you, for your generation.' Grace paused for a bit before she continued. 'Protest is how people communicate in a democratic society. China should respect that if it really wants to maintain "one country, two systems" until 2047.'

'Who do you represent, young man?' an elderly man's voice interrupted the interview from behind.

'The *Herald*,' James mumbled, turning his body only slightly, to shield his eyes directly from the scorching sun rays.

'Oh, you work for that China state media?' the man said, with his face mildly amused. 'Make sure you try to report what you saw today,' he said. 'I was a journalist too. There is always a way to fight back.'

Before James could respond, warnings for protesters to retreat started blasting from police loudspeakers.

'Back off! I said back off or we will fire tear gas,' an officer hollered as the police hoisted the black flag, a signal that they would fire tear gas soon.

James rushed back to the frontline to capture the moment of the scene. Minor clashes were already taking place as both sides were becoming increasingly violent, with the police threatening to fire live bullets as protesters did the same with bricks.

'The extradition law will hasten China's total control of the city,' a protester cried out.

'Back off!' the police yelled.

'Fight for freedom,' the protester retorted, refusing to back off. Tensions were soaring.

Bang! The police fired off the first round of tear gas, leaving most of the street shrouded in smoke and turning the financial district into a swath of the grey battlefield. Under the chill of the gas that spread over the area, James fumbled into his backpack to find the gas mask provided by the *Herald*. The smoke spread slowly like a snake slithering towards its prey. Those around him began to fade away from his sight. Then came the pain.

Cough, he choked as the sting of the tear gas hit his eyes and nose. By the time he tried to put on his mask, the area around him was enveloped by tear gas, burning his eyes, nose and throat. The pain numbed his senses as he could no longer hear people screaming around him. Bullets travelled in a linear manner killing one at a time, but gas spread in all directions damaging hundreds in one go. The police fired tear gas nonstop for the next few minutes, with little remorse or sympathy.

Clang! A tear gas canister fell less than a metre from James, rolled towards him before it was stopped by his right foot. The white fumes began to billow up, the smell of more gas, in combination with the acrid gunpowder pierced James' brain via his nostrils. It was like he had swallowed fire. He instinctively kicked the gas can away from him and began to back away as tears and mucus flowed uncontrollably down his reddened face. Tears blinded his sight and he tumbled. He struggled to crawl away from the chaos as fast as he could, amid the cries and wailings of the screaming crowds.

Clang! Another canister fell within earshot of him. This time, the cloud of white fume was so powerful and close that it struck him out quickly and he lost consciousness.

When he reopened his eyes, he found himself in temporary safety behind a fortress of umbrellas shielding him from tear gas and bean bags that continued to fly over the crowds. Two of the protesters had placed one of their own air filters on him as they tried to fix James' mask where the filter was detached.

'You all right?' one of them asked, offering James a bottle of water. 'Stay low while we fix your mask,' he added.

James opened his eyes weakly. He desperately wanted to see what was happening around him, but the sting in his eyes left him with a blurred vision. He worried about how accurately he would recall what he experienced.

Another protester poured water on James's face to wash away the residual tear gas.

'I think they have put an old air filter here,' a protester said. 'We got some spares. Take this.' The protesters stayed with James for another fifteen minutes before leaving.

'Thank you guys,' James said, grateful to the young protesters.

'You think you're all right now?'

'Yeah.'

'We have to go now. Don't get hurt,' one of the protesters said as they left with their umbrellas as shields.

The protest turned ugly over the next few hours. It became a war zone. The police fired water cannons with blue dye, as well as more tear gas and bean bags. Angry young protesters retaliated with bricks and even petrol bombs, but it was clear that their vulnerability had been exposed.

'Charge!' The police then ran to the protesters with their billies and started to beat up whoever came into sight. The attacks weren't limited to the violent protesters but also included those giving out first aid, food and water.

'Please stop,' an elderly woman cried out to the police who were unmoved by her plea as they continued to beat her up. Her grandson jumped in, cowering over his grandmother as a shield. He was also ruthlessly beaten till he bled, causing the elderly woman to blackout at the sight of the pool of blood gushing out from the back of his skull.

Nearby, a handful of young protesters had blocked the entrances to the Admiralty subway station with plants, cardboard boxes and other objects before torching one of them.

James, astounded at how quickly these events took place around him, collected his strings in the field and wrote his article, filing it to his editors in the office. It was already 9 p.m.

* * *

Speechless. Shock ran through James as he read his published story in the *Herald* the next morning. The distortion began with the headline that read: *Radical core of Hong Kong protesters who trashed the city's legislature was prepared to die for their cause* and construed the protesters as *mobsters* throughout the entire article.

'Unbelievable,' James raged as he smouldered with resentment to how the editors distorted his report. Consumed with acrimony and humiliation, he went to work.

Once back in the office, he pulled his supervisor Byron aside.

'What on earth is going on here?' he asked.

'It was an instruction from the higher-ups,' Byron said, avoiding eye contact. 'Think debate's over here.'

Feeling some sense of guilt, Byron forwarded an e-mail that Theresa had sent to the duty editors.

Dear editors and colleagues,

Please note we should never call anyone taking part in this movement 'protesters', especially when these mobsters are attacking the police by throwing petrol bombs and bricks, threatening our safety.

They should be called 'masked radicals'. Remember this when you write your headlines, edit stories and send out story alerts. This is the final decision made by senior editors and it must be followed.

Best,
Theresa

'There was nothing we could do,' Byron remarked to James later. 'The e-mail was sent to the copy editors as well and they changed the line without telling us.'

Unable to contain his fury, James charged towards Theresa, who was by the counter at one of the common areas grinding coffee beans with her plugged in earpods blaring Karl Jenkins's choral *The Peacemakers*. Boiling, James wasn't bothered that he was disrupting her moment of morning peace.

'I'd like to know what happened to my coverage,' he asked quite aggressively, ignoring any pleasantries whatsoever.

Theresa stopped grinding her coffee beans. His attitude instantly sparked off her anger and the urge to turn the tables back on him.

'I have to say . . . ' Theresa began. 'I was very disappointed in you.'

'Your accounts were problematic; they portrayed a false image of the protests. They legitimize the violence of these separatists and don't give a truthful picture about what's going on here to our international audience,' she asserted despite having not once set foot in a protest zone.

'Your story was lacking balance. What about the 70-year-old who was beaten to his death by protesters? And the man who was set on fire? What about the numerous cases of people being beaten and shops vandalized simply because they have connections to the mainland?' she went on, echoing the editorials of a state media.

'I included those too,' James pointed out. 'My question is why did you take out the other accounts that I saw?'

'That is not my point,' Theresa stopped him.

'Here, look at this,' she said as she took out her phone. 'This is my grandma's place. Look at what the radicals did,' she began showing the reporter a series of photos in her gallery, shots of a vandalized house taken from various angles.

'This is the truth. This is what happened to my grandparents! These rioters vandalized my grandma's place and threatened her life. They are radicals and terrorists. Full stop. No more debate here.'

'Well, I think you can at least try to make our coverage balanced,' James argued.

'I have made my moral judgement. And that judgement is final.'

'A *moral judgement*?' James retorted. 'So what you're saying is that you make judgements about stories before we publish them and get us to only write stories that support your opinion?'

'Get out,' Theresa cut him short. 'Stop wasting my time,' she said, turning bright red as she walked towards the meeting room, one hand with the grinder, another with her empty coffee mug.

* * *

James struggled with boiling anger for the next few days. He could barely breathe. Theresa and her narratives made him feel wretched, lethargic, even broken. What was more infuriating for him during those hot summer weeks was how the *Herald* turned a blind eye to allegations of rampant police sexual assaults on protesters they arrested and took into custody. In all the incidents reported, the police flatly denied all allegations of wrongdoings on the basis of inconclusive evidence. It reiterated that its use of weapons aligned with safety guidelines and continued to label protesters as 'radicals', 'mobsters', 'rioters' or 'terrorists'. 'The Hong Kong police, as always, is committed to protecting the safety of this city, upholding law and order under the "one country, two systems" principle,' said a spokesman at a regular press briefing, in response to allegations that mainland Chinese officers had infiltrated the local force, after videos showing a pair of officers in Hong Kong riot police uniform hollering at protesters, 'Back off! Back off!' in Mandarin went viral.

Public outrage, on the other hand, exploded, setting off some of the most violent face-offs between the protesters and the police. Despite the increased use of violence by young demonstrators, public opinion polls showed that far more people blamed the police than protesters. The *Herald* stood steadfast behind the official line of the force. It also hyped up the argument that the protesters' increased violence inflicted vast economic damage and adversely impacted society, justifying the police's actions to restore order. 'The protests have sent Hong Kong to its biggest economic recession in decades . . . ' appeared in almost every story published on the protests.

'If you compare the Hong Kong police to say, forces in the West in confronting riots, our officers are already very restrained,' Vijay told a group of frontline Hong Kong desk reporters covering the unrest. 'We need to view the situation in proper context and objectively.'

With that, the *Herald*'s effort to give a voice to the police was no longer subtle. As the rift between the public and the police widened, a similar divide was emerging in the newsroom—journalists sympathetic to the democracy cause and those who weren't. Some fought with editors who were accommodating to the government, while another group focused on producing stories that helped shift the narrative to favour the police, the government and ultimately, Beijing. And it all began with a mysterious closed-door meeting between the deputy police commissioner and the *Herald*'s top editors.

* * *

'Welcome to the *Herald*,' said Theresa standing at the entrance, smiling from ear to ear. Her voice was a couple of octaves higher, affectedly lively and energetic, but her body language said otherwise. She bit her lower lip and held her breath, a sense of anxiety hanging over her. Her hands were clasped and she straightened her back a few times as if to demonstrate her respect for the guests.

Three men in dark suits—one in black and the other two in different shades of navy—walked into the *Herald*'s office. They looked relaxed and confident in contrast to Theresa's trying effort to mask her stress. They moved towards her slowly, scanning their eyes around to size up the environment.

'I like your perfume,' said one of the two men in navy, staring at her a little over her shoulder.

Theresa felt a chill down her spine, but she maintained her calm as much as she could to appear professional.

'Thank you,' she said as she regained her composure.

'Gentlemen, this way please,' she picked up her pace and stepped ahead of the group, ushering the guests to the Shanghai meeting room. It was the largest meeting room in the office and located close to the main entrance for guests to retain some privacy during their visits, especially for meetings involving sensitive issues. The editors had held many such meetings over the past year or so, but those were times when political stakes were less high.

As the three guests entered the room, Pax, Vijay and four Hong Kong and China desk editors who had been waiting stood up to greet their special visitors.

'Welcome, a very warm welcome to you all,' Pax told the three men, looking at them intently. Editors who attended then recalled that the room was filled with a strange sense of tension, with the top editors looking nervous and somewhat resolute. Pax grinned, cracking his dried lips while a few of the editors smiled thinly.

'It's our pleasure to be here,' said the second man in a navy suit, whom editors recognized as the Hong Kong Police Deputy Commissioner Ronny Yip.

'Please, sit down and have some tea,' Theresa interjected, not wanting to be left out in the exchange.

'Thank you,' he curtly replied and turned slightly. 'Oh right . . . Mr Yong, it must be your first time meeting Mr Wang. Let me introduce Mr Wang from our national security department,' Yip gestured to the man in a black suit on his right.

Wang nodded, without saying a word. Yip went on to introduce the man who complimented Theresa's scent as Wang's deputy.

Pax and Theresa once again forced a wide smile as they tried to calm their nerves. Of course, they knew who Wang was. Wang Tao was a deputy minister ranking official from the state security department with oversight on Hong Kong affairs. They briefly shook Wang's hands and sensing his aloofness, decided against making small talk.

Wang sat down next to Yip, with his deputy on the other side and crossed his arms. He seemed to be enjoying the strange tension he brought to the room, the editors thought. They, however, enjoyed how Wang's presence—and to an extent, Yip's as well—humbled the masthead editors, especially Theresa who was usually short with her team members when things did not go her way. Yip glanced at those sitting before him, but never gave more than two seconds of eye contact with anyone. He also didn't waste time and quickly moved on to his agenda.

'I have always admired those who work in a newsroom,' he said, but this time staring Pax in the eye. His eyes were cold and restless.

'I think you people have what I call a highly noble profession. Your job is to find out the truth for the prosperity of this country. I fully trust you to do the same during this time of uncertainty.

'I have to say though . . . I am a little concerned about some of the narratives of so-called international media these days. They are writing stories based on fake claims of terrorism and helping the rioters justify their criminal acts.'

Yip then crossed his legs, pulled out his Mont Blanc pen from the inside pocket of his jacket and started pointing it at the editors.

'This clearly is America's propaganda,' he said firmly. 'What we need is objective, balanced reporting here. Let me elaborate on that. We need an alternative narrative against fake news. Victimizing these terrorists only justifies their actions and that threatens our social stability. We must stop that from happening.

'Just look at the economic damage they've done!' Yip raised his voice, appearing emotional. 'Will you really let this continue? Where is your patriotism? Media should play its role to protect our national interests!'

Theresa nodded vigorously and appreciatively.

'Don't get me wrong though,' the deputy police commissioner continued, twirling his pen before it fell on the table with a sharp *smack*.

'All I'm asking here is that you report what is happening in a fair and objective manner, which is one of the fundamentals of journalism, right? Any institution that fails to do so shouldn't exist.'

Pax didn't say a word. Theresa, on the other hand, jumped on her chance to outshine Pax.

'I agree with you completely,' she blurted out. 'These youngsters do not understand what they are jeopardizing. It's their jobs and future that they are putting at risk here.

'I think what we need is an accurate narrative so that international audiences know the sufferings of ordinary Hongkongers. The silent majority, I call it. You can count on us for that.'

The room went eerily silent and no one spoke for the next two minutes. Wang said nothing but continued to look at everyone in the eyes like a human scanner, almost like he was profiling each editor in his mind. The meeting was pretty much a one-way lecture, with brief interjections from Theresa and was wrapped up in about twenty minutes. Pax saw the visitors to the elevator and did not return till another hour later.

'Where is the principle of journalism here?' James asked Mary after he crossed path with the departing officials at the reception area where he picked up a courier delivery. 'How are we supposed to play the role of watchdog when we openly invite those officials to our office and have an editorial meeting with them?'

Mary, with her skinny physique that belied the resilience she had as a reporter, looked tiredly at James.

'I think we're done here,' she said after a long moment of contemplation.

The masthead editors again didn't mention the meeting to the rest of the newsroom, although word got out of what was discussed, which reporters interpreted as veiled coercion from the top law enforcement institutions in Hong Kong and Beijing. No one spoke further or questioned about the meeting after that. This was because reporters had become lethargic after years of seeing similar occurrences in the office. It was definitely an evolving change that mirrored the broader political development sweeping across Hong Kong.

A few weeks later, officials from Hong Kong's China Liaison Office joined in and observed the *Herald*'s 9.30 a.m. daily news conference at Pax's invitation. The editor-in-chief thought the encounter was no more than a harmless relationship-building opportunity, but reporters who saw the visitors listening to editors deliberate on how to report the news that morning were aghast. It went against all the principles of their profession.

'I'd like to have more of these conferences in the future,' the officials said after the meeting.

'That would be our pleasure,' Pax replied warmly.

Where are our ethics as a media organization? Reporters questioned with disgust. Profoundly upset, one of them leaked the episode to a widely-read local media outlet, the *Hong Kong Mail*.

The next day, the *Hong Kong Mail*, pulling no punches, reported the incident with a story to condemn the editors at the *Herald* of compromising journalistic ethics under a headline that read: *The Herald invites Chinese officials to its editorial meeting.*

The *Herald*'s newsroom was downside up the next day. Pax and Theresa boiled with rage, forming a rare alliance.

'Who leaked this?' Theresa yelled across the newsroom, throwing the *Hong Kong Mail* on her desk. 'This is based on fake claims,' she insisted. 'We have never jeopardized our editorial integrity,' she continued yelling into the air.

Her assertion was followed a few hours later with an angry e-mail from Steve.

To: editorial@herald.com
From: steve.hsieh@herald.com

Dear Herald Family,

Hola! Hope everyone's well in this difficult time. As your team leader, I want to make a few things crystal clear with regards to that tabloid story about us. We normally do not respond to these kinds of things, but we thought this was an exception as it was a total lie, a fabrication—everything but the truth.

I have full trust in the independence of our reporting. Also, I fully support our mastheads and their news judgement. I think such distractions will continue as our scope of influence grows in the future. Let's stay strong and pursue our core values of seeking the truth and fairness in journalism.

Ciao,
Steve

Momentarily after Steve's e-mail, Pax also had his shot.

From: Pax.yong@herald.com
To: editorial@herald.com
Cc: steve.hsieh@herald.com

Dear Comrades,

Today, we saw a perfect example of fake news. The Hong Kong Mail published a fabricated fictional story claiming that we have a close alignment with Beijing. We have demanded corrections to be made immediately.

Officials from the Liaison Office in Hong Kong wanted to visit our office first. They contacted us about a month ago, stating one of the officials was leaving the city permanently. We offered them a farewell tour yesterday. The officials arrived at around 9 am, coinciding with our morning news meeting. So naturally, the officials happened to observe the meeting as we run our daily routine. You all know that the reason we have visitors to our office is a reflection of our core value of transparency.

Shortly after the meeting, we invited the visitors to bid farewell to the departing official in a meeting room. We then firmly demanded and pressured them to have more transparent visa policies, which have personally impacted our editorial staff.

Please feel free to reach out to me if you need further clarification on this matter.

Best,
Pax

Pax's claim was only partially true and showed again his comfort with stretching the truth. The office had hosted officials from different countries, but having them participate in the editorial meeting was a rare move. Pax and the other two mastheads weren't bothered about paying extra attention to inviting Chinese officials to the office or editorial meetings, even though the company was already facing heavy criticism for promoting China's 'soft power' since Arcade took over.

Neither did they show any remorse after the *Hong Kong Mail's* report.

'It's hopeless,' Mary told James who came by her desk to get a contact from her.

'Yeah, they're trying really hard, aren't they?' he replied cynically.

'I thought they would be ashamed,' she hissed. 'Clearly, I was wrong.'

'Wait, it was . . . you?'

'Shhh,' Mary shushed him. 'Transparency? They probably don't think it's a problem, or that the media is a watchdog of the government. They couldn't care less about journalism—or rather they only care about their own interests. Period.'

But what Pax and Theresa did learn was they needed to implement measures in a more indirect manner to obscure their true intentions and avoid head-on resistance from reporters to carry out reporting assignments that fulfilled Beijing's agenda.

In fact, five years ago, they faced a similar backlash. Theresa attempted to control the narrative of reporting the anniversary of the Tiananmen Square Massacre by whitewashing the number of deaths in the crackdown, a figure that varied between a few hundred to thousands depending on the source cited. She tried to pare down the numbers widely accepted by international organizations, to fall in line with China's 'official' lower figures. Many reporters thought it was problematic, but Theresa deflected their concerns by questioning the accuracy of some reporters' references.

'We need to have one figure throughout our stories. We can't have figure A in one story and figure B in another.'

Since then, Theresa had taken on a more meticulous strategy. She mixed the pro and anti-Beijing narratives in stories to appease the 'naysayers'. She also started to run what appeared to be pro-democracy opinion pieces in the newspaper's heavily one-sided opinion section maintaining the ratio of seven to three. But when it came to sensitive issues like the Hong Kong protests, she didn't hesitate to take Beijing's side, fully aware of what was expected of her during those times. Her ultimate job was to promote China and reshape international opinion on controversial issues to favour Beijing's interests, such as China's sovereignty in Xinjiang, Tibet, parts of Kashmir, South China Sea, Taiwan and of course Hong Kong.

Strengthening a positive image of China was an insidious crusade that the *Herald* had launched ever since it was taken over by Arcade—to conquer foreign minds with Beijing's narratives and therefore paving the way to pursue the nation's interests. Theresa, who was promoted to deputy editor after the acquisition, was responsible for justifying China's measures of subversion, bullying and pressure, ultimately aimed at attaining Beijing's goal—that the international community would self-censor what they say about China, for fear of losing funding, access or influence.

Interestingly, James sensed that it was also the same fear that drove Theresa to work harder to fulfil her duty inside the newsroom. She feared losing influence and not having political access, he thought, which made her take a more intimidating and encompassing approach to push Beijing's interests. She was pressing the newsroom to dance to China's tune, without specifically being told by Beijing to do so. She assumed her act was impressing the higher-ups.

* * *

The *Herald*'s narrative on the Hong Kong police took another shift following the visit of the three law enforcement officials, eventually converging with the Chinese state media's line to demonize the protesters. It published a mix of stories, editorials and columns based on the line, with Theresa leading the charge. A little more than a week after the visit, she published a 1,700-word analysis highlighting the 'damage' generated by the protesters. In addition, she began to penalize reporters who showed even the slightest sign of sympathy to protesters, convinced, ironically, that they were incapable of impartial reporting.

'James, did you hear about Patsy?' Victor whispered, looking shocked. 'She got suspended from reporting.'

Patsy Kwok was a Hong Kong desk reporter covering the protests. She was one of the first reporters in Hong Kong to learn that Chinese immigration officials at the border checkpoints in Shenzhen were inspecting mobile phones of Hongkongers entering the mainland for sensitive data on the protests.

'We need to break this story,' Patsy had urged her editors, including Vijay and Theresa.

'No, we don't,' Theresa answered instantly, without waiting for Vijay to respond. 'This is a typical example of what I call a hasty reporting based on fake claims. We can't report based on just a few cases.'

'No, Theresa. This is big and this would get attention internationally. We have to break it before others do.'

'I agree with Theresa this time, Pasty,' Vijay said, trying his best to stay relevant. 'How about . . . '

'Bring me at least five more stories on your case,' Theresa said, snubbing Vijay again. 'I want them with the interviewees' full names, ages, where they live and what they do. If you have all that, then we will run the story.'

'Fine.'

Pasty returned two days later with six more cases containing named sources, meeting all the editors' demands.

'There you go,' she said sarcastically with a tint of exasperation.

Theresa frowned for a while and closed her eyes in contemplation. A few seconds later she finally spoke.

'No.'

'What do you mean *no*?'

'This is still based on some people's perspectives of the incidents and that's not enough evidence or representation for accusing Chinese authorities. What we need here is a case based on factual evidence.'

'That's absurd. We have more than enough incidents here.'

'That still doesn't convince me.'

Three days later, another international media outlet broke the news. The *Herald* then followed with its story by Patsy with the same information she had reported to her editors. The editors had dodged the responsibility of breaking what they feared was a sensitive story that would upset the higher-ups.

Pasty was a passionate reporter who tried to understand the protesters in her reporting work. She actively tweeted about the frontline, including posts showing police brutality that caused tremendous discomfort for the mastheads. Theresa was looking for the opportunity to rein her in and it came mid-August.

On her day off, Patsy tweeted that she joined the protests as a demonstrator. The tweet sent Theresa shooting through the roof and she immediately called Patsy to give her a piece of her mind about how inappropriate it was for reporters to take part in the protest.

'It will undermine the objectivity of our coverage of the protest,' Theresa said. 'Your action is a threat to our collective efforts to maintain the coverage as objective and neutral as possible. I won't allow you to cover the protests any more.'

'Fine. I won't,' Patsy agreed without hesitation because Theresa had a valid point.

Another two days later, on her way home from work, Patsy came across another round of protests which erupted into police violence where a group of armed policemen were relentlessly beating up an unarmed protester. She recorded a video of the scene and as she agreed with Theresa, didn't upload it onto social media. Instead, she sent the footage to her desk editors thinking they could use it for publication. Within an hour, Patsy had Theresa yelling at her on the phone.

'You are a disgrace! You failed us again by being at the protest scene and recording the kind of footage that may mislead the public.'

The reporter was stumped but didn't back off. 'I think you should use all resources available to you if you want to produce a comprehensive news piece,' she tried to rationalize with the editor.

'I don't want to hear your opinion,' Theresa roared. 'This is about you violating our core journalistic ethics. You are suspended from work and that starts now!'

Patsy left the company and later joined an international wire service. Her departure signalled the start of a wave of resignations from the Hong Kong desk reporters disappointed by the increasing bias of the coverage. With resources stretched, the editors decided to rope in reporters from all desks to help with the live coverage of the protests.

4

Turning Points

At the *Herald*, police action had been an issue of contention ever since the demonstrations escalated when officers fired their first tear gas and rubber bullets at protesters gathered outside the LegCo building to oppose the second reading of the extradition bill. The visit of the state security official Wang Tao and the Hong Kong Deputy Police Commissioner Ronny Yip a month before the task force was established widened the divide in the newsroom. The masthead editors had always viewed the issue from the government and the force's perspective, backed by the Party. Their political stance came before the fundamental journalistic principle of balanced reporting. Stories on police action in the protests usually omitted the protesters' viewpoints and their side of the story, which enraged frontline reporters, some of whom were victims of tear gas and pepper spray, or had witnessed police action in person and seen how officers had crossed the line. Each day, James saw the nagging undercurrent in the newsroom—that he was also embroiled in—stewing more ferociously, threatening to boil over.

'The kids, including some of our reporters, are so naive and clueless. They think the Western style of democracy is what our society needs and the police are crushing their rights,' Pax lamented to Theresa and Vijay at one of their daily catch-ups after the 9.30 a.m. news conference.

'They don't realize that our power to progress is driven by us being part of China. How many other places have the world's second-largest economy backing them? None!

'And don't forget Hong Kong thrives because the police have protected us well. We are one of the safest cities in the world, 728 criminal cases per 100,000 people. The police are not our enemy. It is the external forces with the agenda to see Chinese people fail.'

Theresa could see that her boss was trying to maintain his usual calmness with increasing difficulty.

Nodding, she said, 'Reporters are sympathetic towards the protesters and anti-police. Some have even lost sight of their position when covering the demonstrations and joined in the protests. They have also been tweeting . . . and I've picked up a few problematic ones by city desk reporters and screenshot a couple of examples. Here, let me show you one.' She pulled up a screenshot on her phone and waved it before Pax and then Vijay.

'This tweet from Suzy Lin, 'Police action: oppression or protection?' That's out of line. She's representing the *Herald*, not on a democratic crusade.

'Vijay, you better keep a tighter leash,' she offhandedly added, ignoring Vijay's glare.

How dare she tell me how to do my job! And in front of Pax, he seethed with anger. He was already incensed by a number of Hong Kong desk reporters who fought with him on the narrative he wanted for the protest coverage and considered them insubordination to his authority. Now he was fuming as it gave Theresa the ammunition against him. Suzy was one of the reporters whom he had a sit-down with for a pep talk only days earlier.

'Suzy, I know you're passionate about your work and the issues you cover and that's a good thing. I appreciate you pushing out stories on social media and going the extra mile to be out at the frontline even on your days off, filing reports for us,' he told her.

'But your enthusiasm has crossed the line. Your tweets are one-sided and biased, and this harms your professional credibility more than it helps. Surely you don't want that?'

Suzy who had been a reporter for five years looked at her boss in disbelief. 'I don't understand how my comments, to create a discussion on the issues, translated to me crossing the line. Do enlighten me, please?' she said with underlying sarcasm. 'Besides, there's a disclaimer to say it doesn't represent the company.'

'Well,' Vijay replied slowly, 'you should know our editorial stance. It's not a simple case of black and white. You're an experienced reporter, you should understand the context here and know what to do.'

A month later, Suzy left the *Herald* to join another media organization, where she continued to report on Hong Kong's political crisis, winning awards for her writing. Her resignation left Vijay relieved, as well as pleased that he had one more spot that he could fill with his own people.

But at the meeting with Pax and Theresa, Vijay wasn't one to let Theresa off easily.

'You may or may not know, I spoke to Suzy a few days ago and the tweet had been deleted. I guess the screenshot you have is dated, Theresa,' he countered, with a slight smug in his tone.

* * *

The question of whether the Hong Kong police resorted to excessive force dominated conversations both online and offline in the city, to an extent, beyond. Just as it was in the *Herald* newsroom, the split was between those who supported the police and the camp who stood on the side of the protesters. James debated on the issue countless times with colleagues. He tried to maintain a certain level of open-mindedness towards how the police had acted, convinced that it was necessary for professional purposes. At a more personal level, he found that it was increasingly hard when what he saw on the streets constantly threatened the balance he tried to keep. The events on the sweltering Hong Kong summer night of 31 August brought months of political unrest to new heights—a turning point.

On that fateful night, scores of anti-riot police and members of the Special Tactical Squad known as 'raptors' tore through the Prince Edward subway station in the Kowloon area to hunt down anti-government protesters after the operator of the Mass Transit Railway (MTR) reported vandalism at the premises. The police ravaged through the platforms and train cars, swinging their batons and guzzling out pepper sprays indiscriminately at civilians and anyone who looked like a protester. It was a long night for the city as millions of people were glued to their mobile phones and devices, watching live recordings of the heart-wrenching scenes showing fearful civilians begging the raptors to stop. For many, the police, which previously held the role of protectors, were now the attackers.

'Please, please, I beg you, stop!' One video showed a group of four people cornered and hunkered down in a train car, huddling together as three raptors sprayed pepper and clubbed them continuously with their batons.

'The police pelted tear gas and pepper spray at close range, no more than two metres away. They didn't care whether we were protesters, reporters or just commuters,' recalled one journalist.

When unrest began to grip Hong Kong in June, the MTR was the reliable mode of transport that carried protesters to demonstration venues, disperse from the scene or shuttle between rallies in minutes. Intensified police crackdown had turned the stations into battlegrounds, strewn with tear gas canisters, broken glass, debris and blood. Over the course of the month, frustrated young demonstrators had begun to take aim at the MTR, which they perceived to have conspired with authorities to stymie protests following a few occasions when riot police fired tear gas at protesters inside the stations. They burnt station exits, damaged ticketing machines and service centres, as well as turnstiles.

The Prince Edward station was a complete mayhem that summer night; by the time medics cleared out the last injured person around 1 a.m. the following day, the standoff had lasted three hours. In an early morning briefing, the police told reporters that officers used their professional experience to distinguish protesters who had changed their clothes to pass off as regular commuters. 'But we concede that it was difficult to be absolutely sure,' said the police spokesman.

The 31 August attacks, as they came to be known, shook the community. Hongkongers felt it was another step too far by the police. The different tallies of injured people from the police, hospital authority and fire services department fuelled speculation that the night took three lives, which the authorities colluded with the MTR to cover up. The force rejected the rumoured deaths as malicious smears and the MTR—a listed company on the Hong Kong stock exchange—refused to publicly disclose CCTV footage that could shed light on what had transpired at the station. Overnight, the already waning police credibility sank to a new low. For days, the exits of the station became makeshift shrines where Hongkongers laid wreaths and flowers for the three people who were perceived to be unaccounted for on the night of the attacks.

Inevitably, the police's excessive use of force widened the scope of the demonstrations and moved beyond opposition to the extradition bill. It triggered the call for an independent inquiry into the force's brutality, which formed the foundation of the protesters' five core demands under the slogan 'Five demands, not one less'. They were the withdrawal of the extradition bill, retraction of the characterization of the 12 June protests as 'riots' by the authorities, release and exoneration of those arrested, an independent commission of inquiry into police conduct, the resignation of the Chief Executive and universal suffrage for LegCo and chief executive elections. In the end, only one of the five demands was met. The bill was withdrawn by the Hong Kong Government.

Criticism against the police reached a fever pitch in the days immediately following the 31 August attacks, shrouded by a widely perceived cover-up of three deaths that night. Pax couldn't stop worrying about the odds in the society stacking up against the force, the government and ultimately the Party.

Just weeks earlier, the *Herald* had published a long analysis lauding how the police, albeit 'embattled', was holding the city from the 'brink of collapse'.

That had hardly helped defused public anger and worse still, it was the start of the newspaper's credibility tailspinning to devastation, James had thought.

'I think we have to write a couple more editorials this week, to support the police,' Pax told the editorial writers, who were responsible for crafting the publication's view, on the Monday after the Prince

Edward station attacks over the weekend. Pax met with these editorial writers daily to deliberate issues to opine and make clear the publication's stance. The other two mastheads participated in these meetings, but it was Pax who decided on the issue and the position to take for all editorials.

The first editorial that he commissioned defending the police dated back to mid-June after the force began firing tear gas. It echoed police appeal to protesters to refrain from violence and gave no consideration to the other side of the story. Thereafter, it formed the basis of the newspaper's position.

'The police are just doing their job to maintain law and order. Without them, we could have more trouble from these radicals,' he rationalized to the editorial writers with a hint of indignation that Monday morning. 'People are blindly blaming the police. They are simply lying when they say the police are behind the coverups.'

'That's easy. We can argue the police's case by advocating for an independent inquiry into police action,' suggested one of the writers, Samuel Lee. 'If the authorities had nothing to hide, an inquiry would clear any allegations.'

Pax raised an eyebrow slightly. 'Appreciate that suggestion, but we shouldn't be seen as giving in to the protesters. If we go on this track, we're effectively saying the police are wrong to be just doing their job. That won't be fair.'

'What then do you think would be fair?' Samuel asked, chafed by what he saw as another of Pax's lame excuses to side with the institutions.

It wasn't just the stance that got to him, but the editor-in-chief's relentlessness to find every opportunity to spin a positive story about the police. A month ago, he published a leader praising the police for its restraint to refrain from bloodshed after protesters had vandalized the LegCo building and defaced the Hong Kong SAR emblem. When there wasn't an incident to fall back on to rave about police work, he commissioned an editorial praising the calmness and soft-spokenness of the police spokesman at the force's daily press conference, during the months of the protests.

The highlight of the leader read:

> *As the voice of dissent rises among young protesters, with demands that underscore their disconnect with facts and the reality that Hong Kong is a Special Administrative Region of China, a sound of calmness is invaluable. That of Chief Superintendent Jimmy Chow is an exemplar of what we need right now.*
>
> *Over the past months, Chief Superintendent Chow has consistently and patiently explained police action at the force's daily press conference, even when the heat rose on some days.*

The editorial made the *Herald* a laughing stock, with not just Samuel's friends in the industry but also those in other professions.

'Sam, the police don't really need a Police Public Relations Branch; they have the *Herald* and you guys have a bigger and global reach too!' a high-ranking civil servant he had known since high school had teased. Samuel let out a small snort at Pax's definition of fairness within earshot of the editor.

Pax ignored his displeasure and went on, 'For today's leader, let's just go on the line that both sides need to take a step back, especially the protesters, fuelling accusations without one shred of proof. John, can you take this?'

Turning back to Samuel, 'Sam, I need you to look at a leader on typhoon preparedness, given that it is typhoon season,' he said with a smile in an apparent gesture to appease Samuel, who gave a slight shrug.

He was accustomed to the editor's self-censorship under the guise of what the writers called Pax's 'intellectual rationalization'. He was more than glad to be spared the agony of penning a police-complimenting editorial he couldn't agree with.

Editorial writers were a handful of Pax's direct reports. His other direct report was the business editor, even though he had minimal experience with business and financial journalism.

Hong Kong was one of the world's leading global financial centres, where news and information surrounding business activities were critical. The danger of Edward Murphy's inexperience and ignorance was more far-reaching than Pax realized. He was happy with the performance of the business editor who was unqualified for the role, but knew exactly how to please Pax with the right words and pro-business coverage.

'We're in the process of getting an interview with the Russian president and I want you involved. We want an elevated point of view on geopolitics,' Murphy said to a senior reporter.

'Right, we should include in the piece the energy and resources companies, the conflicts and issues at stake,' the reporter enthused.

'No, no, no energy companies. It's a geopolitics piece and nothing to do with these companies,' Murphy rejected. His perspective showed his lack of knowledge and ability to connect the dots, the reporter concluded.

As a result, the quality of the *Herald*'s business coverage deteriorated; business stories did not question the soundness of corporate governance and regurgitated what companies wanted to say. They went against the principles of journalism but agreed with Pax's pro-institution stance and how he ran the newsroom. He kept a relaxed supervision over Murphy in contrast to the editorial writers—his conduits to communicating the right messages to the higher-ups.

Pax knew loyalty was foremost for the Party—the world's second-largest political party with more than 90 million members. Membership brings benefits and a powerful network. Like millions of his fellow members, Pax was deeply indoctrinated by the propaganda machine, seeds of deep-rooted nationalism sown from a young age. Such indoctrination effectively dulled one's ability to think critically. By then, the Party had vehemently pledged its support to the Hong Kong police.

An excerpt of the *Herald*'s editorial in September read:

> *Increasingly, criticisms and questions are raised over police actions and therefore its credibility, as the unrest widens in our city. The force has attempted to give answers but many remain unconvinced, continuing to badger and hold the police accountable for the alleged deaths of three people in the Prince Edwards MTR station attacks, albeit the absence of evidence. Such unfounded and irresponsible accusations against the force*

are a contradiction to the strength of the rule of law, a principle that many protesters claim is the bedrock of their movement.

Effective law enforcement is critical amid Hong Kong's unfolding crisis, but public perception and support for the police to do that is just as important to maintain order so that there is normality in society.

While the occasions when police opted for a low-key approach through verbal persuasion to ease tensions have won praise, they are far and few. If the majority of protesters, including the radicals, could be persuaded, the crisis would have been defused. Because that wasn't the case, in reality, officers on the frontline need to rely on their professionalism and judgement on-site to determine tactics and deployment.

Our force is our last line of defence. They can't keep our city safe if Hongkongers work against them in doing their job to ensure law and order.

'How can they?' James growled under his breath after reading the editorial. He looked around at his colleagues seated nearby. The entire newsroom appeared unusually quiet and even subdued, in contrast to the intensifying rage against the police that swept across the city the week following the Prince Edward station attacks. It culminated over the weekend with another round of protests at the Hong Kong International Airport. The earlier protests in July and August led to major disruptions and thousands of travellers stranded. James himself was stranded at the Shanghai airport when his flight home after a reporting assignment was cancelled.

The latest and third round of airport demonstrations spilt onto the roads leading to the terminal. Roadblocks were set up and riot police dispersed some of the protesters. There were many who trespassed onto the tracks of the Airport Express line, causing suspension of the airport train services. Protesters retreated to the closest MTR station—Tung Chung—only to be met with similar action from the police's Special Tactical Squad as seen at the Prince Edward station. Again, the MTR closed the Tung Chung station, leaving protesters stranded. Some retreated, walking 15 km along the North Lantau Highway towards Tsing Ma Bridge, one of the world's longest span suspension bridges, or by taking ferries back to Hong Kong island. When word got out that riot police had been deployed in Central piers to track down young protesters, sympathizers mobilized volunteer drivers to pick up protesters—an effort some dubbed as 'Hong Kong's Dunkirk'. James monitored the events closely on television and his phone at home that weekend, touched by the unity he saw of Hongkongers coming together.

As the police adopted more hard-handed tactics to deal with protesters, the Chinese government began arm-twisting Hong Kong-based companies to clamp down on the people's demands for civil liberties and to take sides. China's aviation authority ordered the city's carrier, Cathay Pacific, to remove any cabin crew who supported the movement from its mainland-bound flights as a measure to 'improve flight safety and security'. Long-serving staff were also fired because of their political stance. Big global multinational, regional and local companies took out full-page advertisement space or issued statements to declare opposition against violence and support for national sovereignty. One example was PwC, one of the Big Four accounting firms.

> *In response to an advertisement in Hong Kong by a group of unnamed individuals claiming to be employees of the Big Four accounting firms, PwC emphasizes that the advertisement does not represent the firm's position. We firmly oppose any actions and statements that challenge national sovereignty. The rule of law and the 'One Country, Two Systems' principle are the foundations of maintaining stability and harmony in Hong Kong. We condemn all violent and illegal activities and misleading statements.*

After days of Chinese state media bashing the MTR for being too soft and an 'accomplice' of protesters, it shifted its stance and began shutting stations around protest zones as a 'prudent' measure. Throughout September and October, the MTR frequently shuttered its gates and suspended services with little forewarning. Daily services for a while terminated at 9 p.m. forcing many employers, especially those in the retail and services industries to close early so that staff can catch the last train. The abrupt and ad hoc shutdowns or suspended services sometimes occurred in the day, usually when stations became battlegrounds between protesters and the police.

* * *

The *Herald* photographer and task force member Alan Choi experienced police brutality first-hand two weeks after the Prince Edward attacks. As a Hongkonger, Alan didn't consider himself anti-China, but he was against the current regime's increasingly hard-handed way of rule, which he believed thwarted the progress of the mainland and in turn his city.

The morning after Edwin Law's body was found—before the task force was formed—Alan was assigned by his editor to photograph detectives and crime scene examiners combing the Yau Tong Bay area for more evidence. A three-hour search yielded nothing and the police wrapped up the operation. Alan headed towards Yau Tong station to take the subway to his next assignment. Photographers usually had back to back assignments and were hard-pressed for time.

At the entrance of the station, a few small groups of protesters were pacing around, their heads vigilantly scanning for police officers. They must have just completed some flash mobbing, Alan thought, as he quickened his steps towards the ticket gate. He wasn't equipped to cover a protest should one break out, having left his helmet and mask in the office.

Barely a few seconds after he tapped his smart card ticket and was about to pass through the turnstile, he felt a loud rumble of thundering footsteps behind him. A group of anti-riot police who seemed to have appeared from nowhere were charging towards the ticket gates. 'Clear out! Clear out!' they yelled to commuters at the station hall, as scores of them leapt over the ticket gates and tore down the escalators and staircases towards the two levels of platforms, firing tear gas unsparingly. Very soon dozens of young demonstrators, choking from the toxic smoke that was clouding up from the platforms, where the police had fired tear gas to impede their visibility and escape, were scrambling up the stairs and escalators, heading towards the exit.

Alan had turned around and run towards the exit, but his photojournalistic instinct slowed down his steps, despite the absence of protective gear. He began to press the shutter button of his camera incessantly, holding his breath for as long as he could to not inhale the gas that had engulfed most of the station hall. A loud continuous warning beep had gone off as an announcement boomed through the station's broadcast system: 'The station is closing because of a very serious incident. Please exit immediately!'

As he continued to snap with his camera, Alan gingerly retreated backwards. Less than ten seconds after he stepped out of the station, the shutters began to drop as the last few protesters slid under the falling gates, with several raptors closing in on them, inches away.

Clang! Alan cringed and felt a tingling numbness in his eardrums, but that was before he realized that one of the protesters was held down by the officers. The young man, whom Alan sized up to be no older than a university freshman, was quickly pinned down on his front by three of the officers, his face smashed hard onto the ground.

One of them held him down pushing his knee onto the young man's upper back, while another officer clubbed him mercilessly on the head with a baton. While the protester gasped for breath and struggled to break free, the third officer grabbed his groin and gave it a hard squeeze. The young man screeched with pain, as tears poured out of his reddened eyes.

Alan couldn't believe his eyes. In the months covering the protests, he had heard numerous accounts of sexual assaults on protesters by police officers. He believed they were grave allegations and however put off he had been with the excessive violence the police had deployed, he held his reservations over such accusations.

He was now totally shaken inside, as he witnessed what had unfolded, the act visually amplified as he viewed it behind his camera lens. Before he could snap another shot, three other raptors had formed a human barricade before him to shield the assaulting officers. To make sure Alan and another photographer from a Chinese language media next to him had zero chance of recording the act, the three officers sprayed pepper at the two photographers at close range.

In less than a morning, Alan had his evidence and verified that the content of many video recordings that had shown officers deploying tear gas against nonviolent crowds and journalists—contrary to authorities' claims that the materials were doctored. He also saw first-hand sexual assault committed by an officer of the law. His eyes were burning from the excruciating sting of the pepper spray, which blinded his vision and had him gasping for air. He felt sick to his stomach, physically and mentally from what he saw, as a couple of volunteer medics came to his aid and guided him to a safer corner away from the police.

Later in the day, Alan received a call from Pax.

'Alan, I'm sorry to hear that you were pepper sprayed,' the editor said, feigning sympathy. 'I've put a call to Chief Superintendent Chow to voice our protest and they have promised to look into it. Take the next two days off,' Pax said, before he hung up, without giving Alan his chance to respond.

Alan heard nothing further about his case, nor did Pax issue a public statement of reprimand as media outlets usually did when its reporting crew were assaulted on the job. The *Herald*'s inaction was a stark contrast to the response from the Chinese media, whose photographer was also attacked by the officers. The Chinese media issued a public statement condemning the police action and demanded an apology.

Eight days later, Alan found himself becoming a member of the *Herald*'s task force to investigate the death of Edwin Law.

* * *

Edwin Law was an extrovert, well-liked by his classmates and friends. He embraced life with energy and enthusiasm. An idealist, he was fresh out of university and had just started work as a social worker, to help the underdogs from the lower stratum of society and fight for the rights of the people in his city. He came from a working-class family and lived with his parents and two younger sisters in a cluttered 400 sq ft public housing flat rented from the government—like more than 40 per cent of the population. His father was a low-ranking civil servant, while his mother worked as a part-time sales assistant in a boutique in the neighbourhood, which was at the brink of closure as business dried up amid months of unrest and the landlord was jacking up the rent.

Life was not a bed of roses for the Laws. They knew they would never be able to afford a flat of their own in Hong Kong's insanely priced property market, but both parents worked hard to give the children a good education. Because of the family's background, Edwin learned from a young age not to take anything for granted and developed a strong sense of right and wrong. The 22-year-old also inherited his parents' optimistic personalities and undeflatable resilience in any adversities.

'Son, you can choose to be either happy or unhappy and the day will still pass. Why not make every day a happy one?' his mother had taught him.

He was grateful to his parents for providing for him, even allowing him to indulge in competitive swimming since he was in primary school. The trainings and swim meets were additional financial burdens that the family could do without. Edwin, therefore, decided the only way he could repay them was to do well in school and be a useful member of society. He thought he had his future quite well planned out, until the late spring of 2019 when the first anti-extradition bill demonstrations broke out and his own political awakening that ensued in the following weeks.

By June, millions of Hongkongers—many who usually stayed out of previous political movements since China regained control of the city—had protested in one way or the other against the government and the proposed passing of the bill. For many, it was likely the last straw that broke the camel's back—the bill potentially subjects Hong Kong residents and visitors to the jurisdiction and legal system of mainland China, which would undermine the city's autonomy and people's civil liberties, as well as infringe on freedom of speech.

Days before the second reading of the bill, one million Hongkongers—one in every seven citizens—marched through the streets of Hong Kong island from the shopping area of Causeway Bay to the central business district. The government turned a blind eye and a deaf ear to the people's demand to scrap the bill. But protesters successfully halted the second reading three days later, which also marked a turning point in the peaceful movement to date—police took to tear gas to disperse the crowds sitting out at the LegCo complex and the government branded them 'rioters'. Police action fuelled anger among the people and the Chief Executive's move to suspend the bill later in the week, which stopped short of announcing a full withdrawal, only fanned public fury, driving two million people to protest a week later.

It was also the time Edwin felt something inside him snap. He had been watching live recordings of the protests, overwhelmed by the people's determination and courage, but maintained a distance literally and figuratively. As he swiped to the YouTube video on his phone the day when the police started using tear gas, the emotions and stress from what he saw made him implode. One particular scene shot from considerable height, where at least twenty anti-riot police with their shields and baton had charged towards an unarmed solo young protester on a street near the government headquarters strewn with debris, tore his heart apart. At least more than ten officers swung their batons at the young man all at the same time for no less than ten minutes. The police recorded that around 150 tear gas canisters, 'several' rounds of rubber bullets and twenty beanbag shots were fired during the protest clearance.

He read in press reports a week later that the human rights organization Amnesty International found fourteen incidents of excessive use of force by the police since that day. The force was criticized for using rubber bullets callously: shooting projectiles directly at protesters' faces; improper use of riot control agents with peaceful, unarmed passers-by being pepper-sprayed; lack of visible police identification; and using force on journalists and medics. The organization concluded that the police's use of force against largely peaceful protesters was unnecessary, excessive and 'violated international human rights law and standards'.

All of a sudden, Edwin felt he couldn't chomp along quietly as he had over the years. The quality of life for people like him and those of similar social stratum hadn't improved. The income gap was widening, as was inequality and competition in the job market. The government's policies seemed inclined towards protecting the interests of the wealthy and property tycoons and increasingly the elites who supported the Party. Land sales were a major government revenue earner. Prices, therefore, rose to astronomical levels, pushed up further by non-stop inflow of mainland Chinese funds looking to divest assets out of the mainland.

He knew the decision to be on the frontline would create a storm at home. Although his parents were born and raised in Hong Kong and felt little allegiance to the mainland, they were ordinary folks resigned to the fact that the city would have to take whatever comes from its communist rulers. As citizens, they had no choice. While over two decades of Chinese rule had improved life for the privileged and a portion of the middle class, as well as mainlanders who had immigrated south, nothing got better for the rest of the locals. They learnt to stay focused on making ends meet and maintaining their peaceful lives. The shift in Edwin's beliefs naturally didn't go down well with his parents, but they feared that if they suppressed his politics, they would eventually lose their son.

'I can't see how you and the protesters can change Hong Kong's fate,' his father said to him one night after dinner. 'I don't agree with your view and I can't support that. But I respect your decision and I know I can't stop you. Just that I want you to never forget your family is always here . . . and stay safe.'

Edwin saw how torn his father looked, which left him with a sense of nagging guilt towards his parents until the moment he died.

On a warm and sunny day in June, Edwin joined his friends and was among the two million marching through the streets of his city, to fight for change—for his future.

Throughout the summer, Edwin participated in the numerous protests and flash mobbings that broke out across Hong Kong island, Kowloon and the New Territories. The demonstrations became more frequent and soon occurred on weekdays and nights. But the bigger ones took place on weekends and they were almost certain to escalate as the night wore on, to hours of violent standoffs between protesters and police—only to end in bloodshed, injuries and arrests.

On the frontline, Edwin felt he found his calling and solidarity among fellow protesters. They often engaged in intellectual discussions on politics, the frustrations of the Party's increasing encroachment of Hong Kong, distortion by the local media whose owners caved in to commercial and political pressures from Beijing, as well as hope for the future. He was scared sometimes, but the camaraderie with other demonstrators gave him comfort and courage, even when he was bashed by police batons, tear-gassed or pepper-sprayed, or when his friends were arrested. There were dark moments, but his optimism always pulled him out of despair and made him never lose hope. Unfortunately, Edwin never foresaw what would befall him in the weeks ahead.

* * *

Meanwhile, two days after the *Herald*'s task force was set up, the editors received officials from Beijing. This time around, they were more discrete and careful that the Chinese officials were kept away from any editorial-related meetings or engagements that may be going on in the newsroom. The short thirty-minute visit covered a short tour of the two-floor newsroom and a closed-door meeting in the Shanghai meeting room with the masthead editors.

The meeting, however, didn't escape the notice of two Hong Kong digital and pro-democracy media outlets. One report was headlined: *Pax Yong's commie background in the limelight* and another went further: *The Herald Under Red Capitalism—Arcade's Media Agenda*. The second piece attempted to explore and analyse Jin's acquisition of the Hong Kong media company. Pax and Theresa never found the leak.

5

The Real Boss

Mark Jin was already a bigger-than-life character before he bought the *Herald*. His rags-to-riches story was nothing short of daytime soap opera material. Born to farmer parents, Jin grew up in the rural areas of Nanjing, the eastern coastal city which has a prominent place in Chinese history and culture. Having served as the capital for dynasties, kingdoms and republican governments, Nanjing also suffered atrocities such as the Nanjing Massacre, an episode of mass murder and rape against the local residents during the Second Sino–Japanese War. The city is now the capital of one of China's richest provinces—Jiangsu.

Growing up, Jin's family had little and he took on odd jobs from his teenage years to help pay for school and worked extremely hard to secure scholarships to pay university tuition. As a student, he cared little for politics or the Party and no one in the family was a member. In fact, he couldn't see how the Party had made life better for farmers or people living on the margins of society. He decided at university that taking an apolitical stance was the best strategy.

Jin graduated with a Bachelor of Science in computer science in 1990 and found employment in a quasi-government firm in Nanjing that made electronic components for a Sino-foreign joint venture. The job was mundane but he relished the opportunity to travel to the US for work. It was during a trip to Silicon Valley in 1995 that he was captivated by the power of the Internet and decided it was where he'd focus his energy on building a career, an empire.

Arcade wasn't the first company he established, but it was the grander extension of his first outfit, Passage, which started in his one-bedroom apartment in 1997. That year, Jin and his two university friends saw the market opportunity to help domestic Chinese companies maintain and run their websites. Those were early days when Chinese companies were just beginning to join the global supply chains, ahead of the nation's imminent entry into the World Trade Organization. Passage's business boomed and Jin and his partners sold the company for a handsome profit. With the capital, he founded Arcade, which comprised two business areas—a social media platform to build a customer base and an online marketplace for B2B and B2C transactions, later supported by an in-house mobile payment system that over time became an online financial powerhouse.

Throughout the 2000s, Arcade grew rapidly as the Chinese economy took flight. Domestic consumption took off as never before and an emerging middle class grew. Technology and the Internet were in hot demand. By the time Arcade prepared for a listing on the Nasdaq in 2013, it was already a multi-billion dollar company. It dominated the Chinese e-commerce and mobile payment markets, as well as operated the biggest social media platform where consumers chatted, shopped and derived entertainment. In the meantime, Jin had carved a niche for himself among thousands of his employees and millions of young Chinese.

James had previously covered Arcade's development years ago, about a month into joining the *Herald*. He remembered that in the early days of Arcade's growth, Jin was never coy about his mantra of conducting business in China as a private entrepreneur, 'You can date the government, but don't marry them'. Anyone operating in China would attest to the nuanced benefits of *guanxi* or connections and sound government relations were vital. He boasted in press interviews of how the company cleverly refrained from working on government projects. 'If there was a time where we can't escape, we'd do it for free.'

So when James had the opportunity to interview the tech tycoon at a media briefing as part of Jin's global roadshow to drum up investor interest for Arcade's Nasdaq listing, he asked, 'Mr Jin, your business holds onto massive personal data. How will you protect individuals' privacy against pressure from the Chinese government for such access?'

He recalled that Jin had chewed slightly on his lower lip, before breaking into a slight grin. 'Arcade upholds the strictest privacy policy, which matches international standards and the fact that we have been approved to list on Nasdaq speaks for itself.' Then in a lower voice, he added, 'But anything that's related to national security, well, that's a different story . . . as it's also the case with Western nations.'

That final quip was telling, James thought. It was the first thing that resurfaced in his head when news broke that Jin bought the *Herald*.

Arcade was a forerunner not only in China's social media and e-commerce sector but also in the country's lucrative mobile and online payment services. It launched a third-party service, partly with the intention to complement its e-commerce business with an escrow account, in which the company held buyers' money until goods were delivered. It came at a time when regulators were still grappling with the concept and formulating rules. By the time regulations were introduced, Arcade's financial business had been in operation and reaping returns for six years.

What went under the radar, however, was Jin's increased allegiance with the Party, contrary to his earlier claim of keeping an arm's length. Many had argued for him that it was inevitable as the power at the top shifted from the technocrats and reformists of the late 1990s to the hardliners who pushed hard propaganda characterized by intense indoctrination. Central to the current ruling regime was the déjà vu compulsory personality cult nightmare last seen during the Mao Zedong era that destroyed most of China's civil societies and slowed the country's progress. *Guanxi* meant another layer of interpretation, one that boiled down to a transaction. Arcade had benefited but would need to pay in due course. When Jin announced in early 2016 he would acquire the *Herald*, a report from a reputable US news publication had revealed he was a Party member. Jin embodied the Party's China Dream and under his ownership, the *Herald* had lent itself more generously to propagate the goals of Beijing as the latter sought a greater role in global affairs. The newspaper's long history of operating in Hong Kong, which had a reputation of press freedom and its English-language base, was the perfect platform.

From a commercial standpoint, analysts found it hard to justify Jin's decision. The media company was struggling to transition to a digital platform in an industry that was overall shrinking and the credibility of journalism was under attack as operators compromised quality and standards to churn out content that drove online traffic and on the cheap. For whatever it's worth, Jin attempted to explain his decision after the deal was closed six months later.

'China needs a global platform that offers an alternative narrative to the Western media and the mainland state outlets. *Herald* is the platform that will let the world see China in a different light and perspective. And the best return for me and the investment is the publication does well,' he stated.

* * *

The *Herald* was established in the early 20th century when Hong Kong was a British colony, with a mission by its founders, a Chinese businessman and a British journalist, to be the people's critical voice to the powers of dictatorship and injustice. That said, for most of its history, the paper had supported the colonial government and in return, been awarded exclusive government policy stories through the decades. It had also dared, to its credit, to question and then upheld what was integral to journalism, freedom of speech. As the newspaper documented Hong Kong's phenomenal transformation from a fishing village to an international city, it also became one of the few English media that the rest of the world relied on for a reading of a relatively closed-up China, especially during the heady days of the Great Leap Forward movement (1959–1961), where millions were starved to death and later on, the Great Proletarian Cultural Revolution (1966–1976). The consequences of the Cultural Revolution were especially damaging and long-lasting. The movement threw the country into political and social chaos that crippled the economy, ruined millions of lives, as well as stagnated social and political growth for more than a decade.

The Cultural Revolution forced another wave of mainland Chinese to flee south to Hong Kong. Many of them, even today, cannot wipe off the vivid memory of brutality that the Party had inflicted on ordinary people decades ago.

The political turmoil in China provided the *Herald* with the right fodder for the kind of journalism to build its global street creds and reputation as a media company with insights into mainland politics. Between the tale of its home city's rise and the story of the political upheaval in China, the newspaper only rose in stature, to become one of the world's most profitable media in the 1990s. In the mid-1980s, the newspaper was controlled by the international media mogul Robert Wellberg, whose empire spanned across continents and medium formats. The opportunistic businessman bought the company with an eye for expansion into China. The end of the Cultural Revolution had led to the normalisation of US-China relations and the country's opening up, as well as economic reforms to draw foreign investments. Under Wellberg, the newspaper expanded its coverage of China, where rapid economic and social transformations were gaining global interests, but always maintained a critical eye on the communist regime. It didn't shy away from issues that mainland Chinese state media considered sensitive or taboo: rampant corruption and fraud among Chinese officials, Chinese dissidents, Taiwan and Tibet and was unsparing in its coverage of the Tiananmen Square Massacre on 4 June 1989. Reporters were not just the first on the ground during that summer, but also the first with the news.

Although James was too young to understand the power of the *Herald*'s coverage, he recalled his university-going cousin rave about the publication and how the Western media called it an authoritative voice. The Party's violent crackdown of the student protests, culminating in Beijing sending in the army and tanks to deal with the protesters and their sympathizers, were met with international outrage and analysts downgraded the economic outlook of the country. The foreign interests and inflows of capital that had gained traction in the past decade came to an abrupt halt. Because of its ability to strike an appropriate balance in its China coverage, the *Herald* won accolades at home and abroad and drew the biggest advertisement revenues and profitability the company had ever seen. In the meantime, the exodus of Hongkongers to countries like Canada, the US, the UK and Australia, to escape from the imminent Chinese rule accelerated. The majority of Hongkongers, however, didn't have the option to leave. Many capitalized on the business opportunities that came with China's opening up. Hong Kong entrepreneurs were the earliest foreign investors in China—since economic reforms began in 1979—so that by the early 1990s, many firms had moved manufacturing operations to the mainland's southern Guangdong province where costs were much lower. A hollowing out of the city's manufacturing base took place.

In Beijing, China's late paramount leader Deng Xiaoping also realized the urgency to regain foreign confidence and assure the international community of the Party's commitment to liberalization. China's entry into the World Trade Organization was already disrupted and would not materialize until four years after Deng's death.

Deng emerged from retirement to make his famous 1992 southern tour—visiting Shenzhen, Guangzhou and Zhuhai in Guangdong, as well as spending the Lunar New Year in Shanghai, using it to reassert his economic policy. The southern tour unleashed a new wave of optimism about the Chinese economy and strengthened the reformist platform within the Party. Hong Kong benefitted tremendously with the start of an economic boom until the Asian Financial Crisis hit in 1997 due to its free trade policy and rule of law. It was the ultimate bridge that connected the international markets with the then-fledgling Chinese economy. Between 1992 and the city's return to Chinese sovereignty on 1 July 1997, the local economy grew by leaps and bounds. The *Herald* prospered too.

In the early 1990s, the Hong Kong media scene could be broadly categorized into the pro and anti-Beijing camps. The Basic Law, or Hong Kong's mini constitution, would safeguard the city's freedom of speech and the local government's autonomy—with the exception of security and defence issues—under the 'one country, two systems' principle, but was never fully bought by many journalists. By then, Wellberg was also looking to expand into broadcast and digital media and wanted to divest. For him, profit had peaked and he didn't want the *Herald* to detract from his other aspirations, including those in the mainland.

So entered another bigger-than-life tycoon with strong ties to the Party.

Henry Kua was a Singaporean businessman with ancestral roots in the southern province of Guangdong. He fled to Singapore during the Japanese occupation, settled down to build a family and a multibillion dollar regional business, from trading commodities and resources to property development. He began doing business with the Chinese in the late 1950s in response to the communist government's call for overseas Chinese to contribute to building 'New China'. Ever since China reopened its doors in 1979, Kua's interests and investments in his birthplace only increased. With less than four years to China regaining control of Hong Kong, Kua was pleased to serve the motherland again by gaining control of one of the media seen as most pro-British government, if not anti-Communist. In January 1994, his Lionscape Group became the new owners of the *Herald*, one of the biggest turning points in the history of the paper's development and editorial direction. The years under the Kua family signalled the beginning of the paper's shift towards being a China sympathizer and pro-Beijing, as well as a gradual decline of its credibility and editorial independence. While the family made up of astute businessmen had enjoyed tremendous success across all their businesses, managing a media company was out of their depth and breadth, complicated by the precarious demand to look out for the Party's interests.

From the mid-1990s through most of the 2000s, the *Herald* remained profitable even though bottom-line earnings were depleting. It had enjoyed a near-monopoly of the city's English language print advertising market until the advent of the Internet. Globally, the media industry was also rapidly digitalizing and moving onto online platforms in the 2000s. But what media operators struggled with was creating commercially viable digital platforms that delivered sustainable growth. It was doubly hard for the Kua family, which came from industries where investments and gains could be measured in predictable business cycles. Returns from the media business were, on the contrary, intangible and came over a longer time span as the title's reputation was built and rested heavily on the quality of journalism and the news content produced.

The dilemma came at two levels for Lionscape: it needed to increase spending on digitalization and to uphold the *Herald*'s credibility; it must be prepared to criticize institutions and the Party to deliver balanced reporting. The company was neither willing to invest with little or no return in the short term, nor offend China, where its business interests far exceeded the investment in the newspaper. To free up the funds for digitalization in a half-hearted manner, it slashed costs aggressively and instituted a layoff programme in the name of restructuring. Under its ownership, eleven editors came through the *Herald*'s doors, with each passing one incrementally more sympathetic to China. By the time Arcade entered the picture, it was an open secret that editor-in-chief appointments must be endorsed by the Party's proxy in Hong Kong. These moves demoralized the newsroom.

When the global financial crisis caused by deregulation and relaxed oversight of the industry hit in 2008, the Kua family felt that they had paid their dues and wanted out. Henry Kua may be loyal to the Party, but he wasn't a member, nor a Chinese national. Up until now, the *Herald* was still seen as a Hong Kong company and not the red capitalist entity the Party would prefer. Taking over the *Herald* wasn't a regular business deal due to the financial pressure that was tied to a media company and the political microscope it came under. It required a buyer with deep pockets who was also a loyalist to the ruling regime, even though such an acquisition in itself argued against all the principles of journalism. But the face of journalism was also changing; the onslaught of social media and digitalisation created a less desirable byproduct—fake news.

In China, two types of companies would have fulfilled such conditions—the giant state-owned enterprises with access to government funds and the tech firms of the new economy. Business-wise, the tech companies appeared to be a better match, given the media industry's need to digitalize and innovate. Arcade was no stranger in pushing boundaries, as shown by its advocacy for mobile payment when the concept was novel in China. It challenged traditional banking that was monopolized by the big state banks and smaller government-backed institutions, and opened the way for tech firms to enter China's highly-guarded financial industry.

The *Herald* ran a series of stories delving into the issue years earlier, initiated by Pax's predecessor who assigned a team of reporters including James to look into the vested interests and implications involved in the game-changing sector.

'We don't see the mobile payment sector as a death threat to traditional banking, 'eating up their business' as the media put it,' Arcade's spokesperson for the mobile payment unit told James in an interview. 'As Mark stressed, it is a game changer that'll push our banks to innovate, be more efficient and profitable. We can coexist and complement each other to collectively expand the business pie.'

The game-changing move did ruffle feathers and planted the seeds of political rifts among different factions. Acquiring the *Herald*, Jin thought, was his attempt to appease disgruntled vested parties he crossed paths with and earned political currency with the Party. Owning a media also played to his vanity and allowed him—China—to influence opinions. *And why not?* Arcade then declared its expansionary plan to pour in money into the media company, as others around the world downsized operations. China wanted to be liked and understood. The *Herald*'s mission under Arcade was to do just that.

* * *

Arcade's first moves were to assure the *Herald*'s staff it was committed to editorial independence and to remove the paywall to make the newspaper accessible to many more readers across the world, bucking the trend where a growing number of news websites were now charging for subscriptions.

In the first two years under the new owner, James observed that visible changes in the newsroom were minimal. Jin stayed away from the newsroom and by the time the protests broke out, he had only visited twice: for meetings with Steve, Pax and Theresa. In contrast, the three and sometimes Vijay made numerous trips to the parent company's Nanjing headquarters. Still, there were times when Pax, Theresa or Vijay would slip and reveal how the 'invisible hand' was at play.

In the summer of 2017, the *Herald* retracted a column by a veteran financial journalist Kelvin Ko who wrote extensively about under-the-table deals in China's financial world. The commentary alleged that the relative of a top aide to one of Beijing's leaders was shifting assets out of the country and building up a multibillion-dollar portfolio abroad as the Party clamped down on illegal outflows. The piece survived online for less than twenty-four hours before it was taken down, accompanied by Pax's apologetic note that it was removed for 'failing to meet journalistic standards', while the print version published a correction in the newspaper the second day. Pax made a scapegoat of the journalist who was forced to resign. On the other hand, he let the business editor, Murphy, who edited and published the article, off unscathed in what he described as a 'minor misstep'.

'I can't tell you how grossly disappointed I have been with your last column,' Pax lashed out at Kelvin after his own 'rectification' failed to appease Jin and the Party.

'You have been in this business longer than I have, but you've produced such a sub-standard piece of work filled with serious accusations against a senior official without hard evidence to back up your claims.' James, speaking to a colleague outside the meeting room, overheard the editor raising his voice.

'Can you be specific on what is lacking in the piece?' Kelvin retorted immediately.

'If you're talking about evidence, I don't know if you know, but I've passed on to Edward all my research and documents when I filed my copy; there's an e-mail trail,' he torpedoed back, also raising his voice.

'The business editor is the final gatekeeper; it's as much, if not more of his responsibility to make sure the piece holds up.'

Pax felt anger flood his veins and rage sent his heart racing. 'That's enough! Stop blaming your business editor. Just admit your mistake.

With your attitude, I don't think this is the place for you. You know what to do!' With that, Pax stormed out of the meeting room.

James, who was still chatting with the colleague, darted to one side to give way to the editor. *That's so uncharacteristic of Pax, who's always guarding his nice guy persona. Must have been a big fuck up*, he mused, making a mental note to find out more about the incident.

The incident was in fact more than a 'minor misstep' in the eyes of Beijing and Jin. The top leaders were at the time consolidating their power base and were ultra-sensitive to any speculations—especially ones that touched something as adverse as corruption. Jin was just reaping the initial harvest of his past years of the carefully-nurtured relationship with the senior party leaders. It was highly unusual for Pax to have anyone's back at the risk of angering the higher-ups. But he needed an ally of Murphy in the newsroom, especially in the area of financial news coverage that the editor-in-chief knew little about.

On his part, Murphy took pains to report the Arcade's business activities in a positive light, giving extensive coverage to its special events such as the Singles' Day—China's Black Friday.

'Right, if you guys have no further ideas to add to the story list, I'll consolidate this and send it to the PR folks at Arcade for their review,' he said at the end of a conference call with reporters across China bureaux covering the event one year.

When China's economic numbers began to reflect that a fallout from the US-China trade war was more severe than what Beijing might have anticipated, Pax told Hamster, the economy editor, to counter the negative outlook with a series of stories on China's growth sectors and the prospects of the tech industry.

'Mark said there are numerous industries doing well, like e-commerce, modern logistics, medicine, education and so on,' he said. 'He's right! It'd be a good idea for us to look into these bright spots. Balanced reporting, balanced reporting . . . '

Over time, without explicit instructions, reporters got a sense through social cues and patterns of the editors of what to play up and avoid in their reporting. They came to implicitly understand and accept what was acceptable and what wasn't. When the editors were asked about possible interference from Beijing or Arcade, the default response would be 'nay', with the emphasis that the *Herald* had close relationships with different institutions and governments in the mainland.

'They'll call us to discuss if they have an issue with our reports. But Beijing doesn't call us,' Theresa once told her team. The team was amused at her comment yet wondered at the same time if she was delusional. Everyone knew Beijing didn't need to call. There were enough agents in Hong Kong who would voluntarily rise to the occasion and Theresa, whether she realized it or not, was one of them.

* * *

James was under no illusion that the work he would do on the task force wasn't part of a Beijing maneuver. He also saw it as part of Jin's strategy to get back into the good books of the higher-ups, two years after the incident surrounding Kelvin's column. The way Theresa had cloaked it as a battle against fake news once more showed the editors' well-tried but now ineffective tactic to garner support for propaganda assignments. James had also found the best counter was to rely on infallible reporting and hard facts.

Over the years, he had cultivated a source in the state security department, whom he called *Sum Suk* ('deep uncle' in Cantonese) in honour of the *Deep Throat* pseudonym that the American reporter Bob Woodward had given to his source who provided critical information in the Watergate scandal reporting that eventually brought down President Richard Nixon's administration in the 1970s. The state security department was China's intelligence, security and secret police agency, touted as one of the world's most secretive intelligence organizations.

Sum Suk had pointed James in the right direction in a number of exclusive stories he had written but was never quoted or identified due to an arrangement agreed from the outset that evolved into a relationship built on strong trust. Discussions were always off the record, where

Sum Suk often provided him with context and perspectives and in journalism terminology, *deep background.*

As he lined up meetings with Edwin Law's family to learn more about the dead protester, James also set up a meeting with Sum Suk to get a perspective of the state of play with the Chinese government and the Party over the political crisis.

Part II

Blowback

6

The Inside Story

'That's great!' Theresa said drily, subtly raising her voice to the pitch that indicated her discomfort and irritation. Shocked, she unconsciously stepped backwards, as her gaze swiftly shifted away from James, Mary and Victor to the wooden cabinets behind them in the meeting room.

She was fumbling a little for words with the reporters looking at her in the dull and dreary Hebei meeting room tucked away at the far end corner of the lower floor of the newsroom. The reporters had physically ambushed her and asked to meet at a short notice, much to her displeasure. All four of them were standing in a loose circle as they told her they had secured interviews with Edwin's mother and his friend Ben. The reporters had made numerous calls since the first task force meeting to track them down and then persuaded the interviewees to speak to them.

Theresa didn't expect Edwin's family and friends to be brave enough to consent to the interview requests. From her perspective, it would be a reckless suicidal act, given the controversy surrounding the death and at the height of the political unrest in the city. She assumed that the *Herald*'s stance on the protest would have put them off from speaking with the reporters. She was almost certain about these assumptions, which would allow her to use the task force to effectively control the *Herald*'s internal narratives—intercepting stories that hurt the Party without appearing to compromise editorial integrity. But the interviews would quash her plan, destroy her playbook and ultimately threaten her seat. She expected the task force to only be able to score interviews with the police and government officials. But Theresa had obviously miscalculated.

Seeing that Theresa's thoughts were drifting further, Victor brought her back to the room. 'So will you secure a page in the paper for us then?' he asked with a hint of sarcasm, stroking his chin. He stepped forward a bit as he tried to pressure her to commit.

'Oh yes . . . I mean . . . Let's see what I can do,' Theresa answered vaguely, as her body stiffened, with a small and sudden shudder. The interviews, if published, would no doubt cost her her job, she thought, desperately activating all of her brain cells to try to kill the pitch.

James was having a moment, seeing a squirming Theresa being attacked. He doubted that she would agree to their request for a full-page coverage and seethed with renewed bitterness towards the editor.

'When can you get back to us?' Mary chipped in as well, looking straight into Theresa's eyes. A diligent and soft-spoken reporter, she had also been observing the editor's subtle change in body language.

'I'll talk to you again in a few hours,' Theresa mumbled. Her emotional fluctuation was evident in her shaky voice.

'In a few hours?' Victor snarled.

'I have an urgent meeting,' she tried to brush the reporters off, leading them out of the meeting room and shutting the door. 'Off you go. I'll get back to you later today,' she said with her back towards them as she walked off. Her response was mechanical and transactional.

'Do you think she will give us a page?' Victor asked his colleagues, as the three walked back to their seats. The soles of his shoes, which were wearing off, made a squeaky sound as they rubbed against the concrete floor.

'She can't just say no, right?' Mary, her eyes flashing in disbelief, said tartly. 'In the meantime, let's come up with questions for the interviews.'

* * *

Theresa who had pulled herself away from the group felt seized by a mild panic attack after meeting the reporters. She loathed being taken off guard and scurried towards the Shanghai meeting room even though her next meeting would start only in fifteen minutes. She entered the large unlit room and shut the door firmly behind her. She needed the space to recompose herself. She could feel her face turning blue during the short walk between the two meeting rooms, trying to overcome a complicated mix of fury, defeatedness and insecurity, as well as fear. From the reporters' determined faces, she knew that she needed to come up with valid reasons to thwart the interviews. Theresa may act like she was the queen of the newsroom, but that didn't mean she could do whatever she wanted without rational justification. Pax made sure of that. And now, her pride forbade her from discussing this with him. After all, she had taken on the task force project assertively and she must see it through with success. Failing to do so would benefit Vijay, who was always after her crown, and widen the gap between her status and Pax in the eyes of the higher-ups. Vijay was capable of reporting to the upper levels of her incompetence if she failed to build a counter-argument. She desperately needed compelling reasons to sway coverage towards the direction that met the Party's agenda. She leaned against the back of her chair and closed her eyes, knitting her brows closely together.

How should I counter this? I need valid reasons to stop them from adopting any unpreferred, Western media-style narratives. After minutes of contemplation, she opened her eyes. The colour had returned to her face where a smug had begun to form across it. She found her answer.

At that moment, the room was lit up as senior executives including Steve and the Chief Operating Officer Sheldon Lam, as well as Pax began to enter.

* * *

Two hours later when she exited the meeting room, Theresa was a different person. Exuding an air of confidence, she looked relaxed and comfortable. She once more made her way to the Hebei meeting room, as she called her secretary to bring the three reporters back. Theresa was seated on a chair with legs crossed when the three, puzzled and intrigued by her relatively fast response, returned to the room. An air of disquiet filled the space but was quickly broken by the editor's renewed confidence.

'I have some other urgent assignments I need you to work on first,' she said, with her lips twitching.

'I need you to work on covering China's Belt and Road Initiative project in Pakistan. This is actually a very important task.'

'Are you serious?' Victor shrieked. He thought he had misheard.

'China's BRI is facing major scrutiny in Pakistan and I believe this is more of an urgent story,' Theresa reiterated.

Victor rubbed his reddening face with his cupped hands and shook his head.

'Read these,' she continued, pointing to a faded brown-coloured paper box on the table. Slightly deflated, Victor walked over and rummaged through the old, dusty box, where he pulled out scraps of news clippings. They were stories on how China's massive infrastructure development and investment strategy was scrutinized in Pakistan; the most recent clip being six months old. Theresa enjoyed the perturbed and annoyed looks on the reporters' faces with a nasty sneer of her own.

Victor was about to open his mouth to respond, but James beat him to it.

'So you want us out of the task force?' he asked fiercely. 'You can't just assign us a different task when we've secured interviews with the victim's family and friends,' he badgered on.

'Oh no. Don't get me wrong,' Theresa said. 'You still are,' she articulated every word. 'I just think you are the most appropriate reporters to cover the BRI, given your experience and knowledge on the project. I can trust you on this, right?'

* * *

It took a while for Victor to calm down. *How low-handed can she be?* He was enraged by Theresa's demand and made no secret of it in the newsroom. The story caused an uproar among his colleagues, aggravating the broader resentment stewing against the editors' increasingly biased news judgement. Reporters were agitated, some to the point of distraught. The incident between Theresa and the three task force reporters turned into gossip that spread like wildfire in the office. James heard a rumble of voices around him for days. It was the topic of water cooler conversations. Colleagues gossiped about it excitedly, guessing what would come next. Their interest amplified the growing dissatisfaction towards the *Herald*'s juggernaut of self-censorship measures to appease Beijing.

The incident prompted reporters to speak out against Theresa and her deputies' orders and challenge her editorial lines not just on the Hong Kong protests but across different topics. They questioned the authenticity of the Chinese foreign ministry's official statements on diplomatic issues, such as the arrest of foreign nationals for alleged espionage, refusing to just mimic Beijing's claims. They also confronted some Hong Kong desk editors who executed Theresa and Vijay's orders mindlessly in order to survive. They advocated the need for more critical stories if the *Herald* was serious about leading the real conversation on China and to drive the debate from a rational standpoint. This was how the company could help Chinese people, they argued.

Vijay, who had been watching gleefully, sensed the wind of change in the newsroom. The political animal that he was, he swiftly exploited the growing grievances against Theresa to his advantage and slowly inserted himself into the controversy. He quietly observed and listened to the complaints, collected anecdotes and information for ammunition he could use to criticize her when the time was ripe.

He raised his concerns to Theresa one afternoon following the editors' daily editorial meeting. 'Do you have a minute?' he said rubbing his neck. He stood between her and the meeting room door.

'What is it?' Theresa asked, while she sidestepped him and tried to make her way out of the room. She didn't care what he had to say. He was another subordinate.

'Hey, I think things are starting to fall apart these days. You need to pay more attention to reporters' concerns in the newsroom,' Vijay said to her as she walked past, putting on a worried look.

Theresa gave him an icy cold glare and if she could, would have pierced his heart with spears.

'Many are worried about some of the recent measures that have been taken,' Vijay continued, his eyes fixed on Theresa. 'It might drag down our productivity, don't you think?.'

'Mind your own business!' she said, scowling at him. She then retraced her steps aggressively and came to an abrupt halt in front of him. 'And please, surely you don't need me to remind you of your position,' she sniggered.

'You, as my inferior, have only one job to do and that is to support me. Be a loyal supporter to the Party or I'll report your misconduct to the top,' she said as she walked out of the room.

The incident was the start of Theresa's tyranny. It reminded her of the urgency to restore her stronghold in the newsroom. She needed to set an example in order to silence the complaints of reporters. *Shutting down the voices of dissent would also limit Vijay's clout*, she thought, *killing two birds with one stone.*

Theresa announced a restructuring of the China desk. Reporters and editors who had questioned her news judgement and decisions were assigned insignificant roles and responsibilities. She was no longer tolerant of 'rebels'.

'You're incompetent,' she often bellowed at editors and reporters across the newsroom. 'You're delivering the wrong facts about China.'

To home in on the message, she also deducted the salaries of those who disobeyed and veered from her editorial line. Her action petrified the whole newsroom—reporters either practised greater self-censorship or headed for the door. Theresa didn't blink an eye to the resignations; they didn't really matter to her, or to Pax. She quickly hired new reporters to fill the vacancies. She showed, in plain terms, the repercussions of going against her and the tactic worked.

* * *

Cafe Bloom, 8 p.m. Mary left a note on James' desk, two days after Theresa assigned them the BRI story. Mary and Victor were already waiting for him when he arrived. Mary looked worn out, while Victor's fluffy hair was unusually flat, with the fringe stuck on his forehead. It was another long day for all three reporters. They had been mentally drained by Theresa's roadblocks to distract their investigation into Edwin's death.

'What are we going to do with the interviews?' Victor asked. 'I don't think I can work for this company any more. I have half a mind to quit right now!'

'That will only satisfy and benefit Theresa,' Mary disagreed, lifting her eyebrows.

'At least she can hear us then,' Victor said, even though he looked uncertain.

'How about we just work on those interviews on our own time?' James suggested.

'I'll meet his mother and you guys go ahead with your interview with his best friend, get something juicy, then let's confront her again. She probably still wouldn't publish it. But at least the entire newsroom will know whom she really works for.'

'I agree,' Mary said, with some energy returning to her voice, 'and if she still vetoes us, we can just pass the materials to other media outlets, right?'

'Sounds like a plan,' Victor said, standing up to take out his phone from a pocket. 'Let me call Ben now, see if he is willing to meet us after working hours,' he said walking out of the tiny cafe.

A few minutes later, he returned with a grin on his face.

'6 p.m. Saturday. Hang Hau Man Kuk Lane Park.'

* * *

The sun was setting on Saturday evening, painting the sky pink and the wind was dropping when Mary and Victor arrived at the Hang Hau Man Kuk Lane Park near Edwin's office in eastern Kowloon. Ben was Edwin's colleague and friend since secondary school. The two reporters had hopes that a conversation with Ben might move their investigation forward.

A lake stood in the middle of the park encircled by a concrete fence that contained the water from flowing out. *Like a barricade that obstructed Edwin's story from surfacing,* Mary thought. *Just like us, up against a wall that includes the battle with editors. What will it take for the fortress of lies and propaganda to collapse?* She daren't think of the answer. A few pedestrians hustled across the park as if unconcerned that a member of the local community had disappeared and later found dead.

At a corner of the park, though, was a small makeshift shrine with a picture of a smiling Edwin. His friends must have built it to remember him. Stalks of white lilies and chrysanthemums were placed in the front and by the side of the photo. A few young people dressed in mourning black hovered around. The reporters walked towards the group. Mary stared silently for a few minutes at the photo of the young man—who seemed to smile back at her energetically—querying him about how he died. Others in the group were probably asking their own questions; their eyes filled with fury, pain and sorrow, choked her.

'Victor?' a voice called out from behind. Ben, sweating slightly in his white shirt and black pants, jogged towards them with a friendly wave.

'Let's have a seat there,' he said, pointing to a wooden picnic table with attached benches at a corner of the park across from the group.

'Thanks Ben, for agreeing to talk to us,' Victor said, after meeting the young man midway between the makeshift shrine and the bench. Mary took out her notepad from her backpack. 'It must've been a difficult decision to meet us,' Victor continued, as they walked towards the bench. Ben constantly glanced around him to make sure he wasn't tailed, or watched for talking to the two strangers.

The three of them sat down quietly and drifted into several minutes of grim silence. The reporters thought Ben's silence spoke volumes. Mixed emotions overwhelmed him, leading to a momentary ambivalence before he sighed in exasperation.

'He was my best friend,' he finally broke the heavy silence.

'Can you tell us about him?' Victor asked carefully.

'He was a good guy,' Ben replied, muttering.

'And he didn't have any mental disorders. Those claims on the Internet are simply not true.'

'Can you tell us a little more about his background?'

'Well . . . he lived with his parents and two sisters; a normal working class family. And he was always eager to help out those around him. He'd never commit suicide,' Ben rushed his words and then drew a shaky breath. His pause was telling.

'I still can't believe he's gone now. He is definitely not that type of person who would kill himself.' He halted again, trying to keep his composure.

Mary was struck by the sorrow in his voice and the pauses that seemed to suck him into a deeper level of grief. She found herself choking up as well.

'I never bought the police's official announcement,' Ben said, 'as soon as Ed's body was found, they almost immediately asserted that there was no foul play. His family then quickly cremated his body. Don't you think that's strange?

'The investigation's incomplete. There are millions of questions left unanswered.'

'Can you tell us more about him? What was he like in his last few days?' Mary asked.

'He also paid for private guitar lessons, just a few days before he disappeared,' a sharp voice emerged from behind them.

Jessica—also a friend and colleague of Edwin's—had sprinted towards them from a distance and invited herself into the conversation.

'I mean . . . who does that when you are about to end your life?' she continued. 'You must be the journos, right? I heard from Ben that he'll be talking to you,' she said, as Victor blinked in surprise. Jessica's eyes gleamed in enthusiasm and she slipped onto the bench, sitting next to him.

'Also, they said he drowned, right? That's a lie,' she assertedly said. 'Ed was a swimming champion when he was in secondary school. He even won awards in local swimming competitions. As if he would drown to death.

'He also had regular diving training in those days,' she added. Jessica spoke quickly and with firmness. 'I don't know if this helps,' she said as she tossed a small vinyl sack to Mary. 'It's his swimming gear that he left in the locker at work. I took it before the police arrived.'

'Can we hold on to this for a few days?' Mary asked, thinking she might need proof to fight against Theresa. She peered into the sack which had his swimming trunk, goggles, lotions and a comb.

'Sure.'

'When was the last time you saw him?' Mary continued.

'At the protest scene, earlier this month,' Ben answered. 'We went to the protest together. Edwin got separated with friends at Mei Foo district', he continued. 'There were too many people at the protest. It's actually easy to get separated.'

'But Ben received a text message from him at about 10 p.m. to say that he was going home,' Jessica said.

'That was his last message before he disappeared,' Ben said. 'We've checked his home and our ghetto places near Mei Foo, but couldn't find a trace of him.'

'We reported it to the police, the day before they announced that they found him dead, naked in that sea,' Jessica added.

'Did anyone see the police arresting him?' Victor asked.

Ben sighed again, weary that he'd never know the answer to that question.

'No . . . we tried to get hold of the surveillance footage around the protest area, but they wouldn't release it to us. I have no confidence in the Hong Kong police investigating the case properly.'

He told the reporters that the full surveillance footage of the protest scene at Mei Foo was never released, though a few days earlier, the authorities released a part of the recording which showed Edwin leaving his office in Hang Hau and walking towards the waterfront near Tseung Kwan O. The footage had no timestamp, but it supported the police's version of the story.

'Please speak up for Ed on behalf of us,' Jessica pleaded. 'We just want to know the truth. Just look at all these suspicions surrounding his death. We want Ed to rest in peace. Please help us out.'

On the day that Victor and Mary met Ben and Jessica, James interviewed Edwin's mother.

'Please, come on in,' Edwin's mother ran to the door barefooted to let James in. A wisp of grey hair hung over her face.

'Thank you for coming, I'm Vicky,' she said as she quickly pulled her hair back away from her face into a knot at the back of her head, making herself presentable. She was wearing a worn-out, stretched white T-shirt and casual cotton pants that clung to her legs. Her eyes were swollen and tired-looking.

'I am sorry for your loss,' James said, as he walked into her home.

Vicky's eyes immediately filled with tears. 'No, you don't need to,' she choked a little. 'Thanks for ...' she struggled to finish her sentence.

'Excuse me,' Vicky ran to the kitchen. She turned her face up to the warm water running from the tap in the sink, patting her eyes with her fingers to wash away the tears that had welled up.

It was an old public rental flat. Bits of the floral wallpaper had peeled from the walls and the furniture was worn but clean. A light-coloured curtain hung from the back window, shielding the heat from the strong sunlight that flooded into the 400 sq ft flat. Photos of Edwin and the family were hung on every corner of the house.

James sat down at the small dining table, face to face with Edwin's 48-year-old mother. Edwin's father had gone to work and his two sisters to weekend school, Vicky told James.

'Life has to go on . . . ' she mumbled.

She was a picture of a devastated mother, her already small build appeared to have shrunk down by size due to her recent loss. Her big eyes stared sadly into James', hopelessly wondering if there was any future while seemingly seeking an answer. She poured James and herself cups of hot tea.

'I miss him,' she said, her voice was quickly breaking again and she gazed down at her teacup to stifle tears that were beginning to fill her eyes.

James felt a lump at his throat and was lost for words for a moment. He took a sip of the tea.

'I agreed to talk to you because I want to find out the truth,' said Vicky in a soft but firm voice. 'No one and nothing can bring Edwin back. But I think we deserve the truth. The police think it's accidental, but we don't buy that.'

'Can you tell me a little bit about Edwin? What was he like?' James asked.

'You know, Edwin was a swimmer, so drowning is not a possibility unless something else happened before he was thrown into the waters . . . I know there are some people who thought he might have taken his life because he was at odds with us, opposing his politics,' by now, tears were flowing freely past a pair of dark-ringed eyes and down her sunken cheeks.

'We brought our son up to be upright, confident and believe in himself, not to give up when there's opposition before him.

'Let me ask you, he's just won a scholarship to further his studies abroad, something he's dreamt about since he was young. Why would he then just end his life?'

For about a minute or so, they both said nothing. James wanted to give the mourning mother some space before he made his request.

'My son would never commit suicide,' Vicky repeated, breaking the silence with an assertive voice. 'He even sent a text to me that he was coming home on the day he disappeared,' she said, turning her head towards Edwin's photo hanging on the wall.

'Did you tell that to the police?'

'Of course! Many times! They told me not to say anything about that to the media, as it may have an impact on their investigation.'

'Do you have any of his belongings from that day?'

'No. They just said he was found naked without any of his belongings. I went to the MTR myself and confirmed that station cleaners had found my son's mobile phone and some stationeries on the ground near an exit at Tiu Keng Leng station.

'I informed the police and they said the evidence suggests it's a suicide.'

'Vicky, I won't pretend I can understand your pain,' James said carefully, looking straight into the eyes of a bereaving mother. 'But I can assure you I want to find out the truth as much as you do. I know it's a very difficult period for you and I'm grateful that you agreed to see us.

'Please tell me everything, anything you can remember ever since Edwin took an interest in the protests.'

Vicky pursed her cracked lips for a few minutes. Quietly, she nodded.

James began his interview, one that went on for four hours before he left the Law home, with a heavy heart. But what he learned in those few hours about Edwin's untimely death would be overturned two days later, by none other than the young man's mother.

* * *

'My son took his own life and that's the truth,' said Vicky in a live television interview, her voice croaking.

James, Mary and Victor's faces dissolved to shock when they saw her on air. The three froze and stared at the TV screen, their frowns deepening as they grappled with her responses to the questions from a reporter on Hong Kong's pro-Beijing broadcaster.

'What is this?' Victor was the first to speak. They were watching the interview from one of the numerous TV screens in the newsroom.

'I can't believe this,' Mary hissed.

James felt numb; his mind went blank and he couldn't move, like the paralysed prey of a venomous snake. He was dumbfounded by Vicky's comments, which threw out everything she told him two days ago. *How cruel her words were, coming from a mother*, he thought.

She was now spinning a totally different tale, one that he struggled to comprehend. In the TV interview, Vicky said she had checked all the relevant surveillance footage with the help of the police and she was satisfied with the police's investigation.

'I was also initially suspicious of my son's death, but Edwin was emotionally unstable,' she said in a monotone. Her tired face also looked terrified. She kept biting her lips to suppress her emotions and avoided eye contact with the interviewer. Her gaze was fixated at something or someone beyond the camera, as though seeking approval. The sound of her voice and what she said pierced James, lurching his heart into a frenzy.

'He suffered from schizophrenia. He was mentally sick,' she said. 'In the surveillance clips shown by the police, Edwin's look was rather unusual,' she continued, revealing that her son had told her at least three times a week that he was hearing voices in August.

'He told me that a man's voice was instructing him to do things and because of that he couldn't sleep for weeks.'

Vicky continued to question her son's sanity in the interview, even though her stiffened body and the faraway gaze betrayed her discomfort. She then complained about the harassment she faced and the speculation on the cause of her son's death.

'The rioters and some anti-China reporters have been harassing me over the past few weeks. Would you please stop it? Let me clarify this again. He took his own life; he wasn't killed. He suffered from serious depression.'

'Anti-China reporters?' Victor grunted. James, standing next to Victor, was drawing his breath in sharp, miserable gasps.

'My son took part in distributing leaflets of the protests in June but had become disillusioned by July. He thought the rally had changed,' she said, adding that he was tear-gassed by protesters in August on his way to buy groceries.

'He hated the protesters. He would hate them even more if he knew that they are now using his death for their benefits. They are uncivilized mobs.'

Mary, who was shivering by then, was the first among the trio to walk away from the screen. 'I can't watch this any more.'

'Now, would you please leave me alone from all this harassment?' pleaded Vicky, her eyes showing no emotions. 'I dare not go out of my home. Please leave our family alone,' she said evasively. 'I have been doxxed since his death, being harassed at work and being bombarded by phone calls at all hours. I want to live my life and I want my son to rest in peace.'

* * *

Victor stormed back to his desk after the interview ended. He slammed his laptop shut and shoved it into his backpack. He picked up his bag and jacket, exasperated, ready to head for the door.

'Where do you think you are going?' James asked his raging colleague.

'To Vicky's.'

'Too late. There's nothing we can do now.'

Heather watched James and Victor from a distance. Her black eyes glittered and she grinned wryly, then stared at the two of them with scorn. She walked over like a vulture circling above its target.

'What's wrong?' Heather asked satirically, with malice. 'You guys seem a little blown up here.'

'Please, Heather. Not in the mood. Just go away,' Victor said.

'Hope you guys are all right,' Heather said, smiling at her own impetuosity.

She returned to her seat and began to co-write a story with Nancy based on Vicky's TV interview. Nancy was her usual dissatisfied self but she buried herself in delivering the order.

'I had a meeting with Mr Wang the other day,' Heather told James who walked past her as he made his way back to his seat. 'He helped me to confirm Edwin's accidental death on Sunday.'

James was paying little attention to her until she mentioned the timing. It sent a chill down his spine and he broke out in a cold sweat. It was a day after he met Vicky.

'His office is palatial,' Heather continued. 'Hope I can be someone like him one day. He also guided me to find out the truth about the death,' she said, ignoring a stewing James.

'I'm glad I finally met my deep throat. Think I'll win the next Pulitzer.'

James opened his mouth to say something but Victor was faster.

'Bahaha, since when did the Pulitzer belong to the Party?'

'You guys honestly thought you were the only ones meeting secret sources?' Heather torpedoed with a twisted smile.

She knew about our interview with Vicky? James thought, unsettled and feeling sucked to the floor with emotional throes.

'Oh! I forgot to mention! I accidentally overheard . . . don't bother calling the mother again.

'Motherland will do anything to protect national security.'

7

The Alternative Theory

As Theresa walked into the office in the early morning of 1 October, no one was more surprised than the *Herald*'s security guard. It was barely 8 a.m., a small window in the day when the newsroom was an air of near tranquility. The only sounds were the monotonous humming of a vacuum cleaner giving the office floors their daily sweep.

'Good morning Ms Chu,' the elderly guard greeted the editor. Theresa sailed past him; her eyes were far away, she was lost in her thoughts. It was a big news day for her—China's 70th anniversary since the Party came into power and how times had changed. When she first arrived in Hong Kong as a starry-eyed teenager from the southwestern Chinese province of Sichuan almost three decades ago, she had struggled at every front to shake off her mainland Chinese roots. The peer pressure at school was enormous in those days when few spoke Mandarin. Tall and awkward, Theresa never forgot how she was laughed at and ridiculed for her heavily-accented Cantonese and her poor English. She had few friends and even fewer classmates that were from the mainland. The tide had turned. More Hongkongers spoke Mandarin or at least some of it. And if you were in the service industry such as the retail business, you couldn't afford not to speak the language as more than 70 per cent of tourists were from mainland China. As for Theresa, thirty years later, her sense of style remained odd, as did her accented Cantonese and English. But Hong Kong had warmed towards China and those like her who had mainland roots.

The day was meant to be celebratory, she thought, *but it was now marred by the ongoing protests. Those damn radicals and mobster protesters*, she gritted her teeth. Theresa realized her stress level had been on a steady rise lately and she was increasingly short with people around her. The protesters had promised they would do everything to destroy the celebrations, a forewarning that personally pissed her off.

Arriving in the office two hours ahead of the planned live broadcast of China's celebration parade in Beijing, Theresa wanted to make sure the *Herald*'s coverage encountered no hitches; it needed to be perfect. Live coverage of such events were standard offerings of any newsroom and wouldn't require the hands-on supervision of the second-in-command. Theresa didn't trust her team. She met with her deputies and senior reporters just the night before to finalize the coverage plan for the 70th anniversary. The meeting dragged on for two hours and concluded on a sour note with Theresa as usual feeling frustrated by her team's performance. She complained that they had failed to produce story ideas, which in fact wasn't the case as a list was prepared and put before her with the following storylines.

- Where does the Chinese military prowess stand against the US?
- How likely is China to expand its military might and where?
- The extent of the impact of Hong Kong's unrest on the Party's legitimacy
- What do the consequences of deteriorating relations with the US say about the Party and Chinese leadership?

The truth was Theresa had found them to be offensive to the higher-ups but she dared not say so to the journalists in the room. James could see the veins along the side of her throat bulging while she suppressed her anger. He wanted to see how she was going to rationalize and strike out the ideas and he wasn't disappointed.

'Well, this is about China's 70th anniversary so we shouldn't stray away from that focus,' she said slowly to keep her cool. Regaining composure, she picked up her pace and raised her voice.

'You had months to prepare as you knew this was coming and you're all experienced journalists. You should know better than to suggest ideas that miss the mark.

'Well, we have to draw up the plan right now as we're running out of time,' she said, dialling back to a normal volume. She turned her back towards them, picked up a marker and scribbled on the whiteboard in her barely readable scrawl.

'So this is what we'll do . . . '

- Live coverage: from 8.30 a.m. to 12 p.m.
- Central government leaders who graced the parade
- Full speech of the Chinese president
- Military prowess displayed (continuation of the display of military might over the past few days in the run-up to 1 Oct)
- How nationalist films did at the box office
- Foreign and Chinese experts on China's achievements
- Vox pop of Chinese citizens
- The weather conditions, the traffic situation in Beijing
- How citizens celebrate the 70th anniversary
- Special menus offered by restaurants and hotels, exhibitions
- How the international and Chinese media covered the 70th anniversary

Theresa avoided discussing how to angle and present the stories. *It's irrelevant to them anyway*, she thought. What she also played down in front of the team was the attention to the Hong Kong protests, sidelining the issue which realistically was part of the big picture in China's development story. But the Hong Kong desk led by Vijay wasn't within her consideration. In the end, the *Herald*'s coverage of the protests was less than half the volume it devoted to the National Day stories even though 1 October was, by then, one of the darkest days in the four-month movement, where the majority of the city's districts broke out in demonstrations. On the print version of the *Herald*'s front page the next day, 80 per cent of the column inches were on China's 70th anniversary, with a sliver of space given to the protests. To top that off, the newspaper had sold a wrapper advertisement that went around its front page to pro-China organizations.

The ad essentially became the paper's cover page, with the *Han Herald*'s masthead at the top and featured the lyrics of the Chinese national anthem. It was an additional layer of protection to mute the coverage of the protests. The *Herald*, needless to say, had a hand in that—among all things, it sold the ad space.

* * *

The *Herald*'s extensive coverage of the Chinese National Day lasted four days. The masthead editors deployed more people to cover the 70th anniversary than the protests, inevitably pulling resources from the coverage of the unrest. The front page print story on 2 October, hidden behind the wrapper advertisement, was headlined: 'United We Stand' under a half-page sized photo of the parade in Beijing. Coverage on the protests was reduced to less than a quarter of the page with a headline: 'The perils of division as radicals stage the most violent protests'. The 4:1 ratio maintained throughout the week. For its online coverage, the photo editor was instructed by Vijay and Theresa to select pictures of protesters hurling home made petrol bombs and bricks at riot police.

Heather wrote a personal account of her participation in the 60th anniversary celebrations as a student living in Beijing. The lead paragraph of the story read:

> *Ten years passed since I attended the Party's celebration of its 60th anniversary, but my pride has swooned at least a hundred times over for what my country and people have achieved. The road treaded in the decade was not easy if not for the resolute of the government.*

The four-day National Day coverage was best summarized by an editorial Pax commissioned.

> *Modern China is just seventy years old, but it has attained phenomenal achievements in the past forty years of economic reforms—after it emerged*

from the tumultuous Cultural Revolution—that not many other countries in the world have even come close. While there are challenges ahead, the People's Republic of China deserves every credit for what it has done to alleviate hundreds of millions from poverty in a generation.

Challenges, which were more externally than internally driven, have been inevitable and part of the natural course that every country faces following an extended period of high growth, such as the economic structural dilemma China faces. A prolonged trade war with the US and the unrest in troubled Hong Kong weren't its own doing, but are clearly mishaps that could be averted if all parties concerned exercise rationality and aspire to work towards common interests of universal peace and prosperity. Alas, self before all has taken the better of our external trading partner, like the US.

At home, the citizens of the Middle Kingdom have much to rejoice and be proud of, even though there needs to be caution of any misplaced complacency. The world's second-biggest economy and number one manufacturing centre did not come by chance and was a result of a generation's blood and sweat. The emergence of global Chinese corporations and the biggest tech companies are a cause for pride, a testament to the Party's leadership and the president's 'China Dream' vision. Correspondingly, the nation's economic might and tech prowess also fuelled growing expectations from its people and meeting these demands poses one of the biggest challenges the government faces. At the same time, there is also a thirst for an improved legal system to safeguard transparency and fairness, as well as individual assets as wealth grows. Without a doubt, the path to further greatness is strewn with obstacles.

Politically, the success of the Party's ongoing anti-graft campaign to raise governance and weed out evil elements that threaten to destroy its resolute for a fair and harmonious society continues to play out.

The challenge to the 'one country, two systems' model unfolding in Hong Kong will blow over as the Basic Law pledges to uphold 'the freedom of the person of Hong Kong residents shall be inviolable'. 'No Hong Kong resident shall be subjected to arbitrary or unlawful arrest, detention or imprisonment . . . Torture of any resident or arbitrary or unlawful deprivation of the life of any resident shall be prohibited', under Article 28. Protesters' claims are therefore unfounded. Hong Kong needs to be reminded of the gains it has reaped from being a part of the mainland. The city has been arguably the biggest beneficiary of the past forty years of Chinese economic reforms. It can continue to be so. Beijing has mindfully incorporated and acknowledged Hong Kong's pivotal role before and its current status in the national foreign trade strategy encapsulated in the Belt and Road Initiative and the Greater Bay Area technology hub. Peaceful reunifications of all Chinese territories, Taiwan included, will proceed.

Economic expansion, although the pace of it is slowing, still exceeds those in most parts of the world. And such growth, given the size of the domestic market, will provide the fundamental momentum for the rest of the world. It will also even out the unequal development and narrow inequality in time to come.

Modernization and nation-building will continue without interruption as they did in the past seventy years, supported by the advancement of the Chinese military. The trend is aimed towards a better place and a future where China will truly lead the world when the legitimacy and longevity of one-party rule are no longer questionable at home and abroad.

At the end of the week, Pax sent an e-mail to the newsroom which was copied to Steve and Jin.

To all comrades:

I'd like to take this opportunity to congratulate everyone on the comprehensive and insightful coverage of the 70th anniversary, presented not just from the domestic and national levels, but also from the global perspectives. This demonstrates that we have elevated our game to become a global media—successfully and unprecedentedly setting the mark to reporting on China from an objective Asian perspective which no newspaper has achieved.

The collection of inspiring stories presented in varied formats also reflects our advancement in our digital transformation as a media, as well as the strength of our creativity and innovation as a company to leverage technology to tell a great story.

As a token of the mastheads' appreciation for your efforts, there will be free flows of champagne, beer and pizza at the Hub at 6 p.m. today. To another 70 years!

Cheers,
Pax

* * *

In the middle of the Chinese National Day week, James received a text message from Sum Suk with a proposed time and place to meet. It had come from an unknown number. His source always used a prepaid SIM card.

'You can never be too careful,' he said.

Sum Suk had never misled James or told him anything that was incorrect. In the week of June when two million took to the streets and police first fired tear gas at protesters opposing the second reading of the extradition bill, James received a tip-off that the Hong Kong Chief Executive would meet a senior official from the Party to discuss the bill's suspension by the end of the week.

'You would not be wrong; it'll eventually be more than a pause,' his source advised him. The meeting in Shenzhen took place on Friday and the suspension was announced the next day. In early September, the Chief Executive announced the bill would be withdrawn in October.

Sum Suk requested to meet over the weekend at a remote village in the New Territories, in the northern part of the city. The New Territories was the least densely populated area in the city, less than ten and four times the densities of the Kowloon Peninsula and Hong Kong island respectively. James was on weekend duty so he asked Daniel to swap with him. He left his tiny apartment on Hong Kong island early in the morning for the hour-long journey that required changing three trains and a minibus to reach the entrance of the village.

The grocery was no larger than a 200 sq ft provision store that sold basic necessities ranging from toilet rolls, batteries and canned food to a small variety of perishables such as vegetables and bread. Called

Pang Kee, it was named after the family name of the owner who ran the store with his wife. The couple, now in their mid 60s, lived next door in a two-storey village house. Pang had also set up a food stall on one side of the front of the store, serving a minimal selection of Hong Kong-style foods: milk tea and coffee, toasts and instant noodles with luncheon meat and fried egg. Two tables and stools were placed by the stall, for frequent customers who were mostly local villagers and those from nearby villages, as well as the occasional visitors from the urban districts.

Sum Suk was sipping a cup of milk tea. On the table was a slice of thick toast spread with strawberry jam and two slabs of melting butter.

'Morning.'

'Morning. Breakfast? I'm having mine.'

'A coffee and one plain toast,' James answered, as Sum Suk turned to one side to repeat the items to Mrs Pang behind the stall.

'Young man, how are you?' his source asked. 'Things are heating up.'

'I'm all right, I guess . . . adjusting,' James said. It sounded like self-assurance. 'The narrative has shifted,' he looked intently at the older man.

Sum Suk was unlike most of the Chinese officials and party members James had met. A native of the southern province of Guangdong, he had lived in Hong Kong for many years and spoke Cantonese like a local, sprinkled with the latest slangs throughout the conversation. In the time that James had known him, Sum Suk showed he wasn't a blind follower of the Party or thought that the communist regime was always right.

'I've no illusion that the *Herald* is pro-establishment and China and I can deal with this, as long as we maintain the basic principles of journalism, our professional ethics. Lately, the editors are crossing the line frequently, with the intent to distort . . . you probably gathered from the articles,' James scooped two teaspoons of sugar—from the stainless steel sugar bowl with a hinged lid—into his coffee, stirring it briefly.

'The editors have launched a task force to investigate Edwin Law's death. They said it's our responsibility to quash fake news that the

Party is behind his death . . . ' He looked intently at his source and took a sip of his sweetened coffee.

Sum Suk had finished eating his toast while listening to the reporter and he wiped the corners of his mouth with his handkerchief.

'I won't tell you whether it's fake news or not. You've noticed that the Hong Kong police have never been more desperate to dig up who's behind the protests. It's worthwhile delving into this. There's more than meets the eye. Just be careful,' the older man told him and clasped his hands together, gently placing his elbows on the edge of the table, leaning forward. From experience, James knew that was the nonverbal cue for halting further discussion of Party-related matters. With that, his source changed the subject to talk about the overall unrest atmosphere and wondered aloud how long this would hang over the city.

* * *

Back at the office on Monday, James walked to the other end of the newsroom where the Hong Kong desk was located, to speak to Caroline Mak, a reporter on the police and security beat.

'Hey Carol, heard from a source and I wanted to run this by you.'

'What is it?'

'The police have doubled down on their efforts and resources to nail down who may be the potential leaders in the protests; it's definitely more intense than two months ago. You probably heard we're also on this task force to investigate Edwin Law's death. I'm thinking the two issues may be related.'

'Yeah, my sources said it's been exceptionally crazy in the last couple of weeks,' Caroline told James.

'Some of the top guys in the force are apparently freaking out and coming down real hard on the guys below. The order is to find out who's behind the protests, at all costs. It came from Beijing.'

Pausing for a moment, she added, 'It's plausible that the two issues are connected, but I've not heard anything at this point.'

'How about we check this out and see where this leads us?' James said. 'Of course, it may lead nowhere, but I think it's worth looking into.'

'Sure,' she agreed. 'Keep in touch.'

On the Hong Kong desk, tensions between reporters and editors and Vijay continued to boil. The desk was made up of twenty-five reporters, five desk editors and six copy editors. When the protests first broke out, Vijay allocated half of the reporters to cover the unrest live, with the remaining focused on their regular beats. As the crisis widened, by the time August came around, the entire reporting team became involved. The long hours on the ground, some days shifting from rally to rally across the city, took a physical toll on reporters. But it was nothing compared with the mental strain and frustration many felt seeing their published stories construed in ways to condemn protesters as solely responsible for increasingly violent clashes while sparing the Hong Kong and central Chinese governments of criticisms and playing down public sentiments that went against the official line. Any breaking news that didn't come from or wasn't confirmed by the authorities were strongly discouraged.

In early August, a Hong Kong reporter Felix Tam received a tip-off from a friend who worked at the British Council that a UK consulate employee was allegedly detained by mainland police in the southern city of Shenzhen. The reporter, together with Daniel called their diplomatic contacts and found out that the employee was taken into custody by the Chinese secret police. The two spoke to their desk editors about writing a story. The editors—one each from Hong Kong and China desks—thought the story was significant. But without any sources willing to be quoted on the record, the editors didn't dare take a chance and deferred to Theresa and Vijay for a decision.

'How do we know for sure if he was taken by the secret police? Or for the matter, even detained?' Theresa grilled the editors and reporters. 'The Chinese government hasn't made any announcement. Not even the British Consulate has confirmed this.'

'We're not going to spread innuendos and rumours. No story for now.'

Vijay added, 'Guys, let's wait at least for the Hong Kong government's statement. It'll then be a stronger story.'

It was only a week later that the *Herald* published its first stories. The first article was based on comments from the employee's relative.

The second was when Beijing confirmed the arrest of the employee for 'soliciting of prostitution' nearly two weeks after he disappeared and two days before he was released from 'administrative detention', which allowed authorities to detain any individuals suspected of minor offences for fifteen days. But the Hong Kong public knew better. When the employee emerged three months later to reveal on a social media post how he was tortured by Chinese secret police during the detention in August, he declined to speak to the *Herald*, despite numerous requests including one made personally by Pax. During the two weeks in custody, he claimed on his Facebook post, that the secret police interrogated him for information about the protests, his own involvement and the assumption that the UK was one of the foreign forces backing protesters. Chinese officials believed that foreign powers organized and backed the unrest as part of the broader effort to undermine Beijing. Beijing refuted his claims, which made global headlines and the Chinese state media released a 'confession video' of the employee with the headline shame on you superimposed at the start of the footage.

'Now that the ex-consulate staff has given his account, how about we write an editorial?' Samuel, one of the leader writers, proposed on the day the video was released.

'We've already reported those claims as a news story, which by the way, are questionable as there's no hard evidence. We need to be fair,' Pax answered. 'On the other hand, to address your concern, let's publish a letter from one of our non-Chinese readers who's written to give her take on the issue. That'll give it another angle and some balance.'

The reader's letter published with a disclaimer to clarify that the views didn't represent the *Herald*'s position, said:

The case of the former British consulate worker underscored why a million or more Hongkongers wouldn't give up on fighting the enactment of the extradition law and the mounting fear that the city's rule of law will soon be a thing of the past.

The Hongkonger's two-week detention on the charge of soliciting a prostitute in Shenzhen was an all too familiar tale that has been used multiple times by the Chinese police. And like this time, previous cases hadn't shown the 'guilty' person caught in the act; they had been hearsay. This is where the mainland's judicial system differs from Hong Kong and which is why it sends chills down the spine of many foreigners and foreign companies.

The timing of the administrative detention where individuals suspected of minor offences can be held for up to fifteen days, is also uncanny—at the height of the anti-government protests. It could well serve as a warning to foreign diplomats here in Hong Kong to stay clear of commentary that veers from Beijing's narrative on the political unrest.

Even before 2047, Beijing has changed the rules of the game under the 'one country, two systems' principle. But no change can be more damaging than upending the rule of law, which Hongkongers see as the city's last line of defence.

Eileen Chandler, Fortress Hill

The protests had gone on for four months now and the Hong Kong Government was showing no sign that it was capable of diffusing the high-pressure tensions that were mounting, nor the political will to want to do so.

'The day Hong Kong introduced the extradition bill, you knew it was only a matter of time the government became a puppet,' observed one of the Hong Kong desk editors. 'We just didn't foresee how quickly it gave up the little autonomy it had. It didn't even bother to pretend it was still running the show.'

The *Herald*, however, ran numerous stories of the government's sincerity and perseverance to work out a resolution, shrewdly using them as leverage against the protesters for their refusal to engage, omitting the context around the demonstrators' cause.

'Maybe the mastheads believe that if they keep saying this a hundred times, it will eventually become a fact,' Victor said to James, who couldn't help but agree.

A second incident soon occurred in the case of William Wang, a Chinese spy who sought political asylum in Australia in late November. Theresa told the China team it was a one-sided claim that the man was involved in intelligence operatives to intervene in politics in Hong Kong and Taiwan, as well as media coverage.

'This is all bullshit! But we can't not have anything on our website. Let's just run with a wire agency piece, at least that doesn't reflect our position.' To her deputies, she added, 'Let's wait a bit . . . monitor the state media for updates.'

In no time, as she anticipated, a state-run tabloid published a piece saying that Wang was a convicted fraudster previously sentenced to prison for more than a year and had been wanted by the Shanghai police for another case since April 2019. The *Herald*'s story under James' byline led with Wang's claim was a flawed script of a 'fraudster-turns-spy' penned by anti-China forces. The story was padded up by Beijing's argument of foreign interference in Chinese domestic affairs.

James was livid when he read the published article and his fury exploded when Theresa commended him on the piece.

Great job on the story. This is what we call the gold standard—journalistic accuracy and balanced reporting, she wrote in an e-mail to James, copied to the rest of the team.

'Hey, endorsement from the Party's proxy,' Daniel teased James.

'Stop, I'm embarrassed enough! Just pray she leaves me alone . . . at least for a while.' That, of course, was wishful thinking.

'James, we need you to write a piece on the US passing the Human Rights and Democracy Act.' Byron came by to his desk a week later. 'Please frame the piece in the current context, with what's happening in Hong Kong.'

The US legislation would sanction officials seen to be harming civil rights in Hong Kong, under an annual assessment of whether the city was sufficiently autonomous from China to continue enjoying preferential US trade and economic benefits granted via the 1992 Hong Kong Policy Act. The special status enabled the purchase of sensitive technologies, ensured free exchange between the US and Hong Kong dollars, as well as let the city negotiate trade and investment agreements independent of Beijing. The bill was first introduced in the House of Representatives and the Senate a day after the clashes outside LegCo.

James was irritated he had to put aside his ongoing investigation on Edwin Law's death to write the story. Though it was a significant development, Byron could have put another reporter on it. He noticed a recent pattern in his supervisor and other deputies who assigned him with more ad hoc, sometimes minor, stories as if to break his focus on the task force investigation, raising his suspicion by the day. 'There's more than meets the eye', Sum Suk had warned.

Byron saw the look of disdain on his face. 'I know you're swamped with the task force stuff. I tried getting someone else on this, but Theresa wouldn't hear of it. I don't understand her insistence,' he told James. 'Just write this up quickly. If we need more elaboration, we'll take care of it at the editing stage.'

James spent no more than thirty minutes on the story before filing it to the editors. He returned to his desktop research on the task force work while keeping a lookout for his story to hit the website. He had made sure he included enough information in his copy to let the readers understand the chaos surrounding Hong Kong. He included what the bill was about, where it was coming from and quotes from the US Senator Marco Rubio, who started a 'hotline' to accelerate the Senate's approval of the act.

An hour passed and then another went by, but he still didn't see his story on the website. He finally saw the article published when he refreshed the page an hour later.

Headline: China condemns Hong Kong bill as 'sinister intention' by the US

Beijing has lashed out at the US president for signing the Hong Kong Human Rights and Democracy Act on Thursday, calling it an act of foreign intervention intended to hinder China's peaceful growth.

The passing of the new law represented the US' 'sinister intention' to undermine Chinese people and America was the biggest culprit in disrupting Hong Kong, according to official Chinese statements.

The law was likely to encourage radicals to riot and commit violent acts as it allowed these terrorists to take cover behind the act, analysts said. One of the analysts said Trump was 'going to' [sic] sign the bill.

James couldn't read beyond the third paragraph. The editors had turned a straightforward report to one that spoke for one side. His version had read:

Headline: US passes Hong Kong bill as protests and tensions with China escalate

The US president has signed a legislation that authorizes sanctions against Chinese and Hong Kong officials for civil rights abuses in Hong Kong amid the city's increasing pro-democracy protests, as Beijing condemned the move as 'foreign interference into China's internal affairs'.

The passing of the new law came as both sides are trying to negotiate a deal to ease the trade war.

James felt his face flush and placed his palm against his forehead, then covered his face with both hands to calm himself down. *Breathe James, breathe! Don't do anything rash, remember the last time you confronted Theresa? It didn't lead to anything constructive. Stay focused on your strategy. Fight with the task force assignment, with hard facts.*

Nonetheless, he was going to set the record straight, if only for his own sanity. Ten minutes later, with a calmer state of mind, he drafted an e-mail to Theresa, copying Byron.

Hi Theresa,

For the record, I don't agree with how the story on the US passing the Hong Kong bill was written. The few problems for me were:

1. *The lead paragraph of the story was changed from a straightforward angle of the latest development in the current context of the Hong Kong unrest and trade negotiations as was instructed by Byron, to something unrecognizable and was almost a press release for Beijing.*
2. *I didn't speak to any of the Chinese analysts that were quoted in the story and their comments for that matter are highly skewed.*
3. *No one spoke to me about any of these changes or additions to the story. If it was going to be my name on this, I believe I should be looped in.*

Last but not least, I understand that editors are stretched and in the interest of time, they can't be updating reporters on every minor change made. But what we are really talking about is how the story should be framed and presented here, so a discussion would have been warranted. I'd appreciate it if we can discuss this in person.

Thanks,
James

For two days, neither Byron nor Theresa responded. On the third day, however, Theresa replied with a terse note that had a retaliatory undertone and strewn with grammatical mistakes.

Hi James,

I have always found your stories problematic. They generally lack balance and is not giving a truthful picture of what's going on in Hong Kong.

1. *In your latest story, the voice in the story is just one-sided, almost entirely from Rubio - known for their extreme views on HK and China. Even though the atmosphere in the US can be quite overwhelmingly one-sided at the moment, in my experience, not everyone sees this issue this way. I think we need to have more balanced quotes from different people. Otherwise, we are just becoming an echo chamber.*
2. *We just quoted them accusing China of reneging on its promise to let HK have universal suffrage. But we didn't provide any context and background. What they claim is their perception. It is not the reality. We need to provide context and fact-check and not just running people's quotes.*

Such reporting makes us an easy target for criticism.

Best,
Theresa

'Not again,' James murmured with a snort after he read the e-mail. His blood no longer boiled as calm crept in with the time-lapse in Theresa's response. He didn't want to engage and further stupefy himself by countering Theresa's ever-evolving, illogical moral judgement. His time was better spent uncovering new information on Edwin's death.

* * *

Work on the task force investigation gathered pace for James after his meeting with Sum Suk in early October, despite the regular interrupting assignments from Theresa. From the interviews with Edwin's mother and friends, he and his colleagues were able to build a profile of the young man's short life.

After numerous hours on the phone and calls to Chinese public security bureau sources in Beijing and southern Guangdong, he confirmed that the central government had given law enforcement agencies at the national and local levels—the state security department, the public security bureau and the Hong Kong police—a November deadline to establish the mastermind behind the protests. The Party operated a covert network in the shadow of individuals, business groups and associations linked to Chinese provinces in Hong Kong, which had been activated to thwart the protests. The Party's proxy in Hong Kong, the Central Liaison Office supervised the network, which included the city's biggest tycoons whose commitment to backing China protected their investments in the mainland, in what was known as the United Front. The United Front effort in Hong Kong is believed to have started during China's civil war in the 1930s to draw as many Hongkongers to the Party's camp. By the 1980s, Beijing tried to expand its control in the city by absorbing the business elites, whose influence rose as the economy took off. The alliance also included gangsters such as those from Fujian province.

'The network is unbelievably extensive. One powerful example is when all the members, from the top bosses of state-owned companies in Hong Kong and the mainland, academics, officials, state media reporters, individuals fired off a post condemning the protesters for defacing the national emblem on 21 July,' a source at one of China's big state-owned banks told James.

'Look at the post,' the source showed him a screenshot on his phone, '"black terror . . . the illegal acts are a challenge to national sovereignty". It's a united and concerted effort in propaganda.'

In the third week of October, Caroline pulled James aside while he was getting a coffee from the Nespresso machine in The Hub. The two ambled towards a quieter corner to a counter near the window.

'I talked with my police sources,' she said in a hushed tone. 'They confirmed the deadline and have given me some data on the kind of resources that are being poured into ID the leaders.'

'That's great. My Chinese police sources have also verified that November is correct,' James said and his eyes casually scanned around the area to ensure they had their privacy. 'We now also know that Beijing has deployed Chinese officers—paramilitary, state security department and the PLA—to infiltrate into the Hong Kong police force. I think we have enough for a story.'

Caroline agreed. Then with a grim face, she leaned closer and whispered gravely to her colleague. 'That's not all. One of my sources mentioned Edwin Law in passing, kind of a Freudian slip. He said "it was a result of their desperation". When I probed, he freaked out and I could hear his voice quivering and feel him shaking over the phone.

'I think you may be on to something here. I suggest checking it out with the forensics folks or coroners?'

James thanked her and promised to keep her posted.

Through his friends from school and their network, James tracked down the forensic pathologist who was involved in examining Edwin's body.

'Hello doctor, I got your contact from Justin Yeung, thanks for taking my call,' James told the coroner. 'I believe Justin mentioned I'd call.'

'Yes, hi James. He's given me the heads up. This is not a good time and not on the phone. Let's get coffee? I'll get back to you shortly.'

Two days later on a Saturday morning, James met the doctor in a café on a quiet side street in Wan Chai. They chatted for nearly two hours and then said goodbye. James stepped out of the pocket-sized café and walked as quickly as he could the ten blocks to his apartment, oblivious to the sunny crisp October day and hustle and bustle on the streets. He was anxious to get home and in front of his laptop. The doctor had just given him his biggest lead and break in the investigation.

'I don't think the young man died from accidental drowning,' he looked intently at James. 'There were suspicious bruises on his body.'

8

Truth and Dare

It took James several minutes before he could fully digest what the doctor had just said. Never before had he encountered such long intervals of deadly silence in meetings with his sources. The doctor's confession treaded on James' pride as a reporter and pricked his conscience that he hadn't previously dug hard enough for the inside story. He could feel the agony and frustration that the doctor must have gone through since the autopsy and being gagged from speaking the truth. He was also putting his entire career on the line for talking to him.

Have I ever risked my career to publish a story? James reflected briefly before he was seized by a sudden fear that fell upon him, burning his mind into ashes. *What if I end up not being able to publish this story?* His heart sank and he felt being dragged down to the floor, vanishing in vain. He was almost certain Theresa wouldn't easily consent to publish the story. He cupped his neck with his hands to hold his head from dropping further into misery.

'So that means he might not have died from drowning?' James asked, finally breaking the silence.

'Possibly,' the doctor answered without hesitation. His clear eyes reflected confidence and relief as though liberated from the prison of his own moral cowardice. He was ready to share every scientific detail and question he had had during the autopsy, with James. He leaned forward, slowly opened his mouth and articulated every word he spoke, like giving a private tutorial lesson to a secondary school student. It was his manner of talking to non-medical professionals.

'The key in an autopsy for a drowned body is to differentiate between a death by submersion from an immersion of a body. Death of a victim found in water is not always related to drowning.'

'Can you elaborate? So what exactly was suspicious in Edwin's case?'

'There was some evidence that the cause of his death was not drowning,' the doctor said. 'From a drowned body, obviously, you may see water in the stomach. Also, you may see cerebral edema, bloody froth in the airway, petrous or mastoid hemorrhage. But none of that was in Edwin's body.'

The doctor had unconsciously returned to medical jargons that James didn't understand. James also leaned forward to hear better, trying hard to understand.

'So you are saying he was not drowned to death, right?' he asked cautiously.

'I wouldn't say that. Though, highly unlikely would be my answer.'

'Any other evidence, apart from the reasons you've just listed?'

'Oh yes, I didn't see any washerwoman changes in his body either.'

'Washerwoman changes?'

'Yes. It's a change in the skin condition as a result of being immersed in water. It's basically swelling of the skin when you are in the water, as our skin absorbs it,' the doctor said, rubbing his left arm with his index finger to emphasize how water permeates the skin cells.

'But I thought you get that all the time when you are in the water. It means it would happen to all bodies found in water, regardless of how victims died,' James asked sharply.

'You are absolutely right and that's precisely my point. There weren't many washerwoman changes in Edwin's body—as if it was left in the water for no more than an hour.

'Identities of bodies found in water, in some cases, can't be recognized with naked eyes due to excessive swelling of the skin.'

'OK . . . so you are saying this implies that Edwin's body was immersed in water after his death, then picked up by the police shortly after, possibly within an hour?'

'Possibly,' the doctor nodded.

'Also, there are several phases during the drowning process. A breath-holding phase, followed by involuntary inspiration, gasping for air before the loss of consciousness. The death is secondary to the development of cerebral hypoxia, leading to irreversible brain damage.'

'Cerebral what?'

'Cerebral hypoxia. It means your brain is damaged from being deprived of oxygen,' he paused.

'Yes, Edwin's brain was damaged but the damage was rather external. There were some dents on his scalp, which is extremely rare for a drowned body. This means he must have hit his head on something underwater—like a coral reef. But again, as you can imagine, the chances of that are extremely low.'

James had slid into a hunch as he absorbed the information. Straightening up, he now pushed his upper body forward, unconsciously pushing the tea table towards the doctor. The doctor also had to put some weight against the table to find a new equilibrium.

'So did you tell that to the police? I mean . . . you all have to write an autopsy report after the examination, right?'

'That's correct. Our team filed a report for the case, as we always do. We gave it to the police who came to collect it the next day. I also did tell them my conclusion, verbally, that the possibility of death due to drowning is significantly low.'

'What did they say?'

'They said "all right" took his body and disappeared. Never heard anything from them since.'

'I don't really follow,' James said. 'If they weren't going to use any of your findings in the autopsy, why did they ask for it in the first place? They could've just skipped it.'

'Well, it's a bureaucratic protocol that they must fulfil. In Hong Kong, a waiver of an autopsy is not granted if the cause of death is medically not known.

'Pretty much all suspicious deaths must go through an autopsy in many countries and the authorities need to tick that off from their box to end their investigations. And also, it's easier for the authorities to convince families of victims with whatever conclusions they have made if you have conducted an autopsy.'

'Not when your finding contradicts with their conclusion.'

'Well, I'm guessing our report was never shown to his family.'

'Do you mind if I can see that report sometime later?'

'Actually, I brought it today,' the doctor said as he crouched down towards a briefcase he placed on the ground. He shoved his arm into the black attaché case and pulled out a plastic sleeve with pieces of A4-sized papers in it.

'There you go,' the doctor gave the file to James with a resolute look. Once he handed the file over, he looked visually relaxed. His face was no longer shadowed by anxiety, he appeared more certain that he was doing the right thing, standing on the right side of history. Liberated, the doctor took sips of water from his glass and broke into a big grin of victory. It was obvious that he had transcended from fear about the possible consequences of his actions.

The three-page report was divided into different sections, with an examination report for different organs. The first page read:

Office of the Forensic Service Hong Kong	
DATE and HOUR AUTOPSY PERFORMED: *16 September 2019; 8:30 A.M.* *By Jerry Leung, M.D.*	***Assistant:*** *Victoria Wong, M.D.* *** **Full Autopsy Performed***
SUMMARY REPORT OF AUTOPSY	
Name: *Law Chi-wai, Edwin*	***Coroner's Case #:*** *2019-385*
Date of Birth: *21 March, 1997*	***Age:*** *22*
Race: *Chinese*	***Sex:*** *Male*
Date of Death: *15 September, 2019*	***Body Identified by:*** *Johnathan Wong*
Case # *001924-22C-2019*	***Investigative Agency:*** *Forensic Pathology Service* *Hong Kong Government*

The second and third pages included the following sections:

SUMMARY OF CLINICAL HISTORY
DESCRIPTION OF GROSS LESIONS
CLINICOPATHOLOGIC CORRELATION
SUMMARY AND REFLECTION

The gross lesions section included descriptions of the examinations of Edwin's different organs, such as his heart, brain, aorta, lungs, gastrointestinal system, reticuloendothelial system, genitourinary system, endocrine system and extremities.

'Read the description for his lungs,' Leung said.

LUNGS: The right lung weighed 445 grams, the left weighed 395 grams.

'Lungs together normally weigh approximately 1,000 grams,' the doctor said, again slowly articulating each word. 'But lungs in submersions are usually heavier: an average weight of 1,411 grams. It's still a controversial argument in academia about using lung weight as a marker of drowning, as the value significantly varies based on the gender and age of the subjects.'

SUMMARY OF CLINICAL HISTORY: Cause of death from drowning highly unlikely

James read and thought this summarizing line would be enough for the publication of a story. 'Do you mind if I take this with me?' he asked, still staring dry-eyed at the report.

'I'm afraid I would have to take it back. I need to return it to our files,' Leung said. 'I can't print a copy either as it would leave traces in our intranet system if I reprint it. But you're welcome to take some photos if needed.'

James immediately took out his phone and voraciously took photos.

'Are you okay for us to use some of the materials from this report for publication?' James rushed his speech.

'Not a problem. After all, that's why I am here. Feel free to use any of those materials.'

'Wouldn't it compromise you at work, though?'

'Possibly,' the doctor's eyes zoned out for about two seconds before his gaze returned to the reporter.

'But the report has already been widely shared among the members of our team as well as with the police and authorities. As long as you don't publish the photos in the report, which have my watermark on it and make me an anonymous source if you're going to use any of my comments today, I think it should be fine.'

'Thank you,' James said, grateful. 'Just out of curiosity . . . I was just wondering,' he then mumbled in hesitation. 'Why are you doing this? May I ask?'

Leung grinned slightly before he answered. 'I think my job is no different from you journalists when it comes to seeking and speaking the truth. The only difference though is that we speak with medical data. It's data that says it's possible that he wasn't drowned to death. But the police ignored it, silencing our scientific findings.

'I will remember that I remain a member of society, with special obligations to all my fellow human beings, those sound of mind and body as well as the infirm,' the doctor suddenly mumbled, like he was chanting a spell or saying a prayer, barely audible to James.

'It's the Hippocratic Oath. I think it's my obligation as a doctor to let the world know about the findings about Edwin's body and what the data speaks for,' Leung said.

'Thank you. Is there anything else you want to talk to me about?' James said, moved.

'Well, in fact . . . yes. There is one last thing.

'Autopsying a drowned body is a diagnosis of exclusion,' he said. 'It's based on ruling out all other causes of death via complete autopsy and toxicology. So it usually takes two to four hours to perform. But the police only gave me an hour.'

* * *

To the printing room. Now. Emergency. James texted Mary, Victor and Daniel, as he rushed into the office with his laptop clutched under his armpit. His body had tensed up with energy.

He flung his old black backpack to his seat, rolled up the sleeves of his white shirt and rushed to the printing room.

'Come on, come on, come on,' he said, frantically clicking the button on his laptop to print photos of the autopsy report that he had taken. Victor, thinking that James was a nervous wreck, followed him to the printing room.

'You all right?' Victor asked, tilting his messy hair towards James.

'Yeah, I'm fine.'

'What's all this about?'

'I've got Edwin's autopsy report,' James said as the printer started to come alive.

Astonished, Victor stared at the pages that were spitting out of the machine, desperately wanting to read. By the time Mary and Daniel crammed into the small room, the report was already printed and Victor was reading it. He almost shoved his head into the report and looked like he stopped breathing.

'What's going on here, guys?' Daniel asked as he walked in with Mary, looking over Victor's shoulder.

'He's got Edwin's autopsy report,' Victor said, as James handed a second printed copy to the both of them. A few minutes of silence ensued as the reporters flipped through the few pages.

'Can we publish this report?' Daniel whispered, turning slightly pale and the first to break the silence. He glanced around at his colleagues and then through the glass planes of the room at the newsroom which went on with business.

'Contents, yes. But uploading the report, no. There is a watermark of my source on every page,' James said.

'Can we quote him on the record then?'

'Negative.'

'You should've persuaded him,' Daniel said, his voice slightly raised and irritated.

'Don't forget we are going against his mother's words,' he said, lowering his voice down, with Mary and Victor nodding in agreement. Then, he cleared his throat, looked down at the report, 'I mean this is a game-changer. We should unlock its full potential.'

Annoyed, James frowned. 'That would jeopardize his career, safety even. He specifically told me not to quote him. That was the deal,' he said in a shrill voice.

Daniel sighed loudly.

'Can you at least try to persuade him again? You know Theresa would look for every reason to veto this story.'

'Give me one good reason why readers should believe this?' Victor interjected with an impersonation of Theresa in a silly high-pitch holler to lighten the mood. Mary, who saw James fidgeting and sensing his discomfort, playfully hit Victor in the stomach with her elbow. She also broke the awkward silence that filled the room.

'Maybe we can do some more digging, try and get another source and prepare for a bigger piece together?' Mary said, moving closer to both James and Daniel. 'I mean we still haven't used the materials from our interviews with Ben and Jess.'

Vicky's TV interview had brutally cut off any possibility of the reporters writing a story based on the accounts of Edwin's friends. A mother's words were far more powerful, especially when the accounts were of contradicting views.

'If we do find other information supporting our hypothesis, then the story would be more plausible and maybe we don't need to mention the source's name,' Mary said.

James still looked drowned in discomfort. So did Daniel. But they both turned their bodies towards Mary, hoping she could arbitrate. Mary watched their reactions intently. Slowly, she continued. 'I really want to publish our interview with Ben and Jess. I honestly don't think they were lying. That way, we have a scientific report and comments from his friends who are happy to be quoted.'

'I think that's plausible,' Daniel said, clearing away the awkwardness that filled the room.

'How about we divide the labour,' Victor said. 'Mary and I will reach out to Ben and Jess again and see whether they can introduce us to other colleagues of theirs who can speak on the record. Daniel and James can reach out to government officials who can talk to us.

'Then we will start filing . . . '

'Hey, what are you guys doing?' Nancy popped her head into the printing room. She didn't wait for the reporters to respond and opened the door to enter the room, with Heather in tow.

'Leave us alone here, would you?' Daniel said in the most irritated voice. Victor swiftly shoved the autopsy report into a shredder at the corner of the room. Mary slipped the second copy on top of James' opened laptop and slammed the cover down.

'Have a good day,' Mary said, walking out of the room. The other three followed her lead and dispersed.

* * *

James spent most of the second day digging for more information on Edwin's death. It was 10.40 p.m. when he walked out of the grey office building where a cool autumn breeze touched his cold cheeks. He had little success; he reached out to all the relevant contacts he could think of and many of them hung up on him, with an air of indifference that made Edwin's death more suspicious. He felt drained, a walking body that was utterly desiccated from disappointment among the hustle and bustle on the city's streets as people went on with their activities.

Few of these people would have dwelled on Edwin's death, he thought. He was another young protester, someone else's son, but who unfortunately lost his life. James vowed not to lose his conscience at any cost. He pleaded with himself never to compromise his values or ignore the truth if he knew of it. But compromising seemed like a new survival tactic in his home city and it depressed him. Those who fought for what they believed in didn't win; they either lost their jobs or sometimes even their lives. *What am I? A fighter or a survivor?* The question howled loudly in James' mind, stifling his conscience. Sighing in despair, he conceded that he belonged to the latter. After all, he had to also constantly compromise his values—one way or another—to survive. Those who fully stood up for their values and beliefs either left the company when Arcade bought the paper, or when Theresa ordered a series of stories to applaud the takeover. By contrast, James chose to stay, telling himself he could make changes from within. But that vow never realized as he also turned a blind eye to the *Herald*'s columns and editorials that promoted anti-democratic values.

James also realized how he never explicitly fought against Theresa. When he found out she used a fake persona—an imaginary South Asian regional security expert—to write a series of columns to justify Beijing's assertive diplomatic behaviour, he chose to remain silent. Along with other reporters, he simply criticized and talked about it behind Theresa's back when the mysterious expert's Twitter account got suspended as part of the tech giant's investigation to expose fake personas. The *Herald* later withdrew all columns published by the fake persona, claiming that it was also fooled. But James knew that was a lie. He knew the *Herald* usually paid extra attention to check the backgrounds of columnists who wrote for them. But instead of fighting against Theresa, James chose not to raise the issue to avoid trouble.

I'm no different from Heather, he thought. *Maybe I just enjoy standing on a moral high ground over others.* Perhaps it was a natural and perverse consequence that the stories of what he witnessed during the Hong Kong protests and his interviews with Edwin's friends got shut down for choosing not to speak up when he should have. He was an accomplice to the *Herald*'s editorial fallout. *The darkest places in hell are reserved for those who maintain their neutrality in times of moral crisis*, he thought he almost heard the reprimanding voice of his favourite Italian philosopher Dante Alighieri in his ears. *I deserve a place in hell. Or perhaps it's not too late.* Such train of thoughts recurred as he became increasingly driven to learn the truth about Edwin's death. He realized he couldn't avoid colliding with Theresa, which would risk his job security. A fighter, not a survivor, he chose to be this time. As James sighed out his agony, exhaling feeble breaths, his phone rang.

No caller ID. His phone screen displayed. James picked it up immediately, anticipating it might be a call from Sum Suk. He answered the call cautiously craning his head towards his phone.

'North Point Station, Exit A. 11 p.m. today,' said the caller. The voice sounded odd as though it went through a voice changer device.

James couldn't figure out whether it belonged to a man or a woman. It wasn't Sum Suk, as he never used such a device. His pupils immediately contracted in weariness.

'Who is this?' he asked.

'I know Sum Suk. I'll see you there,' the caller hung up.

A fresh rush of blood surged into James' head, soaking his brain. His face immediately blushed in excitement. He felt recharged with a hope that he could break the deadlock in getting additional information on Edwin's death. He jumped off the kerb onto the street to flag down a taxi, ignoring the danger of the traffic that came tearing down. He couldn't wait for the taxi to pull over to the side and hopped into the vehicle in the middle of the street. *Sum Suk might be giving a turning point here*, he thought.

It was just before 11 p.m. when James got off the taxi after he gave—almost threw—crumpled banknotes to the driver as he rushed out in a hurry. 'Keep the change,' he told the driver and made a dash for exit A of North Point MTR station. At 11 p.m. sharp, a young female jogger in a ponytail, wearing a black training suit with wireless headphones, approached him.

'Hello,' the woman, who looked like she was in her early 20s, said as she continued jogging in place. James stood still, without responding.

'A lady in the black car over there wanted me to pass this note,' she said as she tossed him a memo. James' eyes followed the direction of her fingertip which pointed towards a car with heavily tinted windows on the opposite end of the street to where they were standing. He couldn't see anything inside, only the reflection of the street lights where it was parked. The driver started the engine and it purred slowly away.

James opened the half-folded memo, as the jogger covered her head with her hoodie and faded away. The memo had just one line.

Dig into the connection between the Fujian gangsters and the police

While James was racking his brain to decipher what it actually meant, his phone rang again.

He picked it up without looking at the display screen.

'Hello, what does this mean?' James rushed through, trying to scab as much information as he could before the caller hung up again.

'What connection? Whom should I contact? Where should I go for more info?' He threw out whatever questions that came to his mind at one go, as he was pretty sure the mysterious person would hang up again in a few seconds, just like twenty minutes earlier.

'Do some research and I'll reconnect with you in three days,' the mysterious mechanical-sounding voice said. 'I want you to find out something before then.' And the line went dead.

'What the hell?' James hissed in complaint, as he pummelled his fist into his thigh in frustration. He expected the 'deep throat' to give him more than that. *The information, if you could call it that, or was it a statement, or a claim rather,* James thought, *was horrendously incomplete.* He didn't have many sources in the police and he hardly knew anyone from the Fujian gang. It was a mission impossible.

Disappointed and puzzled, James went to the nearest 24-hour Hong Kong-style café—*cha chaan teng*—to think through the one-line message. He drank a cup of milk tea and searched his dim memory about news on the possible connection between the police and the Fujian gangsters in the past.

Michael Fung! A spark surfaced in his mind. Fung was a 43-year-old pro-Beijing legislator in Hong Kong accused of having connections with Fujian gangsters during the Yuen Long attacks on 21 July. A myriad of previously filmed videos suggesting the connection between him and the Fujian gangsters resurfaced online shortly after the attacks, with Fung meeting and shaking hands with the white-clothed group of assailants at a house in Yuen Long. 'You guys are the nation's true heroes,' Fung commended the gangsters in the footage, giving his thumbs-up. 'Thank you for your hard work,' he continued, smiling cunningly. One of the white-clothed men whom Fung shook hands with was later captured in one of the footages of the Yuen Long Station attack. The legislator later defended his encounter with the assailant as one where he was merely obliging to a photo request from one of his constituency's supporters, denying prior knowledge of the attacks. He also dismissed allegations that he was connected to the gangsters, but didn't hide his support for their acts. 'These men were safeguarding our district, where I am also a resident and thus

Hong Kong's rule of law.' James quickly took out his laptop from his backpack and started to search for more information on Fung and similar past incidents.

But then, this doesn't add up. Fung's a legislator, not the police. The instruction was to look for the connection between the police and the gangsters. *Of course!* He suddenly recalled the numerous claims on social media in July that the police didn't show up while gangsters rampaged through the Yuen Long station and attacked the protesters and commuters. James continued his research in the *cha chaan teng*, burying his head into the laptop. It was almost 1 a.m. He pulled out information that the July Yuen Long attack wasn't the first time these gangsters were involved in Hong Kong Kong protests. They also attacked activists in the Mong Kok district during the 2014 Umbrella Movement. The police were similarly accused of not responding in a timely manner and letting the attacks take place. A pro-democracy politician Nick Chow had then condemned police behaviour as a 'clear collusion between police and the gangs'. The one-line message was beginning to make sense to James. He hadn't thought to put the police and the gangs together, but he now felt he had found a new missing piece that could solve the puzzle of Edwin's death.

So does that mean I should approach Nick Chow? But if Nick Chow knew better, he would have made that information public himself, given his political stance. And it was not like he could approach Fung either. If anything, Fung would only report James to his superiors in Beijing, he thought. It would have been perfect if he had a source in the Fujian gang who could just give him some hints about their connection with the police. *Wish I at least had someone who can introduce anyone in the Fujian community in Hong Kong*, James thought, feeling slightly dizzy and exhausted.

He ordered fried rice noodles as he suddenly felt that all the remaining energy had drained out from his body. *Cha chaan teng was mankind's best invention ever*, he thought, as it took less than a minute before they served him with the food. Between the mouthfuls of delicious noodles, he noticed that the neon street signs of North Point through the *cha chaan teng*'s glass windows had flickered out. Looking into the dark street as he shoved the greasy but comforting noodles into his mouth, a name flashed to his mind. *Jeffrey*.

* * *

'Can you give me some of your Fujian contacts?' James asked brashly, as soon as he saw Jeffrey at the office the next morning. Jeffrey was taken aback by the request, but more surprised by the sight of James. He looked like he hadn't slept and had stayed out all night, his greasy black hair plastered to his head and the sweaty outfit that he was also wearing yesterday. Journalists guarded their contacts and sources religiously, they were their biggest assets in this job.

Rude, Jeffery thought. 'What is this about?' he said, astounded, as his nose caught the stinky smell of a dead rat from James, who hadn't showered in more than a day. He frowned in a slight sense of disgust as he saw James scratching his greasy hair. But James appeared oblivious.

'Can you put me in touch with someone from the clan?' James said bluntly, his voice softening as he stepped closer to Jeffery, who in turn moved backwards, holding his breath. He was also baffled by James' request which was so direct. It was unacceptable in most newsrooms to ask for someone else's sources. He began to feel a little sympathetic as the request reflected desperation rather than coercion.

'You know that won't happen,' Jeffrey rejected curtly, but his hardened face displayed a look of intrigue. His pupils expanded as he was figuring out what was going on with his colleague.

'Please Jeffery,' James begged. 'It's got to do with telling the truth about Edwin's death.' James, looking like a semi-maniac now, had a glint in his eyes. Once again, Jeffrey edged backwards unconsciously.

'What exactly is it that you want to know?'

'I got a credible source saying that there is a connection between the gangs and the police surrounding Edwin's death.'

An awkward silence filled the space between James and Jeffrey and divided the two apart. Jeffrey gazed at James with renewed, unprecedented amazement.

'You know they won't just confess to their connection with the police.'

'I know that. But I have to at least try. Maybe I can get some new hints. It's better than not trying at all.'

After a moment of silence, Jeffrey took his mobile phone out and started to search through his contact list. Jeffrey disliked how James had asked him for his contacts, but he liked the recklessness and his colleague's dogged pursuit of a story. *This guy may damage Theresa,* Jeffrey suddenly thought. He recalled a similar request from Theresa about a month ago, to dig into the connection between the police and the gangsters. He was reluctant then to contribute to anything that'd benefit her. Jeffery was also extremely bitter when Theresa sent two young reporters to Fujian in an attempt to show him down—perhaps replace him in the newsroom. *This could be a chance to get the better of Theresa. Make her sweat.*

'Find An Rong at North Point market,' Jeffrey told James, taking his eyes off his mobile phone and looking straight into his colleague's. James saw Jeffrey's dilated pupils were soon filled with perverse eagerness: a yearning for vengeance.

'You can find him at the Xiamen butcher shop,' Jeffery said. 'I'll give him a heads-up that you are on your way. Can't guarantee whether he'd see you though. This is all I can offer.'

'Thank you,' James said in the most excited voice. He then ran off to find his allies—Mary, Victor and Daniel—to see if any of them were available to join him. Mary and Victor, however, were already out to meet Ben and Jess. Daniel was at his desk, biting his nails and drafting a story based on the autopsy report.

'Hey Dan, do you have a minute?'

'Sure. What's new?'

James brought him to the printing room again and told him everything from the call and memo he got yesterday. By the time James finished telling him the story, Daniel was half frozen and confused. He was struck by James' heedlessness, only half-believing what he had gone through.

'So . . . you want me to go there with you now?' Daniel asked, unable to hide his bewilderment and horror, stepping backwards and leaning against the printer behind him.

Was James losing his mind?

* * *

Before he knew it, Daniel found himself walking down the streets of North Point with James.

The two to three blocks of Marble Road and surrounding streets made up the North Point Market. Some shop owners—wearing aprons and rubber gloves—were throwing out pails of dark and slimy liquids onto the main street, where trams and cars ran. The pungent fishy smell first pierced their noses then soon numbed their senses. There was also garbage strewn all over the damp and wet street, hurdling them from walking straight. Water gushing out from big rubber hoses that extended from some shops to the street was pushing the rubbish towards them, making their path even less appealing. Dodging the trash in zigzag steps, the two reporters made their way towards the Xiamen butcher shop. They continued walking through the filthy street for about twenty minutes before turning into a back street where they finally saw the shop, partially visible at the corner at the end of the alley.

From the corner of his eye, James then spotted about five people following them. The tails were talking loudly, sometimes roaring in laughter and swinging baseball bats—opposite of everything portrayed in the movies. It distracted him from focusing on what he planned to ask An Rong in a few minutes. James pretended he didn't see.

'Who would walk all the way for a piece of meat?' Daniel said quietly.

'This is definitely a cover-up business for money laundering,' his colleague whispered. He was also wary of the five gangsters stalking them.

'As a matter of fact, all money laundering cover-up businesses are dodgy,' he said.

'Agreed,' James responded. 'I bet they don't sell decent meat, just like the *Herald* doesn't publish any real news.'

The reporters rounded the last corner towards the shop. Another group of eight men were leaning against the wall, unmoved as though they were expecting the reporters. James' blood ran cold, whilst Daniel turned pale and let out a hiccup.

An unpleasant ammonia-like scent of raw pork wrapped around James and Daniel as they entered the shady shop, a departure from the typical Hong Kong butcher where hanging red lamps light up the storefront to give an extra layer of shine to the meats. A woman in her 40s, wearing a black leather apron cleaning a 12-inch butcher knife stared at them as they walked in. Her face looked sour and her large eyes were pinned onto James and Daniel.

'Hi there. We came to see Mr An Rong,' James mumbled, looking at the floor.

The woman wildly looked around them, before she dropped her butcher knife fiercely onto the big thick wooden chopper with a loud *thud.* She then took off her leather apron and hung it on the wall.

'It's definitely money laundering,' Daniel whispered again. 'Have you seen anyone wearing a leather apron in a butcher shop? What is she, a blacksmith?' he ventriloquized. Daniel's auto-response to anxiety and stress was apparently to talk fast and non-stop.

It's comforting to know that I'm not the only one who's nervous, James thought.

The lady turned around, shutting the two cold-sweating reporters up immediately.

'Come on in,' she said expressionlessly, as she walked through an old iron door at the back of the store counter.

'Do you think we can come out in one piece?' Daniel whispered. 'Now I'm starting to wonder what kinds of meat they are selling here,' he continued his life-risking talk, as he stole a glimpse of the meats in the fridge with fear.

But James had no room in his mind to be afraid or worried about his own safety. He now only had two more days before his next meeting with the 'deep throat' and he needed to find an answer. Ignoring Daniel's question, he walked ahead of his colleague to keep pace with the woman, pulled the door open and skidded inside. Daniel, looking even paler than the blank pages of the notepad he was carrying, hunched his shoulders and followed James' lead.

Behind the door was a flight of endless steel stairs, partially lit by a few flickering naked light bulbs that hung from the ceiling. The stairs descended into an underground level. It was so deep that James felt like it was a tunnel to hell. He took a look around the darkness that surrounded him, in amusement and trepidation. He felt his heart pumping his blood through the veins. It was as though boiling lava was consuming his heart, burning him from the inside.

The stairs were so narrow that the reporters could only tip their toes with each descending step. For a moment, James felt like he was walking in Theresa's ridiculously high heels and broke into a wry smile. Following the mysterious lady's lead, they descended about seven stories and finally arrived at the bottom-most floor where they assumed they'd meet An Rong.

'Here we are,' the lady said at last, with a twisted and mischievous smile. 'Welcome to Fujian.'

The bottom-most floor exuded pretty much the same atmosphere as the stairs they just walked down. It was dark, cold and unpleasant. There was a large open space, where a couple dozen gangsters were watching TV on couches, working out and blowing weed smoke on dead plants. James and Daniel continued following the lady and came to another long alley that started from the corner of the open space. A stream of frosty darkness fell across the paved, tiled floor of the alley, freezing those who walked on it. The alley was even darker than the open space that they left behind. It was basically unlit except for a few half-broken, blinking bulbs dangling from the ceiling. The floor was unpleasantly sticky, making nasty noises every time the reporters stepped forward and it smelt like spits. James just wanted to get his job done as soon as possible and flee. Daniel regretted coming along, his face white as though he had seen a ghost. As they walked across the alley, a few gangsters stood alongside the corridor, smoking Godknowswhat, glazed at them. One threw his half-finished cigarette in their direction, reminding them how welcomed they were.

'Chill, misters,' the lady said to James and Daniel, seeing their pale faces. 'Nothing life-threatening here.'

She stopped in front of another door. 'There you go. He's been waiting.'

When they opened the door, they saw a bold (and bald) man in his 60s, wearing a grey-coloured suit, sitting on his brown leather sofa. He was smoking a Cohiba cigar, flicking the ash onto his expensive-looking purple Persian carpet, which was also an ashtray. The room was designed like an office, uncannily similar to Pax's.

'You kids are brave,' Machiavellian An Rong said, with a devious smile on his face. His face was a lipstick shade of pinkish-red, looking somewhat squiffed. The strong smell of alcohol that was locked within the small room also pierced James' nostrils.

'If it wasn't for Jeff, I wouldn't meet with you kids,' he said as he pursed his dark purple, revolting lips. 'He is part of the Fujian family and families help out one another.' An's cracking voice reverberated through the high-ceiling room, sending a sinister echo that disquieted both James and Daniel.

'So what is it that you want to know?' the triad boss asked, crossing his legs, lifting his chin, whilst looking intrigued.

'We just want to know how you guys were involved in the Yuen Long attack.'

An suddenly cracked himself laughing. A terrible but somewhat mirthless laugh echoed across his office. The horrible laugh—if it could be called that—prevented James from asking further questions. Just like Daniel, he froze and stood like a piece of furniture, barely breathing.

'You guys are funny. Give me one good reason why I should tell you that.'

'For Jeff,' James said schemingly, trying to respond in An's language.

An snorted and looked unconvinced. But he thought the tale was harmless as it would only benefit him by apotheosizing him and his clan. An often enjoyed telling tales of how great he was, boasting about his clout to strangers and enjoying sensing their fears.

'I must say I'm amazed by your recklessness. Deal. I got one condition though. It has to be off the record and I can't be quoted with whatever stories you guys are writing.

'I must not be seen,' he said as he inhaled the last sip of his cigar smoke. 'James, you live in Wan Chai; and Daniel you live in Tsim Sha Tsui right? If you publish my name, I will make sure you don't get another day in your lives. Understood?'

It seemed that the gangsters had already done their background checks of the reporters. James was amazed at how fast his personal information could be leaked. *This confirms my hypothesis that the police are backing them*, he thought.

'Deal,' the cold voice of James said. Daniel looked at James, frowning.

'Our clan is one of the most powerful clans in Southern China,' An said in his drawling voice, as though he was narrating a fairy-tale. 'We have about 10,000 members all across the mainland with more than twenty subgroups.

'We are currently on a long-term project here in Hong Kong since June this year, requiring more manpower. So our comrades in the Fujian headquarters had to come over here to help us out. They first went to Macau, took ferries there and got here on 6 August.'

An Rong's arrogant account helped refresh James' memory. He remembered that there had been rumours flying around the city that some Fujian associations and communities were relocating their relatives and friends from their hometowns to Hong Kong. He also recalled reading a news article around that time of the year when the Fujian clan recruited more gangsters and had a meeting at their clan's premises on Ming Yuen Western Street at North Point. *The United Front—the network the Party used to expand its control of Hong Kong.*

'It was a coalition operation,' An continued talking with pride. 'We made a temporary peace with our rival, the 18K, for the greater good.'

The 18K was another triad group based in Hong Kong. It was led by a man known as 'Cobra', whose identity remained unknown.

'What did you guys get in return? I mean, you can't be doing all these for the greater good, whatever that means,' Daniel torpedoed, suddenly finding his courage.

'What do you think? Money, of course.'

'Who pays you then?'

An's grin faded a little before he summoned. 'The only reason I'm talking to you is because I promised I'll help Jeff when he needs my help,' he said as though it was the greatest kindness he had ever shown to anyone before.

It sounds like Jeffrey has a close relationship with the Fujian clan, James thought. He recalled a story Jeffrey wrote shortly after the Yuen Long attack, in which the police had 'warned' the Fujian clan that anyone engaging in violence would be arrested, quoting the anonymous gangsters. *Hong Kong police have asked the Fujianese gangsters to stop their violence for the stability of the city,* he wrote, quoting a man who refused to be named.

It appeared on the surface as though the police had urged the Fujian clan to cooperate, fulfilling their duties to protect the needs of public safety; but the gangsters also enjoyed the story of the police asking for their cooperation. To them, it meant that the police had acknowledged the clan's clout, feeding An's ego and pride. The police and the Fujian clan had had a symbiotic relationship for a long time. The clan had always served the needs of the police—performing deeds that the force couldn't. In return, the force ensured the clan's survival, becoming their biggest sponsor.

'How do you think we survived?' An said.

'Without the authorities' help, we don't exist. In return, we do things that they can't.

'After all, they need us as much as we need them.'

* * *

It was 11 p. m. when James once more waited for the mysterious woman at the North Point Station. He was wary of accepting her help, but he also knew she was his best chance. Amid the sound of cars driving past, James strained a little to listen again to the recording he made of the meeting with An Rong two days ago. A random pedestrian—a teenager in school uniform—approached him. James instantly looked at his hands for any sign of a possible second memo.

'A lady over there wants you in her car,' the boy said, pointing to the same black vehicle he saw three days ago. James walked across the street and hopped into the car. The lady, who looked like she was in her 50s, was also sitting in the backseat. She was in a tailored navy pant suit, reading a thick report. A man in his 30s in a black suit was in the driver's seat.

'Have you done your homework?' the lady asked, as she lowered her reading glasses to the tip of her nose and looked directly into James' eyes.

'I have.'

'Talking to An Rong was a bold move. I like it.'

'So you had tails on me?'

'No one at the safe house?' she ignored James and asked the driver.

'No ma'am. It's clear.'

'Then let's move.'

'Where are we going?' James choked.

'To find the truth.'

A tidal wave swept across James' mind. He desperately wanted to decipher what she meant and where they were heading, only to realize he had absolutely no idea who she was. Yet he hadn't given a second thought to the risk that he might have set himself up for. He only had a series of queries about the mysterious woman sitting next to him.

'Who are you? Why are you helping me?' James threw his questions out as he turned his head towards her. 'And who do you work for?' he continued, sounding hysterical.

'I'm Yang from the state security department. There are many different political factions within the agency,' Yang answered calmly, as though she was accustomed to dealing with reporters like James. 'And that's all you need to know,' she added firmly.

It was quite a long drive. After about forty minutes of driving North, the driver finally stopped the car on an empty, remote street in the New Territories. As they got off the vehicle, James saw an old wooden house, ruined, in the middle of nowhere. It was so remote that there were no neighbourhoods in sight, nor any other structure or living thing.

'Come on in,' Yang said, as she walked into the house with the driver, who had doubled as a bodyguard.

The dark house was like a safe house that James often saw in the movies. In the living area, there were several black and white monitors spying on an adjacent room that looked like an interrogation chamber. James walked to the very room that he just saw on the monitors. There was a table and a fallen wooden chair on the floor.

'Where are we?' James asked.

'It's where Edwin got killed.'

'You are confirming that he was murdered?' James asked, eagerly. 'You know I'm going to write this, right?'

'Don't be silly. If you write it hastily, you won't be able to publish it. You need proof. Do you have any evidence apart from my words?' Yang said as she turned off the light.

She then turned on a UV blood detection device she was carrying, beaming the blue ray on the floor. A pool of bloodstain in black was exposed under the table and on the wooden chair. A trail of blood extended from the pool, stretching all the way towards the door, as though someone had carried a dead body that continued to bleed.

'It's Edwin's,' she said. 'Fujian gangs interrogated him here.'

'Fujian gangs? Not the police?' James shouted in shock, in a higher octave.

'He was already unconscious from inhaling too much tear gas when the police took custody of him during the protest. A current senior official from our bureau had previously given the police an order to transfer the unconscious people to the Fujian gangs' safe house for intense interrogations.'

'Why the ones who were unconscious?'

'It's simple as hell,' Yang said. 'They didn't see the police arresting them, so they won't accuse the police when they are released. And one more reason, perhaps more important, the police can't use violence during interrogation, here in Hong Kong. But we are really desperate to find out who's behind the protest,' she said calmly.

'So it was the Fujian gangs that kidnapped and interrogated Edwin, but they got the order from a senior official in the state security department? Am I hearing this right?'

Yang nodded before she continued. 'When the official found out that Edwin was from an ordinary family—without any political connections with the Hong Kong Government or the mainland—he allowed a little more intensity in the interrogation than usual.

'There you go,' Yang swabbed some blood samples from the ground with a cotton bud, put it into a test tube and gave it to James.

'I have a recording of Edwin's interrogation too,' she tossed a voice recorder to James. 'Should be enough for your exclusive story.'

* * *

Edwin woke up when the Fujian gang slammed a bucket of iced water on his face. The sharp chill from the freezing water slapped his cheeks as he gasped desperately for breath and coughed to expel the tear gas out. His last memory was inhaling tear gas on the street during the protest. Edwin choked, but the heavy rain pelting on the window and claps of thunder muted the noises that he was making. Two gangsters enjoyed watching him suffering in pain. They exchanged sly glances and giggled as though they were watching a slapstick comedy. It wasn't until Edwin came around that he realized he was topless and tied to a chair in the middle of nowhere.

'Shall we begin?' one of the gangsters said, as they walked out from the interrogation chamber, closing the door behind them.

They sat on chairs in front of the monitors that surveilled the chamber where Edwin was held. There were eight German-made speakers—a complete set of surrounding sound systems—installed around Edwin. As one of the gangsters pushed a button on his laptop, loud heavy metal music blasted in the room, piercing through Edwin's ears. The music played for about forty-five minutes and went into a minute's pause before it was blasted out again. The same song was repeated. 'The noise should not exceed 79' decibels read an instruction note that the gangsters were holding.

During the silent pause that occurred after every forty-five minutes of brutal sonic torture, the gangsters spoke into a microphone to coerce Edwin for information, warning him that any resistance against them was futile and to instill a feeling of hopelessness. He struggled and experienced excruciating pain in coping with the noise that was rupturing his ear drums. The brutal gangsters let the music run and watched YouTube videos in the monitoring room. His body screamed in pain. He bit his lips, as the thundering sound poured into his ears.

After about two hours, Edwin spat before he threw up. At some point, he was beginning to wish for his death, as he concluded that it was the only way to free himself of the extreme suffering and pain. His brain and body functions started to slide, as he no longer could control his movements or think clearly. His eyes were cloudy and they started to lose focus, his mutterings were incomprehensible and ultimately slobbered. Sweating and struggling to breathe, he was slowly losing his mind. But perversely at the same time, it felt good as it meant he was that much closer to death. *Death is perhaps the only thing that could liberate me.* Edwin still had no idea where he was. But he was certain that he was going to die there. As his emotional struggle superseded his physical pain, his willpower to live shattered into pieces. That's when the gangsters walked back into the chamber to begin their interrogation.

'Where am I?' Edwin muttered as they walked in, squeezing his final ounce of energy, last of his will—whatever was left—before his death. His mind was only half-awake, but his survival instinct forced him to milk the last drop of energy he had left to yell.

'See, he's not completely broken yet,' one of the gangsters said to the other. 'Gotta do it for at least twenty-four hours before it fully numbs him.'

'We don't have enough time,' the other dismissed. 'The instruction was to return him within eighteen hours. But you are right, he's not ready yet.' He walked to the corner of the chamber and grabbed a couple of baseball bats, throwing one of them to the first gangster.

'We have to speed up the process,' the second gangster said as he swung the bat down on Edwin's shoulder.

Edwin began to sob, as his tears fell from his brown eyes, running down his cheeks. The two gangsters laughed like psychopaths, taking pleasure in every moment of the young man's suffering. The first gangster walked towards him venomously and started to beat him up with his baseball bat. The two were ruthless, habitually cruel and revelled in gaining the upper hand through violence. After about three minutes of ruthless beating, one of them spoke at last.

'Write down three names of your comrades, then you will be able to go back home,' the first gangster said, sliding a pen and a notepad towards him.

'What do you mean?' hoarsely, Edwin mumbled.

'Write down three names of your leaders.'

'You mean the protest? There's no such thing. It's a leaderless movement.'

'Guess we get to have more fun then,' the other gangster sniggered, raising his baseball bat and threatening to take another swing.

'Let's not waste our energy here. All you need to do is to give us three names. Not the whole list. Just three names.'

'I honestly don't know,' Edwin begged, tears streaming down his face.

'You want us to believe that when you work for one of those civil societies? Give us the names now and you can go home.'

'Burn in hell,' Edwin murmured with a baffling obstinacy.

His curse ignited a deep fury in one of the pair. The first gangster fumed and kicked Edwin against the table behind him. Edwin, tied to a chair, fell and hit his head on a corner of the table. With a jolt of unprecedented pain, he lost consciousness. He never got up. Bright red blood spilt from his head, streaming down his neck and ultimately wetting and glowing on the floor.

'Wake up, get up,' the gangster desperately shook him. 'Shit . . . I think he's dead.'

'What did you do?' the other yelled, giving his partner a hard knock on the shoulders with his fist. He then promptly called An Rong to report the development. About an hour later, Wang Tao kicked the door open at An's office in North Point. Wang was furious.

'What did you do? You weren't meant to kill him!' Wang screamed, kicking and punching everything he could see. Frantic with uncontrollable rage, he threw the file he was holding at An. It flew straight onto the gangster's forehead, leaving red marks as it fell on the purple Persian carpet.

'We never intended to. It was an accident,' An said, looking redder than usual.

'An accident? Are you kidding me?' Wang bellowed, looking about to explode. 'Don't you know how much media attention we have right now? This may bring all of our hard work to naught,' he yelled hysterically.

'Do you honestly have any idea how much we have tried in changing both local and international opinions on the Hong Kong protests? You just turned all of our efforts into nothing. You understand that?'

'It wasn't intentional. Sorry.'

'Sorry? Did you just say *sorry*?' Wang seemed angrier. His face was as red as blood.

'You just compromised our entire operation here in Hong Kong. I am going to report your misaction to the higher-ups so that you won't get your pie in this city any more.'

'I'm afraid we are in the same boat sir,' An said grimly, suddenly sticking his head up with glittering eyes, half threatening. 'Reporting to the Party won't be necessary,' he continued with a crafty look.

'No one at the top needs to know that you've reached out to us to interrogate the kid, right? We have been cooperating for decades. I am sure we can find some ways to solve this problem . . . as we always have.'

Wang stopped talking, looking into An's eyes. He sensed that An wasn't bluffing. After all, An wouldn't have survived in his world if he was easily scared off. He also had a complex network of connections, including officials in the mainland, easily transcending between the black and white terrains of the society. *It's always better off to compromise when you deal with someone like him,* Wang thought.

The official furiously stepped out of An's office and gave a call to his office. An could only make out that Wang was meting out some kind of an order, as the conversation was barely audible from where he was. Thirty minutes later, a group of people in anti-containment clothing arrived at the New Territories safe house and took Edwin's body away.

'Clean this up quickly, on the double. We don't want any of our fingerprints or DNAs there,' the woman, who looked like a supervisor of the team, ordered her subordinates, as soon as she hung up her call with Wang.

The next day, Edwin's naked body was found in the sea near Yau Tong.

* * *

A continuous chorus of 'oh my God' reverberated around the printing room the next day when James shared his story and showed the stained cotton bud in the test tube to his team. Daniel, Mary and Victor let off shrieks of excitement. Flashes of triumph sparked in their eyes, as though they sensed a victory from the cotton bud James was holding. But they all covered their mouths with their hands, hushing, trying to keep this confidential.

'We still need to run a DNA test, making sure it's Edwin's,' Daniel said with a trembling voice. 'Do we have any samples of Edwin's DNA other than the blood?'

'We do,' Victor said, whispering. 'We have his hair from the comb in his swimming gear bag from Ben and Jessica.'

'We'll ask for a DNA test now,' Mary said. 'Shouldn't take too long until we get the result.'

Mary, together with Victor, left the printing room and headed to a DNA test centre in the Central district. James and Daniel started to draft their exclusive story for the next few hours.

Edwin Law was beaten to death, did not drown, sources confirm

A 22-year-old social activist Edwin Law, who was found dead in the sea near Yau Tong last month, was murdered by a triad, according to medical and government sources. Medical evidence acquired by the Herald also supports that Law, who took part in the recent pro-democracy protest, was killed in New Territories the day before his naked body was found.

The story included the accounts of Dr Leung and Yang (although they were both anonymous in the story), photos of the exterior of the safe house, followed by the interview with Ben and Jessica. It gave the context of Beijing's United Front strategy and the aim to increase control over Hong Kong. James and Daniel also made sure they had left space in the story to include the DNA test results, as well as an official response from the authorities.

After carefully crafting the draft, James promptly texted Theresa via the company messenger, requesting an immediate task force meeting. He said they just made *significant progress* with their investigation and *urgently needed* to meet. Theresa replied within thirty minutes—which was very unusual—and agreed to meet in the Sichuan meeting room at 4 p.m. By 3.50 p.m., all the team members were sitting in the meeting room. Victor sat opposite Heather, where they were soon locked in a war of glares and almost ready to pick a fight. James and Mary exchanged glances lifting their eyebrows, both trying not to laugh out loud.

It was Heather who fired the first shot.

'So . . . what did you guys do after Vicky's confession interview?' she asked satirically. 'Nancy told me that you guys were whispering something in the printing room a few hours ago, planning to overthrow our mastheads? Does Pax know about the coup d'état too?'

'We have some solid evidence regarding Edwin's death,' Victor retorted. He looked cemented and unshakable.

'Stop please,' James whispered to Victor, shaking his head.

'What? She'll hear it in a minute anyway,' Victor didn't back off. Turning his head away and towards Heather, he continued. 'So what did you do then? Spoke to another Beijing-commissioned liar?'

'Guys . . . please,' Mary was about to say something when Theresa violently walked into the meeting room, followed by a more relaxed-looking Pax. Heather had informed Pax of the 'secretive meeting' in the printing room and warned that there might be a story that could collide with Beijing's interest.

James and Daniel told Pax and Theresa of their investigation over the past few days, including the autopsy report, photo of the safe house and the blood sample that Mary and Victor submitted for a DNA test.

'We are currently waiting for the DNA test results,' Daniel said, calmly. 'We strongly believe the story needs to be published for the interest of Hongkongers.' He then showed them their draft of the story that they had begun to write.

Pax and Theresa read the copy in silence. Neither of the editors spoke a single word for the next minute. *Perhaps a good sign?* James thought. The glimmer of hope was shattered when Theresa opened her mouth.

'We are not going to publish this story,' Theresa said, fastidiously, twitching her lips. 'There is no credible evidence yet to fully prove it was a murder.'

'Agreed. No real facts are backing your arguments,' Pax pledged his support for Theresa instantly. *The story will seriously damage my reputation among the higher-ups*, he thought. He wanted Theresa's failure, but this story would also jeopardize Pax's chair.

We are now in the same boat.

Victor immediately turned red like he was about to explode. 'So we are not allowed to publish anything that may make the authorities angry?'

'Don't you speak to me like that,' Theresa snapped back, shakily. 'Did you notice that all of your sources are anonymous, apart from those friends of Edwin's—who don't really matter?'

'As if we could name them in the story,' Victor retaliated in a towering rage. 'Since when has the media started to name whistleblowers of such kind?'

'Who is your source?' Theresa cunningly asked James, with her high-pitched and shrill voice.

'I can't say. And you know you can't ask me that' James hissed. 'Revealing who they are would jeopardize their safety.'

'I can name mine,' Heather interrupted the conversation, at perfect timing. 'I had an interview with Mr Wang of the state security department last night. He talked about how Beijing prioritizes the stability of Hong Kong and thus, its people's safety,' she said as she handed to the editors a draft of her story.

Exclusive: Beijing remains rock-solid in safeguarding stability, official says

Beijing remains rock-solid in maintaining Hong Kong's political and economic stability, a senior Chinese official says, vowing to further enhance its cooperation with the Hong Kong Government to protect China's national sovereignty from the [sic] Western interference.

Wang Tao, one of Beijing's top officials on national security issues, told the Han Herald that Beijing fully supports the Hong Kong government's effort in safeguarding rule of law in the city. Beijing has always politically supported the local government's effort in battling the [sic] Western interference and would continue to do so in the future, Wang added.

'I'm sorry. You call this a story?' Victor asked in a mocking voice after reading the headline, bringing the undercurrent with Heather to a boil. 'You think we're Wang's PR office?'

Heather was about to open her mouth to rebut when Pax stood up for her. 'Victor, objectively speaking, I think Heather's piece has far more value than your speculative story,' he said. 'She named her source in the story. If the source is able to identify who he or she is, that means the person is confident in what he is saying. This suggests that he would take full responsibility for what he said.

'By contrast, when the source is unnamed it means we as a company have to take full responsibility for the authenticity of their claims. I don't think we can take that responsibility here.'

'How can you possibly name someone when the person is a whistleblower?' James said tensely, frowning. 'Don't forget we also have the autopsy report. If we can't publish this, what's the point of having a task force team?'

'I have made myself very clear on what this team is about,' Theresa said. 'I said you need to investigate to counter the biased Western narratives, not the other way around. If you don't like the job, feel free to walk out now. I've got plenty of others to supplant you.' James' flourishing patience was lost when he heard Theresa's last sentence. Banging the door behind him, he left the meeting room.

No one dared to stop him. Daniel, Mary and Victor watched him leave silently, in despair. They didn't feel Heather's sneering eyes on them. Exposed to Theresa's frosty stubbornness, James lost all inclination and will to convince her. He went back to his desk and picked up his belongings, ran outside and took the first taxi he saw on the street.

'Where to mister?' the driver asked.

'Just drive.'

'What do you mean?'

'I said just drive,' James said in a most irritated voice, hysterically. 'Just drive around the city for about twenty minutes.'

9

Corruption

Three days went by. James had not recovered from the flare-up with Pax and Theresa. His fury stewed and wore him down mentally and then physically. Going to work sickened him, where the sight of Pax and Theresa and the deputies, as well as Heather, was revolting. His disgust of the newsroom was mixed hideously with a painful regret of seeing and being in the thick of the *Herald*'s editorial demise. He took a couple of days off work to clear his head; he needed to figure out how he could bring to the open the unethical behaviour of the editors and a media like the *Herald* which commanded a certain gravitas in the Hong Kong society. The intent to cover up was corruption from where James sat. *What was the dark force motivating them?* Their responses had brimmed on hysteria and desperation, which piqued his curiosity immensely and he was more determined than ever to get to the bottom of the perverse but strange situation.

Byron, I'd like to take two days off to clear the backlog of annual leave I have. Thanks, James texted his supervisor.

No problem. Is everything ok? Byron replied.

He probably heard about the row with Pax and Theresa and wants to learn more, James thought, but he couldn't be bothered to reply.

Even though Byron was supposed to coordinate the work of the task force, he had discretely stayed away as much as he could to avoid unnecessary wrangling that he could do without. All he knew about the flare-up was the reporters had dug out a potentially explosive story that

Theresa had censored and he was curious for the details. He couldn't ask Theresa as that would be inviting himself to the lioness' den to be chewed and spit out. Theresa had been in a foul mood since the clash with the reporters. He had seen how she had bitten Vijay's head off in an exchange over a minor matter.

Theresa's wrath underlined her innermost fear. The reporters' investigative reporting was solid and if the story ever went out from the *Herald*, it would mean that she had lost control of the situation, which would lead to her fall. *No! It's never going to happen under my watch. I've worked too hard to get to where I am,* she swore to herself.

Pax was anxious too as the findings could cast a devastating blow to the Party's stature and would unravel the network and important ties that he painstakingly built with those in power in the mainland. He believed his agenda was less self-serving than Theresa's, but they both were aligned in their determination to bury the story.

Out of the office, James tried to isolate his anger and emotions. He wasn't going to let Pax and Theresa off that easily. *Where should I look for ammunition to battle?* As he agonized, an e-mail alert popped up on his phone with a preview: *[For internal circulation] Kudos to another milestone - 50 million MAUs!*

The numbers, of course! Online traffic volume and earnings, he thought, the area where the editors and Steve had been obsessing over the past few years. He had wondered about the authenticity of the numbers. Steve told the newsroom that the increased readership came mainly from the US for the *Herald*'s China insights. But James could not fathom how pro-Party narratives and one-sided US-China relations stories resonated with American readers. *From an investment perspective, had the increased MAU (monthly active user) numbers reasonably justified the millions of dollars that the company was pouring into newsroom operations? Or has the spending translated into any revenue, however minimal?* Questions flew around his head. *Since the task force concept was argued on the premise to counter fake news, let's see how real these numbers are,* he thought.

He started going through all of Steve's emails in which he reported quarterly numbers, reading each one of them carefully. It took him half a day to trawl through all the relevant emails but he uncovered little. He decided he would have to work his network of sources within the company and outside. It won't be easy. He made a note to call an ex-colleague who had gone to work for Arcade in Shenzhen.

* * *

The *Herald* held a special place in the hearts of many Hongkongers as a revered newspaper that stood for the city's freedom of speech, a principle that helped Hong Kong to flourish and become the international financial centre it was. The newspaper was also the go-to publication for learning English for generations of Hong Kong students as local schools incorporated the *Herald* as a staple in the mix of language teaching materials.

As a student, James read it daily, progressively covering different sections of the newspaper whilst moving up the educational levels. He was elated when the *Herald* offered him a job seven years ago, but now saddened and frustrated by how the newspaper had fallen by way of professional integrity. The first four years that James was at the *Herald*, Theresa had rewarded him with annual pay rises, largely because of a face issue—she had poached him from a rival Chinese media company and needed to demonstrate the value of her decision. James' strong principles and often unyielding positions had increasingly annoyed her, particularly in the past year as the integrity of the newsroom came under greater pressure amid the political movement in Hong Kong and US-China tensions. The growing animosity between the two was mutual.

The *Herald*'s passage towards decline began with the Kua family's relentless cost-cutting programme more than two decades ago, sowing the seeds of corruption in the company. The pruning that started with the advent of the Internet in the media industry eroding newspaper advertising revenue had decimated newsroom operations to the bones. On average, one staff now carried out five persons' jobs, salaries had frozen for the longest time and worse of all, a culture of distrust and shoe-shining manifested—to survive, suck up to your superiors, as incompetent as they were. If Pax or Theresa liked a subordinate, it was more likely that the individual's actions pleased either of them and less because of the person's capabilities. Favoured individuals could be assured of salary increases and bonuses, as well as a flexible cap on travel and entertainment expenses.

Arcade's entry, despite its red capitalist background, was the oasis for a dried-out newsroom that was surviving on a drip. It brought much-needed funding and the latitude for managers to spend and transform into a global media without the pressure to deliver a monetary profit in the short term. Jin also awarded senior managers and journalists with Arcade stock options to secure their loyalty and therefore stability in the company through the change of ownership. The free flow of capital and the spending spree to expand were almost ending. The payroll of 350 employees had more than doubled to 800 where the bulk of staff came from the newsroom. New hires, especially those with big titles, were paid astronomical sums to entice them to join from bigger international publications. They weren't often the best talent, but they were right by the standards of the three masthead editors wary about bringing in intelligent people who didn't fit their personal agendas. New computer hardware and software were bought, new products invested and developed, and topped with a new address in one of the city's most valuable districts. On the closed and privately-held books, withering earnings sank deeper, eventually into the red, pulling away further the goal to break even. Worse still, the millions of dollars spent bought the *Herald* less reputational credibility than the owners would have hoped for and instead, growing scepticism that it was a fair and balanced media voice.

Steve's two app-based China products were bleeding money by the end of the first year. Even the juiciest story on corruption in China—the ones based on official announcements of course—drew only a few thousand viewers in a month, compared with the hundreds of thousands for the same story on the *Herald*'s website.

'I don't get it,' James said to Daniel. 'What's the point of doubling your resources to cover the same story?'

Yet Steve, with his used-car salesman-like skills, managed to persuade the board of directors that their performance shouldn't be measured by the monthly user numbers alone.

'The two newsletter products plugged a hole in the audience segment that the core *Herald* online product doesn't reach, that is the younger readers who represent our future,' he told the board.

With his youthful look, hoodie and jeans, the CEO was a naturally engaging speaker, with a knack for using analogies and endless personal anecdotes to illustrate the dullest subject matter. In contrast, Pax and Theresa struggled to communicate in an organized and cohesive manner. It bought him more time and so the two newsletters continued to run with expensive teams of editors and multimedia reporters for another two years. What was less obvious to many at the *Herald* was how dire the financial numbers at the company had become by the summer of 2019, as Steve continued to front an optimistic outlook of increased subscriber numbers and new revenue channels in his regular townhalls with staff. Every quarter came with 'awesome' achievements and 'milestones', Steve told the staff, with little explanation on how he would monetize the uptrend. Arcade's Chief Financial Officer Isaac Lin began to breathe down on the *Herald*'s management team sometime after the Lunar New Year holidays.

'I know Mark's five-year period to invest isn't up, but it's nearly four years and your numbers—not just online traffic figures—should be showing a business turnaround, at least covering some costs,' Lin warned Steve and the *Herald*'s Chief Operating Officer Sheldon Lam, as well as Pax. 'In case you've forgotten, it's never a sandbox you're playing in, but we're running a business here. In fact, you should have a feasible business model ready to be put in place to sustain your operations,' he added with a snide.

If Steve and Pax even felt the pressure, they covered it up well as the spending across the company continued as it had in the prior years. In a random meeting with the China team, Theresa told the editors and reporters, 'We are as committed as before to provide you with the best and all the resources you need to do your jobs. I encourage you to travel, to be on the ground to get the stories.'

'Is there any limit on the number of business trips each reporter can make?' James asked. He heard from colleagues in the finance department that the CFO was scrutinizing and cutting costs.

'No, as long as the story ideas you pitch to me are sound and worth writing about,' Theresa replied. 'The rotations for reporters to spend three months in DC and Beijing or any China bureaux will carry on. I'm even looking at setting up rotations at our Brussels bureau.'

The CEO did begin exploring new products such as generating China research reports, a lucrative business area that many of the *Herald*'s competitors had already expanded into as a natural extension to leverage the knowledge base and titles of media companies. The company also tried to rejuvenate its paid conference business that was in limbo. Its reputational decline in recent years undermined efforts to expand its share of the conference market. Still, with Arcade's funding, the conferences moved abroad, beyond the home turf in Hong Kong and China to the rest of Asia, Europe and the US. Many of the destinations coincided with Arcade's market expansion strategy but were less relevant to the *Herald*'s interest as a media company.

The turnout for the expensive overseas events was at best modest, which meant they ran at losses, observed reporters assigned to cover the events. Attendance for its one-day conference in New York City was dismal, where less than half the hotel ballroom was filled and a third of which were *Herald* staff and the working crew, the *Herald*'s Beijing bureau chief who flew in from the Chinese capital to cover it told James. Because of its editorial position, the lineup of speakers was who's who in the past tense: retired politicians and supporters of China and the communist regime, removing any possibility of an open-minded dialogue on the challenges of US-China relations.

'It was a disaster and painful for us reporters who need to milk stories out of a non-event, without coming across as complete idiots,' the bureau chief complained to James.

The *Herald* devoted an entire page in the newspaper to the conference, with the main story whose headline read: *Retired China minister rebuffs China. US decoupling suggestion amid trade war despite analysts saying it is underway*

'It's a joke that isn't funny. The story tells you nothing,' James snorted with laughter as he showed the article to Daniel. 'Imagine, this is the best shot at the paper's high-profile coming-out party in the US! Did you see Pax's self-serving e-mail?' The e-mail had arrived overnight because of the difference in time zones.

Dear comrades,

I'm pleased to report that our inaugural China Conference in the world's biggest economy and the Herald's most important market was a rousing success. We are grateful to our distinguished speakers and guests who brought much insight and perspectives to our understanding of US-China relations, arguably the most important bilateral relationship of this century.

Throughout the day's conference, onstage and off, our team engaged with a wide spectrum of policy-makers, scholars and business elites on issues across the political, economic and social fronts and had the opportunity to communicate important perspectives that would influence how the international community re-evaluate China's peaceful rise and contribution to the world.

To most of you who weren't able to join us in New York City, you are also part of our success here. We wouldn't be here today as a representative of China to lead the China conversation if not for your dedication and diligence to build our warchest of content and insights of the mainland over the years. I've arranged for a free flow of drinks and food at the Social Hive to share the success we have had this week in the US. Please enjoy.

Thank you from the masthead editors.

Cheers!
Pax

The masthead editors and Steve were among the party of thirty that travelled to the US for the conference. They flew on business class tickets and stayed a full week in the Big Apple. Pax, Theresa and Vijay also flew to Washington DC to meet politicians and DC-based mainland Chinese officials and media executives. In New York, they enjoyed a basketball game in an NBA suite. Editors took partying photos of themselves and posted them on their social media accounts. Theresa also flew to California for a vacation with her partner after that. Despite her loyalty to the Party, she harboured a conflicting and secret desire for a life in the US, the land of the free where there'd be fewer restrictions and no watchful eyes from the higher-ups. She had quietly applied for a green card.

'Given that, we've money left from this year's budget, let's spend it on expanding our American network,' Steve had told Pax before they left for the US.

The evening they were at the NBA game, the *Herald* sacked more than a dozen employees from a business unit on the grounds that the company was shutting down the division.

* * *

Corruption—often of the nepotistic kind—was frequently at the centre of Chinese politics and business. The *Herald*, once a critical public voice and the media watchdog against the abuse of official power had, knowingly or not, joined the pack. Furthermore, the thirst for content in the digital era from businesses and companies opened the door for media companies to capitalize on sponsored feature writing as a revenue source.

The firewall between marketing and sales and editorial was crumbling but Steve, who once claimed he was a supporter of press freedom, had become unconcerned as personal interests took precedence. He was more anxious to meet the performance benchmarks that Jin had given him, which was key to his next and hopefully, bigger job. In the near four years at the *Herald*, he saw clearly the old ship was much tougher to change than he had naively thought, but he dismissed his inexperience and ability as the problem. *Nope, the company is a losing battle and I need to get out before it takes me down too!* Steve was agitated and therefore increasingly intolerant of Pax's pushbacks towards his requests to the newsroom like getting reporters to write sponsored features.

'We need to keep that fine line between sponsored features and news stories,' Pax told him. 'The reporters won't buy it. And they are right that it's not their job as journalists to write advertorials. You need to hire writers or get marketing colleagues to write them,' he stressed.

Steve was more amused than angry by that response. *He would be the last person to practise editorial independence.*

Aloud he said, 'Pax, it's your job to manage the newsroom. In the four years I've been here, I have given you, Theresa, your team all the resources you need to do your job. But you and I know very well the financial difficulty we're in. We have a huge hole to fill. Issac isn't going to let us off easily.' His face turned slightly dark as he continued. 'Unless you have a better idea how we can make more money and fast, it's not really a time to take the high moral ground. Just get your reporters on board with sponsored features,' he said.

Pax was flabbergasted by the change in Steve's tone of voice and his resolve. It was unlike him and Pax hated for them to be at odds. *It doesn't serve our greater purpose. It's better to make an ally than a foe of the CEO.*

'Steve, don't get me wrong, we're in the same boat,' Pax began to appease his boss. 'What's troubling you? We can work this out together. Let's have an open conversation.'

Steve looked hard at Pax, pleased that he had once more got the better of the editor's spinelessness. *He's right, we need each other to make this work.*

'Okay Pax . . .' The CEO opened up to the editor-in-chief with his contingency plan or plan B. Pax took five minutes to weigh the proposal and made his decision. He was on board because it served the Party. From then on, the undercurrents between Steve and Pax eased; they became closer work partners.

* * *

In the late 1980s through the first decade of the 21st century, the *Herald* was recognized for laying bare to the world China's culture of doing business. It was unsparring in the detailed coverage of one of the biggest stories in modern Chinese history of the Party's brutality that gripped the world in the summer of 1989. Over the course of six weeks to 4 June, Chinese students and their supporters gathered in Tiananmen Square in the heart of the capital city to grief for the death of reformist leader Hu Yaobang. The massive gathering took on a life of its own as mourning turned into a protest against corruption and repression and a call for greater political freedom. The *Herald*'s Beijing correspondents were on-site round the clock with reports that were disseminated across the globe in an age where there was no Internet. The company also sent more reporters to Beijing before the capital banned entry of the foreign press and blacked out news of the protests. Today, the Tiananmen Square Massacre the world knows of, was merely defined by the *Herald* as a brutal military crackdown against the pro-democracy movement of 1989. James had questioned Theresa at a team meeting on why she banned the use of the word 'massacre' in stories when the editor herself constantly berated reporters to 'call a spade a spade'. 'It's not a massacre, based on the official death toll number. End of story,' she told him and the reporters.

In the years running up to 1997, the *Herald* was well remembered for the series of stories it published exposing corruption among mainland Chinese top officials and businessmen. It won journalistic accolades globally, a wide readership and monopolized newspaper advertising. In 1995, the *Herald*'s exposé on corruption in Beijing led to the downfall of the city's party chief, mayor and vice-mayor. The mayor was at the peak of his power but he was surrounded by widespread whispers about his bribe-taking, prodigious womanizing lifestyle. The former China editor and then Beijing bureau chief spent an exhaustive six months investigating and gathering evidence of the two officials' wrongdoings over years of embezzling public funds to build villas and spend on themselves and their mistresses. The stories also implied the factional infighting within the Party, where the Beijing camp had been upstaged by the Shanghai faction led by the then party boss, who used corruption charges to destroy his opponent.

The relationship between critical hard-hitting stories and securing advertisers' dollars was always dilemmatic. Credible journalism generated readership and circulation that drew advertisers, but it didn't go down well with Beijing and the establishment. It was a tough balancing act and required superb balancing skills of editors and the management of the media company. Such calibre of journalists and stories had ceased to exist in the current-day newsroom; they wouldn't have survived Pax and Theresa's management characterized by misconstruction and misinterpretation. But to the editors' advantage, greater international acceptance of Beijing's argument that stability came first for a nation of 1.3 billion people, as well as foreign investor interests in the vast domestic market, had helped justify the shift of reporting emphasis from human rights and democracy to economic issues.

Kong Chi-fai was one of the experienced China reporters that Theresa shoved aside, eventually leading to his resignation. On 1 December 2018, Chi-fai received wind from one of his network of sources in the mainland that the daughter of Huawei Technologies' founder was arrested in Vancouver, Canada. He filed a short story, which would have been a potential world exclusive. Huawei was itself controversial, being at the centre stage of the technology dispute between the US and China and shrouded by suspicions that its products contained backdoors for Chinese government espionage that would be consistent with mainland domestic laws subjecting its citizens and companies to cooperate with state intelligence when warranted.

'Chi-fai, we can't publish your story as it is now. You don't have anything,' Theresa openly reprimanded him in the office. 'We don't know for a fact if she was even arrested. Has Huawei or Beijing confirmed? You also don't know why she was arrested,' and censored the story.

An hour later, she published a piece by an international news agency about the arrest without explaining the reason. During this time, Chi-fai found out the arrest was made at the US' request for alleged defraud with multiple financial institutions in breach of American imposed bans on dealing with Iran. He didn't bother to update his copy.

'Let them update with another wire story. They don't care if we have our own story or not,' he told James, deflated.

In early 2019, the *Herald* published a confession interview with the detained Chinese-Swedish author Gui Minhai, which was arranged by the public security ministry. Gui was also one of the five Causeway Bay booksellers who disappeared in 2015 in Thailand. He subsequently resurfaced in China and served two years in jail until October 2017, having confessed to being involved in a fatal traffic accident more than a decade earlier—a confession that activists alleged was forced as it was common with such cases in the mainland. After his release, he was arrested again while travelling to Beijing with Swedish diplomats. Gui was a naturalized Swedish citizen, obtaining residency after the Tiananmen Square Massacre. In the interview, the author-bookseller accused Sweden of 'sensationalizing' his case and making him a tool for political wrangling with China.

The *Herald*'s publication was met with a backlash despite its disclaimer that the authorities didn't restrict the questions it could ask Gui during the interview. It was not unusual for Chinese criminal suspects to appear in scripted 'confessions'. In agreeing to the arranged 'interview', the paper gave in to pressure from China and reiterated its position as a mouthpiece for the Party, as human rights activists and some foreign press outlets pointed out.

When reporters confronted Theresa about the accusation, she reacted in her typical fashion—furious and then dismissive.

'Geez, you guys, who cares about the views of a few foreign commentators in Europe who can't tell the difference between news and propaganda? They are pissed off that they didn't have access to Gui in person.' Just listening to Theresa even then had moved James to bitter anger.

* * *

As CEO, Steve focused heavily on ramping up the *Herald* website's user numbers. His first task was to form a brand new analytics team, consisting of data engineers to build a reliable infrastructure for collection, processing and storage, transforming that data into a useful format for data scientists to analyse and add value to the business. He brought in his university friend Matt Gao from the US to lead the team. Steve and Matt pushed for editors to make news judgement calls based on the analytics team's recommendations that were derived from the designed automated digital metrics to measure how readers consume news. Steve's obsession with the traffic numbers cascaded down to the editorial floor. The masthead editors who knew next to nothing about digital media, compounded by their personalities, bought whatever the CEO pressed for wholesale.

'It's important that we shift our news judgement decisions based on intuition to one based on data. The data that the analytics team puts together tells us with certainty the kind of content our readers want. It will empower us to make informed decisions that help the company's digital transformation,' Matt told the newsroom.

Steve and Matt were only half-right. The prototype the *Herald* had built only showed what types of content were popular, it wasn't equipped to analyse why the stories did or didn't strike a chord and how they influenced the reader.

'How will we know whether 'we are leading the China conversation'?' James asked an analytics colleague, even if it was propaganda.

'We won't,' the colleague shrugged. 'I suspect we don't have the ability to visualize and develop such a set-up.'

All too soon, editors began making story decisions based on 'traffic-generating news topics', or 'such articles don't pull in enough page views, spike'. The reporters were dismayed that they were assigned the silliest and most embarrassing stories all the time. The pursuit of online traffic sometimes came at the expense of breaching journalistic ethics, like when editors ran with a story quoting a foreign fortune-teller predicting a mega-earthquake in Hong Kong, which lay far away from the boundaries of crustal plates where earthquakes occurred. The backlash was overwhelming and the article, later withdrawn, drew plenty of mockery from readers.

Steve and Matt claimed that the *Herald*'s monthly active users surged tenfold to 40 million over the past four years. But the management spared in discussing paid subscription, after Arcade's high-profile move to allow free access to the *Herald*'s website. This went against the industry trend of media companies charging readers. Their increased digital media subscriptions showed that the public was willing to pay for good quality journalism.

Just as the *Herald*'s user numbers couldn't be verified as the company no longer conducted independent third-party audits, the financial numbers were also a mystery to staff. Sometimes, monthly revenue numbers that reflected little of the company's financial health were made available, despite Steve's promise of a transparent workplace. As weeks progressed into months and to years, reporters gathered from the piecemeal data at townhalls that the company was struggling to even meet revenue targets every quarter and then, growth in user numbers—if they were even monetized—began to plateau.

'I bet you the losses must be huge,' remarked the Senior Business Reporter Charlie Tanner to James as both men watched Steve gave one of his upbeat forecasts in a monthly town hall in October.

'In the four years of mindless spending, you hardly see any income inflows. Print ad sales are shrinking, maybe bits and pieces of revenue from recruitment and job boards the company runs and plus events. But that's about all. And being a private company after Arcade's takeover, we don't have to disclose any numbers.

'We're just lucky that papa has deep pockets. But would any parent endlessly indulge a child who doesn't perform?'

'I guess not,' James agreed. 'If I were Steve, I would be anxious, even desperate. Is there any way we can look at the numbers?' He was on his investigation. Charlie let out a chuckle and shrugged as both men continued to listen to Steve's positive projection.

Steve told his colleagues that the company was advancing according to 'our strategy and plan', albeit the 'black swan' in the Hong Kong protests.

'It's been an awesome year so far. Our coverage of the protests is world-class, pushing up our user numbers to hit a record high, including an impressive increase of views for our videos. The biggest rise came from the US market. Folks, what this means is 1. we are on the right track with the kind of content the market wants, 2. we've become a truly multimedia operation and 3. we are a global media company.'

The more trying Steve was in spinning a rosy tale, the less convincing it sounded to James, by now a seasoned journalist with fifteen years of experience in the bag. The years had trained him to be more sceptical than he needed. What James didn't know at the time was his hunch was partly spot on.

A little over three months after Issac Lin's warning, Steve was called to Nanjing for a meeting with Mark Jin. It was unexpected but not totally out of the ordinary as Jin had an emotional side to him and sometimes acted according to his whim. It was springtime in Nanjing and the flowers were blooming across Arcade's sprawling headquarters campus. Steve didn't remember enjoying the colourful blossoms, or the sway of the willow trees blowing with the afternoon breeze by the bank of a man-made lake. He felt a slight unease as he walked towards Jin's office; he couldn't find out why his boss wanted to see him.

Hi Mark, Rebecca said you wanted to see me in Nanjing. Happy to fly up but wanted to see if there's anything I need to prep for before we meet? he texted Jin three days ago. Rebecca was Jin's personal assistant.

Nope, it's cool, just come, Jin responded two hours later.

Steve couldn't stop pondering. *Was it the budget for the coming year? That was done and approved two weeks ago.* Nor were there any *problematic* stories he was aware of. He reached Jin's office suite which was on the top floor of the only high-rise, a twenty-storey block on the estate. The suite's windows overlooked the entirety of the campus.

'Hey Steve, sit down, sit down,' the Arcade founder said. 'Coffee, tea, what would you like?'

'Black coffee please.'

'How was the flight? And how's Hong Kong? It's been a while since I was there.'

Steve returned the pleasantries. He told his boss that Hong Kong and the *Herald* were doing well. It would be a 'fantastic year', he projected cheerfully at the time as wide-spread anti-government protests had yet to hit Hong Kong.

Rebecca entered the room with Steve's coffee and Jin's Longjing tea, breaking the two men's small talk. Jin took the cue to launch into his agenda.

'I wanted to talk to you about where the *Herald* is going,' he stared right into the young CEO's eyes. Then grinning slightly, he asked, 'Where is my investment heading?'

Steve—who usually had a quick response to any question thrown his way—felt a sudden sense of discomfort creeping into him. Jin's direct and somewhat blunt manner surprised him. He held back his inclination to respond instinctively as he usually would, so as not to appear defensive and waited for his boss to continue.

'The monthly user numbers you sent through have shown that the growth percentage has fallen to single-digit level, while costs are increasing at a double-digit pace. In addition, revenues have been dropping and forget about profit.'

Jin went on to point out that the quality of the stories and writing were lagging behind that of the top international media outlets that Arcade had wanted the *Herald* to be on par with.

'I know that editorial quality isn't your main responsibility, but you need to make sure Pax and his team perform because that's part of your job.' Jin picked up his Chinese teacup, slid the lid to a slight angle to gently brush aside the tea leaves as he took a sip. He returned the cup onto the saucer on the tea table between them and looked expectedly across at Steve for a response.

'You're absolutely right Mark,' Steve began hesitantly. 'The uptrend is tapering off. I'm also sure you know that in the media business, selling information is not a straightforward process where you produce a product, sell and monetize it,' he said, finding his words carefully as he observed his boss' reaction. Jin's face relaxed and leaned back more on his chair.

'How well we can monetize rests on our reputation. But like you've alluded to, the quality of journalism, our brand equity, doesn't reflect our rich century-old heritage. Our top editors whom we inherited aren't our best bets. But we have to make do with them, as the team was endorsed by the higher-ups.' Finding his mojo back, Steve assured Jin.

'I'm not making excuses here. All I'm saying is, we have planted the seeds, with the right infrastructure and foundation. The results are coming and I assure you by the end of the year, we will be at a different place, the numbers will show—not the subscriber numbers, but real revenue.'

Jin shifted in his seat, rested his left elbow on the armrest. 'What do you suggest? We need some benchmark figures to evaluate your work. I've watched you grow up from a young age, but I'm also a businessman. Your current revenue is what, HK$1 billion? Let's set the target at 5 per cent more. I'd say it's very generous and very fair, wouldn't you? It's not profit, just topline sales.'

'Sounds good Mark. You won't be disappointed,' Steve answered.

'Good,' Jin stretched out his right hand to shake Steve's.

* * *

The funny irony for Arcade was the months of pro-democracy protests that went against the Party's interests boosted the *Herald*'s monthly user numbers to new records. The growth faltered as the unrest weighed on, along with the newspaper's increasingly skewed and unbalanced narrative, which also drove readers away. At protest zones, graffiti condemning the credibility of the paper were often found. 'Don't trust the *Herald*; it's the newest Party mouthpiece!' Reporters who requested to interview passers-by on the street were often rejected once people learned of the publication that they worked for.

The sustainability of the political movement caused unprecedented uncertainty that financial and investment communities and companies had never experienced before. So businesses trimmed spendings. The first to go were cost centres like marketing and advertising, which was the *Herald*'s biggest source of revenue. Without the unrest, Steve might just have managed to attain the revenue target agreed with Jin. Any hope of that could very well be wiped off now. Naturally, the young and ambitious CEO was angry, but he wasn't done yet and the *Herald* wouldn't be the place to mess with a future that hadn't even started. Steve activated his plan B.

In July, Steve made a one-day trip across the border to Shenzhen to see an old friend and roommate from university. Jason Liao was a Taiwanese-American whose parents immigrated to the US when he was three years old. Drawn by the potential opportunities in China, Jason moved to the southern Chinese city ten years ago to work for Huawei and in 2016 founded his own start-up. A decade in China had moulded Jason into a typical Chinese businessman, comfortable treading a fine line or working within the grey area with 'extreme flexibility'. His firm developed mobile apps for companies, but its tentacles extended beyond such a scope. 'Let's just say we provide professional services to new economy firms' was how he described it to Steve. Steve thought he could use Jason's services.

'Jase, my business and operational numbers aren't looking good and I think I need your services to dress them up. You think it's something you're cool with?' he asked his friend, who looked much older than Steve, worn down by the weight of doing business in the mainland. His hair was greying and thinning.

'Yeah, from what you told me on the phone, it's not complicated. Tell me exactly what kind of numbers you need and when you need them by.'

'Thanks, I owe you one.'

'No worries man, any time.'

* * *

In early November, James received a call out of the blue from his friend from university and the *Herald*'s Shenzhen-based correspondent Iris Yip. He had confided in her that he was trying to dig more into the *Herald*'s numbers. Iris had news.

'James, a friend of mine who's in the tech business here said he ran into Steve in Shenzhen a week ago, with the founder of a firm that develops mobile apps for corporates.'

'What's so odd about that? Maybe it's just a business meeting, or maybe they are friends,' James pointed out.

'Hmm, I'm not so sure,' Iris said. 'The guy's infamous and I mean the tech community finds him dubious. Rumour has it he also offers creative services and moves easily across the black, white and grey business terrains.

'There may be something there. I know another guy who works for Jason Liao's firm. I'll ask around. But check out Liao if you have time.'

'Thanks Iris, I will. Keep in touch.'

10

Follow the Money

In the middle of November, James took the high-speed train to Shenzhen, China's Silicon Valley. The rail service, a Chinese national pride, which departed from the controversial West Kowloon Station, was the fastest way to get to the mainland, all in less than twenty minutes.

Wasting another minute travelling was the last thing James wanted, as he felt constantly chased by time. If he didn't act quickly enough, Theresa would do whatever she could to erect more roadblocks ahead. Dressed down in a white T-shirt and worn-out jeans, he sat in the station's waiting area for his 8.35 a.m. train to Shenzhen. The quietness of the waiting area didn't soother his nerves. A renewed fear, anxiety and excitement on what he was about to face in Shenzhen consumed him. He snugged his clasped hands between his knees to hide his vulnerability. James was off to the Chinese city to meet Iris—the first step in his journey to expose the internal corruption at the *Herald*. Undertaking such a mission in China's mainland sent his heart pounding and breathing rate skyrocketing. He tortured himself with preposterous riddles in his mind. He closed his eyes when a wave of nausea hit him.

'Passengers travelling on train G6574 to Shenzhen, then to Guangdong, please make your way to platform 5.' A marvellous, pre-boarding recording came through the public address system, echoing through the pristine hallway of the grand terminal. Seemingly dazzled by the voice, James jumped up from his seat while picking up his black backpack and made a beeline for the platform, along with tens of other passengers who were sitting around him. Their manner of walk and attire indicated their social status. They were all walking fast in assiduously rigid postures; all wearing suits and carrying different-sized briefcases.

Why are they all wearing suits? he wondered mindlessly. But of course, they were off to the mainland—the world's second-biggest market—to impress, to make money. James looked at his casual outfit, intended to ease off any unnecessary attention on him and he let out a small laugh. As a journalist, he had developed a habit of analysing what went on around him to discern Hong Kong's societal changes. It again confirmed that Beijing's strategy of economic luring was working. Many were already relying heavily on the mainland for their economic survival, as those in their dressed-to-kill armours busily walked past him.

I wonder whether these people could openly take part in the protests. If their businesses are heavily tied to the mainland, would they be able to freely voice out something that's against the Party? If not, perhaps they've traded off economic prosperity for political freedom. Maybe it's already too late to burn the Trojan Horse. Endless thoughts continued to bug James as he walked towards the platform, wearing him out before his day had properly started. Sudden onset of lethargy struck him. Looking at his watch and realizing there still was about fifteen minutes before his train would depart, he headed to a coffee shop.

'An Americano, please,' James said inattentively before he shook his head to wake himself up.

As he rotated his neck and tilted his head upwards to relieve the tension on his shoulders, the grandiosity of the station's interior with its leaning steel columns that supported a floating roof awed him. Stupefied, James couldn't take his eyes off the splendour and magnificence of the geometric forms and sweeping curves that laid before and above him. A large collection of cultural, entertainment spaces and a massive green garden across the roof area was luring passengers to socialize and connect to one another. The station was linked to other MTR stations and the city's arts centre, the West Kowloon Cultural District. As the hub station, it symbolized the new heart of Hong Kong that connected to mainland China.

The high-speed rail terminus project was an integral part of Beijing's plan to integrate Hong Kong into China before 2047. The opening of the railway in 2018 deepened the city's connectivity to the mainland, especially its ties to southern Chinese cities under the Party's strategy of building a regional economic bloc known as the Greater Bay Area that comprised Hong Kong, Macau and nine cities in Guangdong province. Around eighty pairs of high-speed trains were running between Hong Kong and Shenzhen each day. More than fifty destinations all across the mainland could now be reached via bullet-trains from Hong Kong.

'Americano,' a dark-haired coffee shop staff said, as she slid a cup of coffee to James before she busily swabbed the coffee machine.

'I was just wondering . . . ' James mumbled. 'Do you remember the protest that happened when they were building this station?'

'I do. I was there. I was at the frontline,' she answered with a sense of pride. 'The government was breaking its own rules, showing no respect whatsoever to the "one country, two systems" principle.'

'Did that somehow make you feel a little awkward when you were getting your job here?' The question startled the staff and her face went blank for about two seconds before she caught herself and resumed what she was doing.

'It did actually,' she said, wiping her chin with her sleeve. 'But life moves on . . . and guess we all need to live our lives here.'

Her sentiments would have echoed many others in Hong Kong, including myself, James thought. *The station connects us all but it represents the mainland's growing influence in the city. The feeling of helplessness.* Pockets of the Hong Kong society felt the principles of democracy in Hong Kong were marginalized under the name of the greater good during the later years of the construction process. It was when the city had experienced the 2014 Umbrella Movement. James had covered stories on how the Hongkongers felt about Chinese immigration and customs checkpoints being installed in the station, where mainland laws were to be applied in the immigration area.

'This is a violation of the "one country, two systems" principle, breaching the fundamentals of Hong Kong's Basic Law!' James could still vividly hear the desperate plea of a citizen he interviewed for his story. The 67-year-old retired businessman stressed that he wasn't opposing the idea of being connected to China, but was demanding the authorities to respect Hong Kong's own legal system and civil liberties to stay unbreached until 2047.

'Also, we want our tax money to be spent on our welfare, not on some infrastructure projects serving political purposes!' The citizen's plea then turned into a cry of rage, James recalled.

Hongkongers had also accused the government of using the project as an excuse for draining the city's tax money to the mainland. That irritation rapidly turned into bitter anger when the construction became a massive cash black hole, as the outlay for the West Kowloon terminus and the Hong Kong section of the rail line eventually exceeded the budgeted cost by more than 26 per cent. Besides the high-speed rail, other integration projects undertaken included the Sha Tin-Central Link and the Hong Kong-Zhuhai-Macau bridge, where costs overran by billions of dollars. The public's protests and pleas to spend their tax money for their own welfare fell to deaf ears and over time, they were marginalized and tapered off.

What is happening at the Herald is a microcosm of what Hong Kong faces. James hissed as he grabbed his coffee and boarded the train. He arrived at Shenzhen's Futian station in no more than twenty minutes. It was even faster than him getting to work from his home. The comfort and convenience of the train slightly eroded his love for Hong Kong, numbing his sense of duty as a reporter for the people in his city. The short-lived guilt was quickly overtaken by a surge of anxiety that hit as he stepped out of the carriage. From the platform to the station hall, multiple surveillance cameras were scanning and monitoring every person there. It reminded James to switch his Hong Kong phone card with one of the prepaid SIMs he brought along. He always carried more than one prepaid card when he crossed the border.

China's world-class facial recognition system was in full display, promptly classifying passengers into different categories according to their *social credibility* as defined by the authorities—marking green, yellow and red squares around the arriving passengers' faces on the monitors. 'Down with big brother', the catchphrase from George Orwell's novel *1984* flashed in James' mind immediately, raising his paranoia on surveillance. He felt himself flush, dropped his head down and trotted quickly to pass the *big brother zone*. He hated the idea of being watched; he ramped up his speed and soon dashed out of the station, tightening the straps of his backpack, slightly panting.

China's social credit system, an integral part of the Party's surveillance, was a numerical ranking system designed ultimately to control how citizens would behave. Hundreds of cameras in the station were detecting citizen's faces and were classifying whether each posed a threat to the regime—dictating how they should behave. Failing to retain a certain level of *social credibility* may result in punitive measures imposed, which included banning one's mobility, access to the best schools, well-paid jobs and high-speed Internet subscription, as well as being publicly shamed as a *bad citizen*. The Party said the social credit system was only aimed at reinforcing the idea of 'keeping trust is glorious and breaking trust is disgraceful'.

The system, monitoring every aspect of daily lives, allowed the Chinese government to silence those critical of the regime, shutting down any kind of resistance before they even started. James' fear had amplified when he learnt that it was a collaborative system between the public and private sectors, where local city authorities across China partnered with tech firms to conduct monitoring work. If you were a foreigner working in a country where the right to remain hinged on a work permit from the government, it meant another hurdle to overcome as you now needed to meet a certain score level under the social credit system.

James made his way to the connecting subway station. He was beginning to get accustomed to the multiple surveillance cameras overhead at every corner he turned. The next thing he saw was a few giant propaganda banners that hung on the walls of a long corridor to the subway. The slogans in Chinese were written in yellow paint on bright red fabrics, in the same colour combination of the Chinese national flag. They stuck out like an old-fashioned sore thumb to the modern world-class facilities of the station.

> 'No Party, No New China'
> 'Follow the Party, Make China Prosperous'
> 'Practise the China Thoughts'

They once more reminded James of slogans from the 'Ministry of Truth' in Orwell's *1984*.

> 'War is Peace'
> 'Freedom is Slavery'
> 'Ignorance is Strength'

James noticed that the TV screens in the station were playing a video of a recent speech delivered by the Party Leader.

'We must demonstrate the anti-American spirit shown during the Korean War,' the Leader said firmly. Intrigued, James stopped and listened. 'That war shattered the myth that the US Army was invincible. It showed that the Chinese people must not be provoked. If you do, be prepared to bear the consequences. We will fight for peace.'

The speech made him recall a phrase from Orwell's other novel, *Animal Farm*. 'Four legs are good, two legs are bad.' The phrase in the novel is uttered by pigs to show the need for animal unity in the face of oppression by humans—ultimately aimed at continuing their rule in the midst of external threats. *The propaganda slogans in the station were inciting a sense of patriotism from its people, telling them how they should think—almost justifying the heavy surveillance and the Party's control,* James thought.

He picked up his pace. Everywhere he went, James felt like he was travelling with an invisible official minder assigned to keep taps of his every move, one whom he couldn't shake off. Strangely, however, it seemed like no one around him felt the same way. They all looked perfectly fine.

* * *

It was an hour later when James arrived at the Shenzhen National High-Tech Zone where he was to meet Iris. Tall, new, fancy buildings towered over him, as a fresh cool breeze calmed him down a little. Shenzhen was known as China's tech hub and the zone housed many of the companies in frontier industries—artificial intelligence, integrated circuits, robotics, life science and new materials—that Beijing was counting on to propel the nation to tech superpower status. The feeling of the district was no different from that of West Kowloon Station. It was grand and structurally magnificent.

As James walked along, he saw a number of people were chatting, smiling and taking breaks at the cafés dotted across the high-tech zone, some within the buildings and others outdoors. They seemed unperturbed by the heavy surveillance and the tool that could control their behaviours in the name of national security. *Maybe I am the one who's being too critical here?* The thought made him laugh and he shook his head, amused. *I mean . . . people look perfectly happy here. Who am I to judge what's right and wrong when people are happy with the system?* he went on, sort of challenging himself mentally, as he arrived at the café where he was supposed to meet Iris. His phone rang momentarily, as soon as he walked into the cafe. *Iris.* The display screen read.

'Welcome to Shenzhen James,' Iris said. 'Do you see the fountain near the café?'

'I do.'

'I'll meet you there.'

James turned around and retraced his steps back to the fountain he had just passed. He saw Iris sitting by the ledge on one side of the gigantic structure, facing the café.

Iris had seen him and waved for his attention, but James was preoccupied with his mental deliberations to notice his colleague. Iris, with a short bob haircut, was in jeans and a white shirt, now waved forcefully again, with a brown folder she was holding. The fountain was in the middle of an open space, with at least a 400 m radius that was free from surveillance cameras. The sound of the gushing water was so loud that James had to shout to say hello. But it was a perfect venue to avoid tapping. It slightly irritated James though, seeing her there when they agreed to meet in a café. He was a little short-fused as of late.

'Hey Iris,' James said, raising his voice to penetrate the sound of water shooting from the jets. 'Why the fountain? Let's grab coffee at the café. It's on me.'

'It's really easy to be tapped in this city, didn't you figure?' Iris said, shaking her head. Her rigidness told him that she was deadly serious.

'James, the surveillance capability here is beyond your imagination,' Iris said, clearing her throat, aghast. 'If you're targeted, it's a piece of cake for them to monitor every movement, every conversation of yours. Also, the surveillance is a collaborative effort of the government and tech giants, you know that right? It means tech giants also have a full capability to watch you in every part of this city. And what are we doing? Digging some dirt on the almighty Arcade. I'd rather play it safe. Not take any chances.'

'All right sure.' James said, tersely. *She had a point,* he thought. 'So . . . who really is this Jason Liao you were talking about over the phone when we last spoke? I couldn't get much about him online.'

'Here,' Iris—looking desperately anxious—said, as she tossed the brown file she was holding to James. 'He is a college mate of Steve's from the States. Found out he's working for Steve under the table.'

In the file, there was a one-page profile report on Jason, including his photo, date of birth and educational background.

'Where did you get the information that he's working for Steve?'

'From a source.'

'A single source?'

'Yes.'

'And that source is from . . . ?'

'Governmental and corporate.'

'Huh?'

'You heard me right.'

'A single source that's both governmental and corporate? That's odd.'

'You can trust him. He told me Jason has been cooking the numbers for Steve for quite a while.'

'Cooking the numbers?' James yelped in shock, looking incredulous.

'Would you please keep the volume down,' Iris said, busily looking around her, seriously irritated. 'Yes,' she whispered. 'They fabricate numbers to boost the *Herald*'s performance.'

'What exactly are they cooking?'

'Traffic numbers for internet viewers and revenue numbers too. The Arcade headquarters also holds that information, apparently.'

The pieces of the puzzle were coming together for James. When Jin acquired the *Herald*, he assured Steve that he didn't have to worry about making profits for the first five years. But that time was coming to an end as 2019 was the fourth year. This must have pressured Steve, as he was yet to come up with specific plans on how to monetize the business.

'Steve and Jason are going to meet up this afternoon.' Iris said. 'That's his address,' she continued as she pointed at his address in the file.

'When exactly?'

'Don't know. My informant told me that Steve crossed the border last night.'

'So what exactly do they do there?'

'To be honest, I don't know much about that either. Maybe Steve is reviewing the numbers cooked by Jason?' Iris speculated.

'Who's the informant?'

'Can't say.'

'Is it Chi, 'cause I'm meeting him tomorrow.'

'No, it's not him. All I can say now is that my informant is close to both the government and Arcade.'

'How does he know they are having regular meetings at Jason's place?'

'Well . . . that's why I gave you the address. We can verify the information.'

James' heart pounded again from a renewed excitement. This was the opportunity. He closed his eyes and imagined the management's faces when claims exposing corruption at the *Herald* would be aired all over Hong Kong. But first, he needed to catch Steve at Jason's place and find out what the meeting was about.

* * *

The sun was right above James and Iris' heads when they arrived breathless at Jason's mansion. The property was near Yang Tai Shan Forest Park, surrounded by forests of litchi and mangrove trees. James and Iris hid nearby behind a group of mangrove trees on a hill that provided the altitude for a clearer view of the front of the mansion, which was surrounded by high walls with security cameras along the ledge and two more hanging above the main gate.

It was a four-storey luxurious mansion. A patterned, postmodern looking concrete panel design with some timber cladding was used as exterior walls, covering the entire first two floors. The third floor, uncovered, boasted of a terrace with sliding glass doors. Through the glass, James and Iris could partially see the interior, which had multiple computer screens and a large open space—like the Hub at the *Herald* office. It appeared to be some kind of work space.

'God . . . it smells of money,' James said. 'And how much does he earn to own a place like this?'

'I'm sure he got at least a quarter of his income from the *Herald*,' Iris quipped.

'Did you get that from your informant too?'

'No. Just another wild guess.'

James and Iris waited for at least six hours. Staking out near the house, they had a picnic lunch of sandwiches and Japanese rice balls, bananas, canned coffee and tea they had bought earlier and packed into James' backpack. They passed time chatting and discussing the *Herald*, the protests in Hong Kong and Iris' experience working as a journalist in China. She had been based in the mainland for five years, the first three in Shanghai and now coming to the end of her second year in Shenzhen.

'The Party's control in China is getting tighter. You experienced the surveillance yourself,' Iris said. 'They're pushing down harder ideological indoctrination. It's a real pressure cooker here and I wouldn't be surprised if it explodes soon.

'I feel there's been some degree of implosion already, the impact from the trade war. This is why the Party is coming down so hard on Hong Kong. It's afraid the Hong Kong crisis will affect sentiments in the mainland.' She told James she was planning to return home to Hong Kong soon but hadn't decided if she wanted to stay in journalism.

'Yeah, it's a tough one. To be honest, I am asking myself the same question . . . ' James empathized.

Their conversation fell into a lull as the sun started to lose its luminosity in the sky. At that moment a black Range Rover approached the mansion, snapping the sombre mood.

'Shhh! Here he comes. Jesus Christ, it's about time,' James said, half-relieved, half-complaining.

Steve in his usual hoodie and dark jeans got off from the vehicle. James rapidly took his phone out and began taking photos of him from a distance. Steve slowly walked towards the gate and pressed a bell, while thrusting his face towards a camera above him, chuckling.

'Who is this?' Jason's voice came through a speaker.

'Very funny, just open the door,' Steve squawked before he disappeared into the estate.

About fifteen minutes later, James and Iris saw Steve on the third floor, through the glass doors. The two men talked in front of the sea of monitors, looking quite serious before Jason closed the blinds on the glass door. James and Iris looked at each other.

'Great. Now what?' Iris asked.

'We wait till Steve comes out, I guess.'

'What's the point? We need to hear what they're saying. The fact that Steve visited his old friend won't be a story.'

'Guess we don't have much choice here. How about we go somewhere closer . . . into the house maybe?'

'What? Are you out of your mind? Breaking into the house? Bad idea,' Iris revolted.

'As you said, we need to find out what they are saying right now. This is our one and only chance.' James, indefatigable, ran towards the mansion before Iris could even react. Iris blinked and her eyes started to track his path. After a moment of hesitation, she followed slowly.

* * *

'Great to see ya bro,' Steve said as he walked into the mansion, opening his arm to his old friend.

'Hey man. Good to see ya! How have you been?' Jason said as he walked out from a glass-made, transparent lift at the centre of the ground floor, holding a can of beer in his right hand. Wearing a maroon coloured varsity hoodie and black shorts, he hugged his old friend.

As a computer programmer, Jason made his living by breathing data, 'with creativity' as he liked to say to his friends. He had clients throughout the country, including those in corporates and municipalities. Corporate executives and municipality officials in China were always under political pressure to achieve performance targets, whether it was during an economic downturn or upcycle. The low performance came with political ramifications that often meant a demotion. Data fabrication was common across many parts of the country but authorities, albeit aware, could be selective in who they punished, picking out those who failed to toe the Party line. Jason saw a business opportunity there.

The ground floor of Jason's mansion was full of hi-tech gadgets.

'What on earth is this?' Steve asked, pointing at a cufflink-sized AI-programmed drone displayed on the ground floor.

'Yeah, I made that one,' Jason showed off, lifting his eyebrows and rubbing his knuckles on his hoodie.

'Are you selling this to the PLA? To spy on the US officials here?' Steve joked.

'Nope, precisely the opposite. It's for spying on fellow Chinese officials.'

'Whooa, wait a sec. So you are selling it to a foreign government? You should watch your back, man. That's treason.'

'Nope. I'm selling it to local authorities in China. Many officials these days are extremely conscious of what their political enemies are doing outside of their offices. I see there might be a market there to track them down.

'Own your inspector gadget,' Jason suddenly yelled, throwing his arms in the air.

'How's that sound? I even thought of an advertising line. Well, you're one of my clients, so please do let me know if you do need this service.'

'No thanks,' Steve replied idly.

They then took the bubble glass lift up to the third floor. As the lift ascended, a quick view of the second level once again astonished Steve. The second floor was full of servers. An aura of blue lights was glowing from the servers. The floor included backup components and infrastructure for power supply, data communications connections, air conditioning, fire suppression and various security devices. It looked like a data centre for a tech company.

'Man, did you add more of those servers? ' Steve said, simpered. 'Are they all really necessary?'

'I need all of those for my business continuity.'

'How much electricity does it use up?'

'As much electricity as a small town,' Jason grinned with pride. 'But one of my clients from a municipality is taking care of the power supply.'

The third floor was Jason's working space. A dozen monitors showing undecipherable javascripts were pinned to one wall. Another wall was also covered with eight TV screens playing different news channels and surveillance footage around his fortress. A terrace with marble balustrades extended from the glass door.

'Shall we get to work?' Jason said as he threw himself onto the chair in front of his workstation. 'So how many readers do you want next month, boss?'

'Er . . . shall we have the blinds closed first? Just in case?' Steve, looking slightly anxious, said cautiously.

'Sure thing,' Jason pressed a button in a remote control on his desk which automatically turned the glass door opaque. 'So back to our business. How many readers do you want next month?'

'Might have to slow down a little,' Steve said, looking worried. 'We don't want any unwanted suspicions. Also, the bigger the number gets, the more pressure I get from the above on a monetization plan, which I don't have right now.'

'As you wish.'

'How about we make it about 55 million MAU?'

'Sure, why not. And how much of it do you want it coming from the United States?'

'About 45 per cent. Let's increase by about 3 per cent.'

'Woo . . . wait a second. Don't you think that is a little too drastic? I mean you're the one who said you don't want to draw any attention.'

'None of your business,' Steve said jerkily, massaging his knuckles. 'Just do it.'

'You seem a little obsessed here with your American audience. What's the big deal?'

'Well . . . increasing American readership is a priority of the higher-ups, as it means we are selling our narratives to them, not the other way around.'

'Okay, if you say so.'

Jason swivelled his chair around to face the computer screen and spent the next ten minutes typing in a series of codes. When he finished, he turned around and grinned at Steve.

'Done! Time for a beer.' The two friends then walked to the fourth floor, which was the living quarters. Jason took out two cans from the fridge and tossed one to Steve.

'Cheers!'

'Like old times, bottoms up.'

The two cheered in triumph.

Clang! An ear-piercing alarm suddenly went off causing Jason and Steve to immediately dig their heads into the sofa they were sitting on.

'What is this?' Steve asked, with his pupils moving fast to figure out what was going on.

'It's an intruder alarm,' Jason said as he dashed for the stairs.

'Someone sabotaging our work?' Steve said, following Jason downstairs.

Two intruders identified, Jason's AI system answered Steve's question. The message beamed on one of the many monitors on the third floor, as it automatically zoomed into the faces of the two intruders. The system instantly ran a facial recognition programme to identify who they were.

James Lai – 38-year-old, Male, China reporter at the Herald. Iris Yip – 39-year-old, Female, Shenzhen correspondent at the Herald. The identities of the intruders were flashed on the screen. The adjacent monitor showed the real-time footage of James and Iris trying to open the backdoors of the mansion and of James attempting to climb up a sewage pipe to the second floor along the back wall.

'What the...?' Steve muttered, looking shocked.

'Looks like you brought company from Hong Kong,' Jason said in a strangely low-pitched voice.

'What the hell are they doing here?' Steve roared, feeling cold sweat trickling down his back.

'Well, you tell me.'

Frustrated, Steve threw the beer can he was holding on the floor.

'Think we've been exposed here,' he said, beginning to lose his cool. Jason, on the contrary, was unperturbed. Keeping calm, he scrutinized the screens connected to the estate's surveillance cameras, replaying the footage captured of the intruders.

'Don't worry man. It's impossible to break into this building,' Jason assured his friend with a cold smile. 'Also, there is no way that they would find out anything we talked about today.'

'I'm going to make Theresa do something about them when I get back.'

'You might also have to have your eyes on them from now on. Do you want my drones?'

'No thanks,' Steve laughed, looking slightly relieved. 'Don't try to scab more from me.'

'Fine.'

'It looks like I might have to stay spend the night here. But before that, I have a job to do.' Steve then made a phone call as he trotted back upstairs, two steps at a time.

'Follow them. I want every single detail about them, what they do and who they see in this city,' he said to an unknown person. Then he and Jason relaxed with a second beer.

* * *

James and Iris returned to the city centre a little after 8 p.m. They had run for a very long time after their attempted break-in set off Jason's security alarm system, before reaching the main road where there were taxis. The pair had ridden silently back to town, rattled by the hair-raising episode earlier and were relieved to be back in surroundings that were brightly lit.

'Now what?' Iris asked tartly, the first to speak.

'I have a meeting with Chi tomorrow'

'And what information does he have?'

'Don't know yet . . . But I asked for his help in digging some dirt on the *Herald* and he got back to me a few days later on an unknown mobile number, saying he'd meet me. I'm assuming this means he has something.'

'So where are you going to see him?'

'He said he'd get back to me.'

'So . . . you don't even know where you're going to see him?'

'Well . . . I know he wasn't lying. He has a bitter history with Theresa too.' During his time at the *Herald*, Chi had faced Theresa's repeated accusations of generating 'fake news' for the numerous critical stories he wrote about the Party.

Meet me in dongmen old street at 4 pm An anonymous number texted James then.

'It's from Chi,' he told Iris.

It was a skill Chi often used in the mainland to avoid being tapped when he was a reporter. He used new prepaid phone cards to talk to his sources in the mainland, then disposing of the cards immediately after the contact.

'Should I come with you?' Iris asked.

'No,' James answered flatly. 'Chi doesn't know that we're working together on this. I'll let you know afterwards on what he's got after I see him.'

'No worries. Keep me posted,' Iris said as the two parted ways.

The next day James arrived at the Shenzhen Dongmen Old Street just a few minutes before the agreed time. It took him more than an hour to arrive at the busy, lively street as he chose to take a taxi. It was a bad decision as the taxi and he were trapped in traffic for more than an hour for a ride that was only 8 km in distance. But James didn't mind languishing a bit in the snail traffic. It allowed his mind to rest and wander aimlessly as he felt liberated from the heavy surveillance of the city. At least he didn't detect any cameras in the vehicle.

Since the morning, James had a strange feeling of being stalked. A man, in a khaki cargo jacket and jeans, was watching him having breakfast at the hotel from the corner of the restaurant where he sat. James immediately stopped eating and was about to flee back to his room when he questioned his own mental condition of being somewhat delusional these days. *Maybe it's my anxiety that's making me overly conscious*, he thought. Nevertheless, he couldn't completely dismiss his suspicions as the day wore on and thus decided against taking the camera-armed Shenzhen subway.

Even when he was in the taxi, he constantly looked behind through the rear windshield, checking whether he was being tailed.

'You got a problem there?' the driver couldn't help asking. He noticed that James was nervously looking behind him.

'No. Nothing,' James replied. The two repeated the same conversation throughout their trip.

After an hour on the road, he finally got off at the Old Street. The vibrant and slightly chaotic walking street, which had been a traditional Chinese shopping district for over 300 years, was as usual full of people. Department stores, street stalls and street-food stands spanned across several blocks. There were food streets where people were eating outdoors. Ad hoc stalls were all tightly packed with crowds of people. Groups of local residents and tourists all mingled together, busily shopping at the market stalls. The stalls were overflowing with merchandise of clothes, shoes, jewellery and handbags. People were haggling with the sellers for a better deal like a rhapsody of lively arguments and banters. Many surrounding buildings were undergoing renovations, some receiving a facelift. Nearby, construction workers were taking their afternoon tea breaks. Some looked as young as twelve years old.

James snaked through the sea of people and made his way to the particular terrace café where Chi had asked to meet. From a distance, he could see Chi, with an unfamiliar looking man sitting beside him. His former colleague looked somewhat anxious, scanning around as subtly as possible to make sure he wasn't being watched. The other man, on the other hand, his legs crossed, was sipping from a cup, looking relaxed and confident. As James was about to wave, the face of the cargo jacket-clad man at James' hotel glanced off the shop window behind Chi. He was speaking on the phone, looking like he was taking instructions.

So he has been following me, but why? When Chi caught his eyes, James vigorously shook his head in desperation.

'No. No. No,' James ventriloquized, frowning desperately. Chi instantly looked away, sensing something was amiss. With the unknown man, Chi stood up and walked out of the café acting totally normal, as though they were trained for such circumstances.

James also turned around and moved away from the café, but headed in the opposite direction to where Chi was going. The tail who seemed to have realized that he was exposed picked up his pace to narrow in on James. His assignment was to find out who the reporter was meeting and why, using 'all means necessary'.

By the time James turned his head around to check the whereabouts of his chaser, he was already in motion. The man yanked a handcart before him blocking his way, bewildering those around him as he charged towards the reporter. James instantly hunched his shoulders and ran through the street market, in and out of alleyways. He dashed through the maze of streets and buildings, with some bystanders and passers-by watching in amusement, wondering if he was a pickpocketer on the run. As he continued running through more alleyways in the old town, at the same time trying to catch his breath, his phone rang with a *no number* call indicated. It was Yang, the state security official who took him to the safe house where Edwin died.

'Hello Yang, I'm slightly busy here.'

'You are being chased.'

'What do you think?' James said pointedly. 'We can't talk in an open line. Think we're being tapped.'

'I'm using a safe line here. Come to 3564, Renmin S Rd, at Guo Mao Shi Dai Guang Chang.'

'Copy.'

'Repeat.'

'3654 Renmin S Rd, at Guo Mao Shi Dai Guang Chang.'

'No, it's 3564.'

'3564.'

'Dump your SIM card after this call. We don't want any tails,' Yang said calmly before she hung up.

James went into a multilevel shopping mall to shake off his pursuer, but the building was under partial renovation, with a few shops open and a handful of shoppers. He saw through the window crowds of tourists, approximately 300 of them, on the opposite side of the road. James dashed out of the building and ran across the roadway where cars were rushing through. The cars honked and their engines whined. Whilst the chaser got caught up in the road, James hid among the crowds, wandered through the tens of tourists to a nearby stall where he bought a hat, sunglasses, as well as a jacket. After swiftly changing his clothes and putting on his hat, James jumped onto a bus. Through the grey haze, he could still see the man vigorously searching for him. He got off the bus a few stops later, bought a prepaid phone card and texted Chi.

3564 Renmin S Rd, at Guo Mao Shi Dai Guang Chang. Now.

* * *

It was a local hamburger shop. When James walked in, two shopkeepers glanced at him and one of them took him to the basement of the building through a back door of the shop, just like the Fujian gang's ghetto place in North Point. The basement was a huge, luxurious bunker, with massive jade-like pillars across the dark-coloured timber floor. After an hour of tedious waiting in a meeting room surrounded by glass, Chi and the mysterious man discreetly walked into the safe house. Sweating and shaking, Chi in his checkered shirt and jeans eyed the second shopkeeper who had shown them to the basement warily. Again, the unfamiliar looking man—wearing a navy suit and glasses—was unfazed.

'Hi James. I brought my colleague here. He's one of us, can be trusted,' Chi said, hiding his nervousness.

'James, Tristan. Tristan, James.'

'Hello James. I'm Tristan Zhang from Arcade,' Tristan reached out his hand to the reporter. 'I heard a lot about you from Iris the other day.' James straight away knew that he was Iris' source, who provided the information about the collusion between Steve and Jason.

Intrigued, James stared at Tristan for about a few seconds before he answered. Tristan looked familiar, but he couldn't recall when they had met.

'Hello Tristan. I was just wondering . . . have we met before?' he asked in a sharp voice.

'You may have seen me in the *Herald*'s office a few months ago. I used to work for Wang Tao,' Tristan said silkily. 'Ring any bells?'

'Oh my -' James almost exclaimed, flabbergasted. *Bloody hell.* He choked. He stood still and stared at Tristan, dumbfounded. He realized that he saw him at the office, walking out of the Shanghai meeting room with Pax and Theresa a couple of months ago, when the *Herald* had a closed-door editorial meeting with enforcement officials. He was one of the three officials including Wang who visited the office, pressuring the *Herald*'s editors to provide 'an alternative narrative against those biased Western reporting' on the Hong Kong protests.

James should've known better. It was an open secret that the Party embedded communist cells in corporates' operations. Arcade was no exception. The measure to reinforce the Party's grip on the private sector, was more strictly applied to China's tech champions, especially when their market values far exceeded that of state-owned companies in recent years. The Party was always wary of high-profile entrepreneurs who might present a challenge to its hold on society. In addition, just a few years ago, Beijing also required foreign companies involved in joint ventures with state-owned Chinese firms in China to have communist cells and provide them with an explicit role in the decision-making process, including approving investment plans or personnel changes. What's more, it was now a common practice in China for local governments to assign officials to corporates, under the name of 'tighter links between the state and private sectors'. One municipality described the measure as a part of its 'New Manufacturing Industry Plan', where the government officials actively serve the role of 'enhancing the communication' with corporates and thus higher productivity. Planting someone like Tristan in Arcade, the privately-owned tech group would become a Party-overseen enterprise.

'So . . . what do you do in Arcade?' James asked, jerkily. He couldn't trust Tristan, not yet. As far as he knew he worked for Wang just weeks ago. 'Why are you helping us?'

'I'm Yang's guy,' Tristan answered shrewdly. 'My job was to spy on Wang.'

He had worked for the Chinese secret police for about seven years before Yang recruited him as her informant, he explained. The political faction Yang and he belonged to—a rival of the current regime—promised Tristan a promotion if he successfully completed his mission. He spent the past five years under Wang before gaining the senior official's full trust, ultimately becoming one of Wang's informants at Arcade. A step closer to their goal: regime change. But James seemed rather unconvinced. He stared at Tristan with suspicion, creating an awkward silence.

'I still don't quite understand why you are helping us,' James continued to question tartly.

'My mission in Arcade was to dig up dirt and report it back to Wang,' Tristan said.

'And why would he want that?'

'Wang needs to strengthen his faction's grip over the company.'

James still didn't fully buy Tristan's story, but his instinct told him that Yang wouldn't have let Tristan step into her safe house if he was untrustworthy. He decided to bet on Yang.

'That's enough self-introductions,' Chi said, siding with Tristan. 'Let's get to work.'

He took out a file from his tote bag. 'This is a balance sheet of Arcade,' he continued, 'so basically there are a few serious accounting misconducts that you might be interested in.'

'Accelerating revenues, channel stuffing, delaying expenses and off-balance-sheet items,' Tristan elaborated as he sat down, moving his sight away from James and crossing his legs.

'The *Herald* booked lump-sum payments from its advertisers as current sales when the advertisements are actually to be published over a number of years,' Chi said, rolling up his sleeves. 'Last May, the management received an upfront payment of HK$136,800,000 from five different casino groups in Macau, making a four-year advertisement contract, but the company recorded the full payment as sales for this financial year that the payment was received. Staggering, eh?'

'It's called accelerating revenue,' Tristan explained. 'Not amortizing the revenue over the contract period is definitely a misconduct.'

'We also found channel stuffing during our internal audit,' Chi said coldly. The *Herald* sent shipments to distributors of its China forum tickets both in Hong Kong and elsewhere at the end of the last quarter, according to Chi's file. The company then recorded the shipment as sales. The distributors, however, sent back the unsold tickets just a few days before the forum started and that accounted for about 90 per cent of what the company had originally sent. On paper, the management neglected all that.

'This means that the *Herald* lied to Arcade as well right?' James asked.

'Well . . . actually . . . it is a win-win for both companies,' Chi said. 'Arcade made the *Herald* as its separate subsidiary so that it could hide the group's liabilities that it doesn't want to disclose, using the *Herald*'s financial book.'

'In other words, money laundering right?' James asked, combing through the financial tables from the few sheets of paper that Chi had given him.

'Yes,' Tristan answered. The file showed that the Arcade did not have to record the *Herald*'s liabilities and incur expenses on Arcade's financial statements and the group could hide the records from Arcade investors.

'Actually, we've also managed to find out that there are funds coming in from shell companies,' Tristan said. 'We believe they are Arcade's money-laundering attempts. But unfortunately as of now, we don't have any significant evidence to prove that.' James nodded, but he was slightly confused.

'The next is delaying expenses,' Tristan continued.

'The *Herald* spent a total of HK$1,224,230,000 in expansion over the past few years. They marked the expense as 'long-term investment' and capitalized the costs. But they transferred those from its income statement to the balance sheet where the expansion cost would be expensed over a period of years,' he explained. 'An appropriate treatment of this would be to expense the cost in the period when the expenses were actually made.'

'Well . . . these are some of the things we found out,' Tristan said, as he tossed another heavy report to James. It was a seventy-one-page anonymous report on this in detail.

This is a bombshell! James thought. But Tristan's next line disappointed him.

'We will give it to you first, but please note that we will leak it to other international organizations too.'

'What do you mean by other international organizations? You mean the media?'

'Foggy Weather Research.'

The US research firm, also a short-seller, was famous for exposing frauds and had highlighted questionable accounting and scams at several companies, primarily in China. A few weeks ago Foggy Weather Research exposed—after receiving an anonymous report on a Chinese local coffee chain Haohe Coffee—that the company was cooking up its revenues. The report claimed that the authors had documented 24,847 hours of store traffic surveillance video that suggested the coffee chain had fabricated its revenue, inflating the number of items sold per day by 70 per cent in the first quarter of 2019 and 88 per cent in the second quarter. Haohe initially denied the allegations, but three months later the company admitted the misconduct, saying that an internal accounting investigation revealed that COO Xiao Ting had inflated RMB 4.2 billion in total sales.

James wasn't too surprised that the *Herald* was fabricating its books. It was somewhat predictable. Arcade had poured in enormous amounts of capital to compete with other renowned international media organizations such as the *New York Times* and the *Financial Times*. One of the reasons that Steve was hired was to turn the *Herald* into 'China's New York Times'. To do that, the management spent massively in expanding overseas and hiring foreigners from other renowned foreign media outlets. It also removed a paywall and scrapped subscription fees to expand its readership. The deficit was bound to grow.

As the production cost of news amplified, the management of the *Herald* lobbied the Chinese authorities to allow the newspaper greater access in the mainland to boost the number of readers and hence, its revenue. However, Beijing was wary of the limited control it could wield on the *Herald* and its journalists, especially some of its foreign employees. They were concerned that however much self-censorship and care the management and its editors exercised, there were bound to be news reports critical of the current Chinese leadership because after all, the newspaper operated out of semi-autonomous Hong Kong. So no matter how hard the management tried to appease China, the *Herald*'s website remained blocked.

'Well . . . good luck,' Chi said.

'And also, take this,' Tristan said, tossing a USB to James.

'It's a recording of a conversation between Steve and Jason from last night. We planted a bug at the immigration when he was crossing the border.

'Leak it to Hong Kong media. It's only a matter of time before the other faction finds out what we're doing. If it takes too long, we should have to move on to plan B.'

'And that is?'

'You'll see.'

* * *

'No way in hell,' Theresa bellowed in the Sichuan meeting room. Her reaction was unsurprising and expected, but James enjoyed watching her face reddening as she went ballistic.

He torpedoed her in the meeting room, saying that he would publish the *Herald*'s corruption. Theresa glared at him with renewed fury. His calm and composure, unaffected by her emotions, maddened her more. James knew well that no organization would want to air its dirty laundry in public. All he wanted was to infuriate Theresa and see her crumble. He had a good reason. The anti-government movement in Hong Kong had reached another turning point while James was away. The protest had intensified and the police brutality on the streets had dramatically ramped up, fogging Hong Kong's rule of law. Among the protests that broke out across the city, the twelve-day siege of the Hong Kong Polytechnic University enraged James the most.

It started with protesters setting up a roadblock at the entrance of the Cross-Harbour Tunnel, an important traffic link between Kowloon and Hong Kong island, next to the university. Protesters took the university as the base to defend against attacks by the police. Just days earlier, protesters bitterly faced off the force at the campus of James' alma mater, the Chinese University of Hong Kong. Some citizens attempted to remove the roadblocks at the tunnel entrance but were stopped by the protesters, which led the police to fire tear gas, rubber bullets, bean bag rounds, sponge grenades and water cannons with blue-coloured water mixed with chemical irritants. The protesters retaliated by throwing bricks and petrol bombs. The police then blocked all campus exits to prohibit the protesters from leaving or face arrest. The force also tried to drive an armoured vehicle through campus, but the students retaliated by throwing bricks and petrol bombs. Hit by the petrol bombs, the vehicle was forced to retreat. Later when the police charged the university, they also arrested first-aiders, medical service volunteers and reporters near the site. The city's hospitals were flooded by the number of students requiring urgent medical attention.

The *Herald* focused on justifying the police's action and use of violence as a necessity for the stabilization of society. *I've had enough!* James thought as he read the stories. The top editors had also misrepresented his story of the US passing the Hong Kong Human Rights and Democracy Act with Beijing's reaction without giving him any prior notice, which only fuelled his anger. James marched towards Theresa's seat to confront her with the seventy-one page report revealing *Herald*'s financial misdoings in his hand.

'We need to talk,' James said to Theresa who was playing Tetris on her computer.

'I'm afraid that won't be possible,' she responded, without looking at him, her eyes fixed on her screen. 'Got an important meeting in five minutes.'

'Another one of those with Chinese officials?'

'What is your problem?' she turned around to face him, slowly standing up.

'I honestly think we are becoming a state media,' James torpedoed. 'When was the last time we were critical of Beijing? Serving China means serving its people, not its regime. You really don't know our problem here?'

'Where's this coming from?' She realized that their exchange, becoming a shouting match, was drawing curious looks from reporters in the newsroom. She led James towards the nearest meeting room.

But James didn't stop. 'This is about editorial integrity. All media should be an enabler for democracy. Any organization that fails to do so is no longer media, it's propaganda. You should know better.'

'No. We also do publish stories critical of Beijing,' Theresa defended. 'The reason we might appear biased right now is because our society needs to regain overall objectivity, an equilibrium.

'It is obvious that external forces are trying to destabilize our home. We need to debunk those Western forces, to lead our public in the right direction.'

'You're not making any sense,' James refuted, his voice rising. 'Do you have any evidence of those so-called external forces active in Hong Kong?'

'Well, do you have any evidence against it? We are a fully transparent organization. If you have solid evidence on that or on anything, we can publish them, even if it's critical of China, or the *Herald*.'

'Okay,' James said, tossing the seventy-one page report under Theresa's nose. 'Let's publish this then.' Theresa spent a few seconds reading the front cover of the report, as her pupils got bigger, out of shock.

'I'd like to publish this story today,' he continued.

'No way in hell,' Theresa cried out. 'This is absolute nonsense. Who publishes their own misdoings in their paper? Even the *New York Times* wouldn't do that.'

'I knew you would say that,' James said in a cackling voice to Theresa who was about to explode. 'Why can't we publish it?'

'Where did you get this information?' She looked genuinely puzzled.

'I can't say.'

'Are you begging me to fire you?' she snarled.

'Oh well,' James gave a fake sigh before he said in a tone of mock sorrow. 'I think if someone else publishes the story, it would look much worse. Better to be transparent as that is one of our company values, right?' he quickly pounced back at her brazenly, half-threatening.

'No. There's no more debate here,' Theresa said as she walked towards the door, partly drawn by the commotion outside.

Fired with rage, Theresa stepped out of the room, only to see Steve and Pax being led away by plainclothes officers carrying cardboard cartons filled with files and documents.

Victor, who was sitting at the corner of the office, raised the volume of one of the TVs.

'Hong Kong's *Han Herald* has been fabricating its revenue numbers in an attempt to evade tax, according to a report released by Foggy Weather Research. Relevant Hong Kong authorities are investigating,' a news presenter said.

11

Déjà vu

The backs of the *Herald*'s two most senior leaders looked sunken and shrivelled as they were led away by the police officers, along with boxes of documents and the men's computers. Theresa and James who had emerged from the Sichuan meeting room, as well as a few others, watched them from a distance. Theresa was shell-shocked from the turn of events: James' fraud allegations, her own fury from his suggestion of a story and then the raid and arrests. The morning in December wasn't even over but it felt like a traumatic week had gone by.

An unprecedented frenzy had also swept across the two-floor newsroom, clouded by anxiety and disbelief. A media company whose business was built on integrity was now accused of having none. A fraud by a Hong Kong media company was unheard of in recent history. Media reports flooded the Internet. Some of the headings read:

> *Arcade's Han Herald in Hong Kong may have inflated its earnings; Arcade-controlled Han Herald fabricates its numbers as losses mounted, sources say; Hong Kong's century-old Han Herald cooks its books to cover up massive losses.*

Reporters and editors were getting calls and text messages from curious friends and peers.

Theresa's mobile phone didn't stop ringing and the screen was continuously popping up with messages. Twenty missed calls and many more text messages. She quickly called Pax's personal assistant

Wendy, asking her and the *Herald*'s in-house Legal Counsel Derek Lam to meet her in the Shanghai meeting room. *What was going on? The news report didn't say there would be arrests.* Theresa was struggling to piece together the pieces as she walked towards the empty meeting room. Wendy entered the room after her, followed by Derek. They told her that the police had come with their arrest and search warrants at about 8.30 a.m. They spent about an hour searching Steve and Pax's offices.

'The police said Steve and Pax committed accounting fraud,' Wendy went on.

'Fuck!' Theresa slammed the table hard and jumped up from her seat. Her fury had been simmering since she set foot into the office that morning. 'What were they thinking? They screwed all of us?' she cursed loudly.

Taking a moment to catch her breath, she turned to Derek. 'Did they do it?'

'We don't know,' the lawyer answered. He was taken aback by Theresa's hysterical behaviour. 'Steve has his own counsel and I've referred a lawyer friend to Pax. The Commercial Crime Bureau will usually hold and interview for several hours. Hopefully, we'll learn more by late afternoon or this evening,' he said carefully.

Theresa was less concerned about her bosses' predicament than the political impact it could have on her. *And what would the Party think?*

'Has anyone spoken to Mark or folks at Arcade?' she asked. 'And where the hell are Sheldon and Vijay?'

'Sheldon's on his way to Nanjing and Vijay is on vacation in India,' Wendy said quietly.

'I don't care, get him back. This is a crisis! He needs to . . . '

'Theresa, calm down,' Derek, seeing that Theresa wasn't going to regain her composure, interjected. 'Here's what you need to do. Address the newsroom ASAP. Your colleagues are journalists and their natural instinct is to dig for information and then speculate on what they find out,' he said firmly. 'Give them the available facts and tell them that we are investigating the matter and will provide updates when we have more information.'

Before she had a chance to respond, her phone rang. It was Sheldon calling.

'I've got to take this,' she told Derek. 'Sheldon, are you at Arcade in Nanjing? What the hell is going on?' she fired away, her face flushed.

'I was summoned really early today, they sent the jet. Derek has looped me in on what happened at the office.'

'Have you spoken to Mark? What did he say?'

'Not yet. The few senior guys I met so far were furious. I'm seeing Mark in ten minutes. It won't be pretty. Just think of all the implications for Arcade and the impact on its stocks tonight . . . Look, I need to go now,' Sheldon's voice trailed off.

'Oh, just one more thing Sheldon, let Mark know that we'll be putting out a story, just a basic factual report and . . . '

Sheldon got off the phone quickly.

Theresa's apparent hysteria was not helping and he had more than enough of it. But her hysterical voice reverberated in his head and weighed on his unease as he stepped into Mark Jin's office. He was prepared for an earful from the tech tycoon. Arcade's CFO Isaac Lin was also in the room.

'Morning Mark,' he said, 'Isaac.'

'Sheldon, it's been a while. You don't come as often as you should,' Jin said, as Lin nodded with a half-smile. 'Sit down.' Sheldon took the seat on Jin's left. Lin sat at a right angle, on his right.

'So . . . I know news itself can be unpredictable,' Jin said wryly. 'But I don't expect my business to be as unpredictable. Explain.' The founder's face was taut and his lips were in one line. He was containing his rage. It was the first time Sheldon had seen Jin like this.

'Believe it or not, I'm just as shocked,' Sheldon began gingerly. 'I'm not trying to shirk from my responsibility here. All I know is that our revenue, ad revenue, has improved in the past six months or so. We are getting more sales. They were Steve's leads, which he claimed were mainly from Guangdong companies that want to reach a global audience.'

Sheldon explained that Steve wouldn't divulge more when he asked for details. 'He said he was on top of it and ordered me to focus on the restructuring of the IT department and back-office functions; we've been downsizing to cut costs. I've seen some of the sales contracts and they appeared legitimate.

'Pax also said the advertisers were reputable. Steve's the boss; there was no reason for me to challenge him when it all seemed to be in order.'

A brief moment of uncomfortable silence ensued before Jin asked, 'Where are Derek and Maria on this?' Maria was the chief financial officer of the *Herald*.

'I believe they only know as much as I do. We're just executers; Steve wanted it that way,' Sheldon, who had chalked up his own grievances, said.

'It's not a blame game now. We need to be very clear with what we're dealing with to contain the damage and best protect the group's interests,' Jin told him. 'The board will meet after lunch; we'll decide on our next step and the interim plan. We need to get this out in the open before New York opens tonight.'

Sheldon sighed under his breath and his mouth felt dry. It was clear to him that Jin's sole concern was safeguarding Arcade's interest. His head started to throb hard. He didn't hear Jin's remaining instructions for Isaac to brace for the worst when the US stock markets opened that evening.

'Let's hope investors won't use this news to come for our blood,' Jin said, with a groan, 'Those bloodsuckers.'

Arcade's shares had been on a steady decline since the trade war broke out between the US and China, as well as the nagging issue that its e-commerce platform facilitated the sales of counterfeit goods and more recently, allegations that its hot-selling video game was a rip-off of a Swedish offering two years earlier. Jin, the largest individual shareholder whose personal fortune was being chipped away, wasn't pleased. But he was also losing patience with the *Herald* and its managers; it had been one bungle after another. *Almost like Hong Kong itself, always asking the central government for favours and concessions, but not really wanting to work for them,* he thought.

Jin ran a tight ship and all his senior managers knew. He set harsh benchmarks for all his employees and pruned off the worst performing

10 per cent of the team annually. The *Herald* was an exception to the policy and Jin was lately beginning to regret the decision he made four years ago. He was new to the media business then and assumed journalists were a different breed of talent, and should be measured differently. What he couldn't discern was the quality of journalism and the calibre of talent he had inherited at the *Herald* when he bought the newspaper. The media industry in China—where his knowledge of the industry was based—was another ball game, controlled by the government and its editorial could also be bought by corporations who naturally also toed the government line. Whereas in the West and in semi-autonomous Hong Kong, the media was a bastion of freedom of speech and journalists were assets that oiled the wheels of this machine. But the latitude and unconditional resources Jin and Arcade awarded the *Herald* seemed only to be repaid by trouble. *Pax and Theresa's self-censorship hasn't shifted the narrative to influence global opinions,* he thought. And the incapable people they hired were liabilities to his personal political profile. Jin never forgot how much the commentary by Kelvin Ko in 2017 cost him. His relationships with those close to the top Party leaders were majorly severed and for the last two years, he had to invest massively in repairing and regaining their favour. By now, he knew more about the media and he saw clearly the extent of the mastheads' capability. *They are just crudely suppressing coverage they think the Party doesn't like. They just don't get it.* Instituting any change was equally tedious and would entail the involvement of Beijing. He had liked Pax for his extreme flexibility in accommodating his needs. *Obedient and easy to manipulate.* But that was about it.

Within Arcade, staff resentment towards their peers at the sister company had simmered and was coming to a boil against the *Herald*, dissatisfied with Jin's leniency and the double standards.

'Mark, we set high benchmarks for the Arcade team, they have to perform or they are out. And they bring in the revenue, sales. But the same set of measurements doesn't apply to the *Herald*. Our staff see themselves subsidizing the media guys, who enjoy all the perks and can spend whatever they want. We need to correct this balance.' Arcade's human resources director had advised Jin a few months ago when she realized that the disgruntlement on the floor was widening and the group had to deal with spurts of resignations. Isaac reported the worrying financial numbers and had told Jin he noticed too many unjustifiable expenses.

'I don't know what Maria was thinking, but as a finance person, I would have rejected half of those expenses; they made no sense. One-third of the management team was travelling at any one time and on business-class tickets and staying at six-star hotels. Seriously?' These exchanges were coming back into Jin's mind as he now sat down at his desk to prepare for the board meeting.

In the Hong Kong newsroom, the mood was tense, wrapped in eerie quietness that the sound of a dropping pin would have been heard. Most of the reporters had heard the news by now. Everyone was glued to their computer screen waiting for updates either from third-party sources or internal emails and busy chatting online with one another or with media friends in the industry. They didn't care if those chats were recorded and could be scrutinized by the company. The volume of chat data was so staggering that morning that any scrutiny by the higher-ups would be a mammoth task.

James, Mary, Victor and Daniel were busy exchanging notes on their own group chat on a platform that was out of the realm of the company's software and hardware. Their vigilance and paranoia had increased since they worked on the task force.

Wow, we knew these guys didn't have editorial integrity, but fraud is a whole new level, Daniel texted.

The only thing consistent about this place is there's no bottom line. Every day is a new low, texted James.

Theresa's going to give an update in 20 minutes, heard from my friend at corporate communications. Their phones haven't stopped ringing, Mary wrote.

She got her wish, didn't she? Taking charge for once, incoming interim editor-in-chief. Boy, I bet you she's freaking out, Victor sneeringly texted, which incited the other three to send more laughing-out-loud emojis.

I wonder what papa is going to say or do, James added. No one had the heart to respond to that.

'Good morning everyone,' Theresa began to address her colleagues at the Hub. 'I wanted to keep everyone abreast of what has happened, in the spirit of transparency. As in the world of news, there was an unexpected development and we have little details of the investigation at the moment. Police officers came to our office this morning with warrants for Steve and Pax on allegations that accounting fraud had been committed. They have taken documents and computer hardware from Steve and Pax's office and brought them back to the headquarters for interviews. We are keeping track of the development and will update everyone as and when we know.

'Now as journalists, we all know there'll be plenty of speculation, rumours from all quarters, especially from our peers outside this newsroom. I know because my phone hasn't stopped beeping with messages or ringing. I ask that you be professional and not add to the rumour mill. Please forward any enquiries to corporate communications, copying me. They will handle all queries. Also, do not and I repeat, do not forward any internal emails you get starting from today.

'The newsroom will be business as usual. We will go about as we've always done. Our job is to lead the China conversation and we will continue to do that professionally. Any questions?'

'Theresa, what was the accounting fraud exactly that Steve and Pax committed? What kind of numbers or scale of fraud were they involved in? Will there be a change in the management team?' asked the Senior Business Reporter Charlie Tanner.

'Charlie, I don't have the details and until we know for sure, let's not speculate,' Theresa replied, annoyed, sending him daggers with her eyes. 'As a senior journalist, you should know better.'

'Have you spoken to Arcade and Mark? Is this alleged fraud related to the parent company?' asked James.

'Again, let's not speculate,' answered Theresa, visibly impatient, irritated even. 'The board is aware of this development and I will update you as soon as we know more. If you have more questions or concerns, come see me separately. Let's stay focused on our work and get on with our day.' As the reporters dispersed and trickled back to their desks, Theresa sent for Byron and Heather, as well as the Business Editor Edward Murphy.

'Byron, I want you to be in charge and coordinate with the relevant desks on this alleged fraud story. We need to keep the coverage as balanced as possible. Edward, I called you in because there will be implications to the business side of things for Arcade. We are going to be mindful of the market reactions tonight and analysts' calls on the stock. I want you and your team to only cover the bare essentials and nothing more. There is absolutely no need for us to analyse or speculate. Just straightforward stories.'

Turning to Heather, she instructed, 'Heather, I need you now to write a news story about this morning's arrest. It doesn't have to be long, based on the corporate communications' team statement which should have been out five minutes ago. Keep it to 300 words maximum. Got it?'

* * *

When the *Herald*'s story hit its own website one hour later, the international news agencies and other Hong Kong media had flooded the Internet with numerous more accounts. Journalists naturally had a greater interest in stories about their own industry and a media story connected to someone like Mark Jin and Arcade always sold well, viewership wise. What's more, it was a scandal. Most stories included the arrests and raids. Many went beyond to speculate the implications for Jin and Arcade's stock price and business. The *Hong Kong Mail* quoted an analyst raising concern about a culture of stretching the truth among Arcade companies. 'There's always unverified reports of double reporting of Arcade's Singles Day sales and the group could never shake off the cloud of inflating its numbers. Is this culture spreading to the *Herald* too?' By the time Theresa reviewed and published Heather's story about the arrests and raid, she was pining for the bad dream to end. *Be careful what you wish for, as they say.* Theresa had yearned to take charge, but not during a scandal that threatened her own standing, along with the owner and the Party!

Her body told her she needed to step out of the office for some fresh air and to think.

James watched Theresa rush out of the newsroom ignoring Wendy's attempt to get her to look at some documents. He felt detached about the turn of events since the morning; he was more curious to know who had spilt the beans. Victor had asked if he were the whistleblower.

'Are you kidding dude, why would I do that?' he retorted, feeling a little hurt. 'I can ask the same of you; was it you?'

'I don't know, 'cause you're pissed with Pax and the *Herald* and this task force crap?' his friend shrugged. 'No, it's not me. I would if I had the details and the story. Who do you think leaked the story to the wires?'

At her favourite Café Nobody, Theresa sipped her black coffee and tried to get a grip of what had happened. *If Steve and Pax fabricated the records, how did regulators get wind of it? Who had ratted them out?* She hated the uncertainty that she was unwittingly thrown into as much as she wanted to be the queen of the *Herald*. It was no longer just the usual politicking with Vijay or Pax in the office. The stakes were much higher, too many unknown variables that she feared were beyond her control. *Would I be implicated?* Even though Pax may be ousted, for the first time Theresa's interest to step into the editor-in-chief's role waned a little. The fact was being second-in-command now already meant she would have to be dragged through the mud. She was smart enough to realize that this would stick around for longer than she liked. *But I can also take this opportunity to perform and score before Vijay jumps on it.* She gulped down the last of her coffee; her thirty minutes were up. As she prepared to leave, James' face flashed through her mind. *Could he have leaked this?* He had pushed to publicize this three hours ago and Theresa knew the reporter had been angry with her and Pax for censoring the story on Edwin's death. She would ask him when she got back to the office.

'It wasn't me,' he looked right into her eyes and stated point-blank. He wasn't surprised by Theresa's suspicion. 'In case you've forgotten, I wanted us to out this ourselves before we got exposed by someone else. That's my definition of professionalism.'

James' sarcasm added fuel to Theresa's fire on an already abysmal day. To salvage face, she explained that her candidness was to uphold transparency in the newsroom.

'Just to avoid unnecessary misunderstandings given our differences on a number of issues,' she added lamely.

'Okay, now that we're clear. If there's nothing else, can I go? I'm sure you have bigger issues to deal with today?'

'Of course,' Theresa stood up to leave the meeting room before James.

The newsroom stayed unusually quiet most of the day. The TV news channels continued to loop news of the arrests and the *Herald*, as well as Arcade. Reporters were all buried in their heads, looking like they were working hard, either typing on their keyboards or speaking on the phone. They were trying hard to focus and maintain as much normality as possible. Though it didn't look like it, beneath the facade, many of the journalists were hit by a range of emotions—most of all anger and embarrassment. Heather was shell-shocked when she first learned of the arrests. A China desk colleague overheard her confiding on the phone that she felt a sense of betrayal from Pax, whom she loosely looked up to as a role model, and told James. He let out a small laugh.

The army of young reporters on the China desk was churning out routine and ineffective yarns on China's progressive development and achievements, copies to meet the daily quota of stories that went online. Theresa tried to slide back into her usual daily routine but was constantly distracted by her own fears of how the scandal would affect her position. Her inbox was jammed with emails, many of them marked 'internal' or 'confidential'. She scanned through the ones that seemed urgent first, sorting and forwarding those which the legal or PR teams would be better placed to handle. Then she began to review stories that required her editing, which was 80 per cent of the daily output. She was agitated with the enormous load before her. But Theresa had only herself to blame. She had ordered for at least half of the stories to be sent to her before they were published as none of her deputies were up to her standards. Today, she couldn't look at all the stories. She'd have to be selective, focus on the major US-China relations story. She felt that she had no choice but to ask Byron to share the 'important' editing responsibility.

'But if it's anything related to US-China relations, or about the *Herald*, make sure I look at them before they're published.'

Byron nodded flatly and turned to walk off before Theresa could continue her rant. At that moment, her phone rang. It was Derek.

'Theresa, this is Derek. Can you meet me in my office?'

* * *

'I just got a call from Pax's lawyer,' Derek began. 'They have enough to charge him and Steve, but they could be released on bail. The picture is not looking good. Looks like the police have hard evidence.' Theresa gasped and Terence Fu, who ran the *Herald*'s corporate communications team and was also in the room, frowned.

'Also, Arcade's board has decided to fire Steve and Pax,' Derek said. 'Our priority is to protect the *Herald*'s reputation now. I'll be speaking to Arcade's legal in five minutes. They will put out a statement before Wall Street opens tonight.'

Derek went on to give firm instructions to his colleagues. He told Terence to draft a press release that will be distributed with the statement that evening while instructing Theresa to synchronize the update report of the investigation with Arcade's communications team and Sheldon. There was to be no mention of the sackings before the statement was released, he stressed.

'Since we're all here now, how about we call Sheldon?' suggested Terence.

'Good idea,' Derek agreed and dialled on the polycom in his office.

'Derek?' Sheldon's voice came through shortly.

'Yes, I've got Terence and Theresa here.'

'Good. You're on speaker by the way; I'm with Katrina and Ryan. We were just discussing the communications plan.'

'What's the game plan?' Derek asked.

'Mark's instruction is that we say absolutely nothing about the termination until the statement and press release. We think that the market will be speculating intensively and there might be leaks. But we hold our grounds from our side, clear?

'Theresa, I know we need to update our news report. Mark has no issue if you ran a story on the progress of the investigation. It is what it is. Beyond that, we don't have anything else to say. The board's priority is to protect the *Herald*'s reputation but also to be implicated as little as possible. The same goes for Arcade's reputation and valuation,' Sheldon said.

'Derek, I'll ring you later. Some details we need to iron out.' With that, the COO hung up.

* * *

Theresa felt that her bad dream was worsening by the minute as she walked out of Derek's office. It was just past three in the afternoon. The day was long and the night was going to be longer. Terence had stayed on to discuss the distribution arrangement for the press release. In her near two decades in the *Herald*, she had not experienced a December as roller coaster a ride as the one she was on now; though in her capacity, she had to suppress her desire to scream out the stress. The news cycle traditionally slowed in December as business activities wound down for the holiday season in Hong Kong, even for 2019, where most of the year had been gripped by political unrest. After a heady November that saw the protests entered into university campuses for some of the worst standoffs and violence of the movement, demonstrations in December had become less intense. The day-to-day tensions in the *Herald* newsroom eased a little and the masthead editors were relieved. That didn't mean the dispute between some of the task force members after Pax and Theresa banned the publication of the story on Edwin's death dissipated. Except for Heather, the journalists were struggling with ways to reconcile with their anger. Just yesterday, Theresa and Pax shared a conversation about the small-scale demonstrations that were continuing and nothing too major in the bigger scheme of things.

'These kids are like flies that you can't get rid of. Annoying,' Pax had told her. She agreed wholeheartedly. 'But as long as the police have the situation under control, it's not a problem. The Party is going to take a stance on this and it shouldn't be too long.'

Theresa had looked at him, wondering if he had intelligence that he wasn't sharing. But he skillfully deflected her probing look.

'Look, it's just not normal and as with how life takes its course, these unusual times too will pass eventually.' He felt the de-escalation of tensions as Hong Kong stepped into December, with a few odd episodes.

On a chilly December day, a suspect wanted on suspicion of possessing firearms fired one live round from a semi-automatic pistol during the arrest, which protesters tried to obstruct to help the man escape. The police retaliated with tear gas. A follow-up raid of his residence found rifles and ammunition that police alleged would be used during public assemblies. A day earlier, police arrested four people from the Spark Alliance, a group providing financial aid and bail money to protesters, on suspicion of money laundering and seized over HK$70 million in funds. The Spark Alliance arrests reignited protests against HSBC Bank, where the group had kept their funds. A month earlier, HSBC closed a business account used by the group for failing to provide documentation to meet compliance requirements. HSBC tweeted a statement later, claiming that the decision to close the account was unrelated to the arrests. The account was closed in November upon the instruction of the customer, it read.

The relative calm in the city had given the editors days of relaxed manner and comfort. There were few calls from the higher-ups. The Chinese state media was flooding the Internet with yearly review stories on the accomplishment of the Party. Pax and Theresa felt 'burdened' by story ideas from these reports and assigned a string of stories to reporters. In a twist of fate, the *Herald* broke the traditional holiday news cycle lull for its competitors with its fraud scandal. Byron and Heather had filed an updated story that included the information that Pax and Steve were released on bail. After it was published, Theresa wrote a short e-mail to the newsroom with the link to the story.

Hi all,
Further to my earlier briefing, the police have finished interviewing Steve and Pax earlier and they have been released on bail. There are no further details at the moment and as the case is now in the hands of the authorities, the Herald will fully cooperate with the investigation. I will update you further when we have more details. Our updated story will be your reference.

Cheers,
Theresa

She pressed send and sank deeper into her chair. There seemed to be an increasing disconnect between her brain and her body that she was struggling to keep a lid on. *Didn't John F. Kennedy say that in a crisis, be aware of the danger but recognize the opportunity? Pax was done.* Theresa's spirits lifted instantaneously at the thought. *Focus, focus, focus.* Meeting Jin to secure his blessing was her most pressing task, she decided. *Not today as Jin's attention was on Wall Street and investors*, she thought, but she'll try to book a time with his personal assistant to get on a call with him tomorrow. Then she went on with business as usual, to push the 'Greater China narrative'. It was the only thing she could do. She wished she could show Jin her value, especially in desperate times like now. In one of her rare occasions, Theresa forced herself to be patient and wait for the right moment.

* * *

At 7.30 p.m. before Wall Street opened, Arcade announced that the board of directors of the *Herald*, a subsidiary of the group, had terminated the newspaper's Chief Executive Officer Steve Hsieh and Editor-in-Chief, Pax Yong with immediate effect in a filing to the American regulators. The *Herald* and Arcade accompanied the statement with a joint press release that was disseminated to the media via a global distribution platform.

Arcade Group Announces Termination of Han Herald CEO and Editor-in-chief

Nanjing, China, 23 December 2019: Arcade Group (Nasdaq: ARC) today announced that the Board of Directors of the Han Herald, a subsidiary of the group, has terminated Steve Hsieh and Pax Yong from the positions of Chief Executive Officer and Editor-in-Chief respectively. The termination takes immediate effect in light of the ongoing investigations by the Hong Kong authorities into an alleged accounting fraud. The board also demanded and received Mr Hsieh's resignation.

In order to ensure continuity, the Herald's Chief Operating Officer Sheldon Lam and inhouse legal counsel Derek Lam will share the duties of the office of the CEO until a new leader is appointed. An executive search has begun and no changes in the Herald's goals are planned.

Arcade's stocks took a dive as soon as the markets opened, recording its biggest one-day plunge by the end of the trading day. Jin's personal wealth was wiped off by 20 per cent in a day, spelling millions of dollars lost. Editors granted stock options also watched with dismay at their book losses. The hedge funds also had a field day, as did the media. As Asia closed, European media picked up where the story left off and then the US when Europe went to bed. Nearly every investment bank—big or small—released a research note. Half of them recommended a 'sell' on the Arcade stock, with another third giving it an 'underweight' and the remainder a 'neutral'. In short, the stock was not attractive to accumulate.

Jin stayed up through the night tracking the equity's performance, speaking to his co-founder and shareholders around the world. He tried to appease investors that the *Herald* was a drop in the bucket in Arcade's investment portfolio and its operations didn't directly impact China's biggest social media and e-commerce company.

'Listen Stu, first of all, this is definitely an independent, one-off, by these two individuals. We had absolutely no idea this went on for six months and we had cut them loose immediately after we knew about the problem, within twenty-four hours. They are gone, history,' Jin tried to persuade the CEO of the world's biggest private equity fund, Arcade's cornerstone shareholder.

'Arcade's business is sound and our bottomline is growing by double digits, everything is sound. As for the *Herald*, you're a longtime reader, you know it's good stuff. We can't let a couple of bad apples destroy what we have.'

There was a pause on the other end. The fund manager then said, 'Mark, you and I know very well that's not how the market works. We have been friends long enough, so off the record, let me say this.' Jin held his breath a little.

'The *Herald* is becoming a liability from the American investors' standpoint. Not from the financial perspective—it's insignificant as you pointed out—but your paper is now a Party mouthpiece and that is weighing on how Arcade is valued. What's on the Internet can never be wiped off. You need to bite the bullet.' Jin didn't like what he heard but when it came from his biggest shareholder, he knew it was time to make the hard decision.

Arcade's stock recorded its biggest one-day loss that day. By the end of the week, the stock had dropped by more than a third, adding to the 20 per cent decline since the beginning of the year. For 2019, Jin's personal fortune in the company had halved.

* * *

Theresa woke up the following day calmer and with some excitement. Topping her to-do list was the call with Jin. The previous evening had gone by quietly in the wake of the scandal. The volume of calls and text messages dwindled as the day progressed. After the *Herald* story was updated to include Steve and Pax's termination, she cleared a few more emails and went home. Wendy reached Vijay who said he'd come back as soon as he could from India, where he was holidaying. The rest of the newsroom hummed along most of yesterday afternoon. The 'most problematic' reporters stayed out of Theresa's way and she was perversely glad that the distraction of the scandal presented the circumstances for her to avoid dealing with the task force team and their findings. As for the accounting fraud report that James had, well, it was no longer an issue. Theresa heaved a sigh of relief. At least it was one issue less to deal with James. But today, the reporter could wait. She decided to do the call with Jin at home, where there was privacy. Theresa had drawn up her talking points in her head that pointed to one objective. She would steer the newsroom through the storm and then she wanted to be elevated to the top job. She also had a list of her contributions and personal milestones achieved for the *Herald* ready to share with Jin. Rebecca called her mobile at 8.29 a.m.

'Morning Theresa, I have Mark on the line. Please hold.' Jin came on the line at 8.30 a.m.

'Good morning Mark. How are you today?'

'Thank you, it has been a busy twenty-four hours. What is it that you can't talk to Sheldon and need to talk to me about?'

'Thanks, thank you for your time, very much appreciate it given the circumstances,' Theresa said, fighting her nerves. 'I wanted to let you know that the newsroom is under control. I'm doing my best to ensure continuity, so therefore, I am hoping we can discuss me possibly taking over the editor-in-chief role. You know where I stand on regional issues and how news should be told. The last few years . . . '

'Theresa, now is not the time to talk about this,' Jin cut her off. 'We should focus on the big picture. If there's nothing else, let's talk another time. Speak to Sheldon if you have further questions. He's in charge.' He paused before adding, 'We need you to focus on what's most pressing, okay?' With that, Jin hung up.

The conversation lasted for a whole five minutes and ended in a worse way than Theresa could have imagined. She felt sick, afraid that she had blown her only chance with Jin. She wasn't as naïve as to expect an affirmative response but she thought it could table the agenda for further discussion. *But he said he needed me, so it's not a dead-end yet.* Holding a glass half-full mentality, she left for work.

On the face of it, the newsroom looked like any other day. But beneath that surface of calm, apprehension and anxiety seized reporters and non-editorial staff. Steve and Pax's accounting fraud allegations were a crippling blow to the fragile morale among reporters at the

Herald. On the demonstration frontline, they often faced ostracization by protesters for 'spinning the Party's narrative'. Back in the office, battling their editors on the slant and tone of the narrative didn't cease. The reporters resonated with one of the numerous graffiti that was sprayed on the wall of the Hong Kong Polytechnic University, which became a two-week battleground between students and the police in November.

Don't trust the Herald, their narrative is controlled by Chinese propaganda.

In some ways, James found solace from what had taken place overnight, that Steve and Pax's coverup of the *Herald*'s losses by falsifying the numbers was exposed. *At least the world knows of the corruption*, he thought. But the truth of Edwin Law's death, he found, was still a burden to carry and he remained deeply troubled about the story remaining censored. He had a nagging feeling it wasn't just exposing a Chinese secret police blunder, but he also feared that bigger and darker forces were at play. He reached out to Sum Suk, ignoring their agreement that he would not call the official at his office. This time he almost pleaded with urgency to meet his source as soon as possible.

'You shouldn't call this number.'

'I'm sorry, but it's urgent. Can we meet tonight?' A momentary silence followed.

'All right,' his source hung up. Minutes later, James received a text message from an unknown number with a place and time.

* * *

Meanwhile in Nanjing, Jin and his senior team continued a second day of back to back meetings with his senior executives, including a lunch session with his co-founder and longtime friend Gordon Bao that extended into a three-hour discussion and review of their business.

'Lao Bao, I know you have a soft spot for the *Herald*,' he looked at his friend.

'I think it's time we let go. It's brought us more headaches than benefits. The stakes have increased beyond our calculation; we wouldn't have known . . . the Hong Kong protests, the trade war.

'And the half-assed job these editors did with my assignment to shift the narrative with that Hong Kong kid's death. They couldn't even control the reporters; the reporters were able to get to the real story. At the moment they are able to ban the publication of the true story, but you can't wrap paper around a fire. It's going to trace back to politics at the very top. It may not be something we can stomach and do we want to take further risks?' Bao's eyes narrowed.

'Lao Jin, I think you're right. The good thing is there are parties who'd be interested to take over. So this could move very quickly. Let's get our people together and move forward.'

* * *

James met Sum Suk at 8 p.m. in a tiny Chinese eatery in Kowloon's Kwun Tong area. The area, one of Hong Kong's first new towns developed in the 1950s, was one of the most densely populated in the city. His source picked a hole in the wall restaurant in one of the many back alleys in the area. James arrived on time, but the older man was already seated, always a step ahead. His source broke into a smile when he saw James. The reporter smiled back ruefully.

'Sorry about the short notice,' he told Sum Suk, 'but I needed some perspective. It's increasingly out of whack.'

'Have some tea and see what you'd like to eat,' the older man poured him some tea and slipped the laminated menu card across the table. The pocket-sized restaurant held five small round tables. Apart from them, there was another table of three diners.

'Don't worry, it's quiet here,' Sum Suk told James, sensing his uneasiness. 'Let's order some food first, then we can talk.

'What's troubling you?'

'I feel like I'm working in a den of thieves. You've probably read—the CEO and chief editor have been arrested for fraud. I had been investigating and pieced together the puzzle just days before the police stormed into the office yesterday. I told my editor—the deputy editor—that we should write the story but of course, she freaked out.' Then he shrugged, 'Anyhow, just glad it's out now.

'What I really want is your take on the case of Edwin Law's death. We found out that his death was definitely not an accident, nor suicide. Edwin was tortured, but it's likely that someone made a blunder. I have evidence but of course, we can't publish it.

'Our deputy editor claimed that the task force's job to find out the reason behind his death was to counter fake news—presumably the rumours suggesting that the Party was behind the death. Now that we have proof that it was unintentional, that should clear the speculation. I don't understand.'

Sum Suk listened to James patiently without interrupting. He then gave it a couple of minutes after the reporter finished before giving his perspective.

'I can't say I have all the details. It has now gone beyond what your editors say. Forget about eliminating fake news. The *Herald* was supposed to shift the narrative, make the rumour that the Party was implicated go away. Instead, you reporters uncovered the truth, which as journalists, I have to say—good job. But it's not about journalism here. Never was. And so, your bosses probably got orders from the higher-ups to bury the truth. You've covered China long enough, you should know.

'Because it's about the interests of those at the top within the Party. You said Wang Tao was involved. Wang's connection is with those close to the Party chief. I'm sure there are already whispers in the corridors of power in Beijing. But if this—accident or not—goes out publicly, the one in power will definitely be implicated. How will that play out? It can erode his power base and give his opponents in the Party a gap to attack, even openly.

'Your story wasn't going to see the light of the day. I think your editors faked this whole task force. But they were not smart and sophisticated enough and thus didn't deliver to those in charge. Jin is believed to be in the camp of those around the Party chief. Now with regards to the fraud, Jin is the one in deep shit. I'm sure he's desperate to exit before the higher-ups discard him.'

Their food arrived. Sum Suk had ordered steamed fish, stir-fried mixed vegetables and deep-fried sweet and sour pork ribs, as well as steamed rice. In silence, the two of them began to tuck in. It was a lot for James to take in. Distracted and oblivious of the dishes on the table, his chopsticks mindlessly picked up grains of rice from his bowl. Sum Suk picked up some fish, vegetables and pork ribs and put them on James' side plate.

'Have some food, we can talk more later.'

The clouds suddenly cleared for James. He was less affected at that point by the political implications, but more concerned about how to find a way to write Edwin's story.

He voiced that concern to his source.

'Have some patience, you may get the chance. Change will come,' his source said.

They continued with dinner, chatting more about the political landscape in China and Hong Kong and had a beer each before parting ways.

* * *

Two weeks had gone by since Steve and Pax were arrested. The *Herald* went about as it always had, with or without the men, as it lived off its own historic fat. Theresa assumed the role of defacto editor-in-chief with little prompting needed. She felt invincible almost, at the top in her self-created farce, as Sheldon was busy managing the crisis. The fraud had created more suspicions from advertisers and Sheldon was working round the clock to dissuade companies from pulling out their advertisements. Business partners and vendors were calling the company on payments and loans. Terence, the company's corporate communications director, was answering enquiries nonstop. It was not pretty and the business executives were burnt out.

After her call with Jin the day after the arrests, Theresa had dropped into Sheldon's office a few days after his return from Nanjing.

'Hi Sheldon,' she breezed in after knocking on the door frame before he could respond.

'Er, Theresa, hello,' the COO was surprised by her unannounced appearance. 'Didn't think we had anything on the diary for this . . . '

'I know, I know. Just wanted to touch base quickly. How are things and the meeting with Mark and the management team in Nanjing?'

'Well, given the circumstances, I would say it's fine,' Sheldon said. 'If you don't mind, I really need to get back to things. Really stretched here.' He turned his head back to the papers on his desk. He couldn't be clearer that he wanted to be left alone.

'I won't be long,' Theresa said as she walked towards the couple of chairs in front of his desk and sat down on one. Sheldon was forced to look up again. This time he just stared at her, trying to hide his annoyance.

'I have been holding the fort and I think it may be appropriate to discuss the possibility of me taking the editor-in-chief role. I know we are in this whirlwind of a mess, which also means the sooner we re-instill stability the better for the newsroom.'

For once, words failed Sheldon and he could only stare. *I can't believe this! I'm slogging to make sure this company survives now so we all still have a paycheck and all this woman can think about is her elevation.* He took five seconds before he opened his mouth.

'Theresa, I hear you but honestly, this is not my decision. And this is not the right time. I'm going to have to ask you to leave because I really have more urgent matters to deal with.' He stood up and ushered her towards the door. Then he shut it behind him.

Vijay witnessed the episode with quiet interest. He was forced to cut short his holiday and came back to work three days after the arrests. But returning to an office where Theresa was calling the shots was certainly unappealing and Vijay felt himself drifting along. With Pax out of the picture, Vijay lost his zest for life at the company and any chance, however, remote it might be of rising up the ranks. *Time to move on maybe?*

* * *

The arrests laid out to bare the dark side of the *Herald* and the losses accumulated, sending shudders through the company. The *Herald*'s staff welcomed the New Year with little fanfare. Until then, the dire straits were simply hearsay, but now that it was in the open, it made everyone fear for the security of their jobs. The biggest worriers were the experienced journalists given the senior editors' preference for young impressionable minds.

The task force reporters didn't know what to think. The fraud allegations had come so fast that they hadn't had time to come around. With the exception of Heather, they felt deflated somewhat after Theresa and Pax's rejection of Edwin's story, defeating the purpose of the assignment. They were also angry at the editors' decision to cover up the story.

'It's quite clear to me now what this whole task force was about,' said Alan, the photographer.

'Whatever their agenda is, I say we find a way to get the story out,' Victor said.

'Agreed. But how?' asked Mary.

'Theresa's not going to agree now, even if we continue to push,' James pointed out, then turned to Mary, 'what are the odds if we talk to Vijay?'

'Vijay's pissed that Theresa's now in charge. He can either try to go against her or feels that it's not to his advantage to oppose. I can try to suss him out. He didn't know about the story, right? He was on holiday.'

'No harm in trying,' Daniel said, while the others nodded in agreement. 'If it doesn't work out, we'll wait for an opportunity. It's too important a story not to publish,' James added.

Each day after they were done with the daily assignments, James, Mary, Victor and Daniel continued to put together the inside story to Edwin Law's untimely death. Alan searched the archives for photos and videos. Mary had also sounded out Vijay's inclination and concluded that he was not about to get himself into a confrontation with Theresa.

'I agree with the editors that the story doesn't stand, your sources are all unnamed. Too risky, it'd put the *Herald*'s reputation on the line,' he told Mary.

'Isn't the reputation on the line already?' Mary responded in her quiet voice.

* * *

News around the *Herald* scandal began to die down. The company hired external forensic accountants to conduct a thorough investigation into its books to salvage some of its lost reputation. It also organized community events with local non-profit organisations to engage with the local communities and regain trust. A semblance of normality was returning, Sheldon reported to Jin in mid-January. The first whispers of a deal came in the wee hours of Tuesday morning in Hong Kong, from the afternoon trading session in New York where Arcade was listed. The rumour drove the Chinese tech giant's stocks up to regain some of its accumulated losses over the past year. Reports of Arcade's plan to sell the *Herald* continued through Tuesday when Asian markets opened. News articles headlined *Arcade to sell scandal-hit media unit the Herald, sources say* and *Arcade may dump fraudulent Hong Kong media firm* were published.

The senior editors had no inkling that this was coming. Business journalists, including the business editor, were usually the first to get whiffs of such a deal but that didn't happen at the *Herald*. Murphy and the merger and acquisition beat reporter, therefore, scrambled to match the exclusive story that was published by an American news agency. Theresa was hysterical when she learned of the news. Her personal stake in a potential change in ownership was much higher with her current position, four notches up from four years ago when Arcade entered the frame.

'Did you know about this?' she grilled Sheldon in his office.

'Theresa, as COO I don't have to report to you,' Sheldon stood up from his seat and steered her towards the door. 'So calm down and let's get back to our own work. I have a full day ahead, as I'm sure you do as well.'

At 7 p.m. that evening, Arcade announced that it had agreed to sell the *Herald* to a private equity firm for US$195 million, a 20 per cent discount to what Jin had paid for when he bought the newspaper. The newsroom was abuzz with excitement when the announcement was released.

OMG guys, Arcade is calling it quits! Have you seen the news? Victor wrote in their group chat.

Yep, Mary replied. *Didn't expect them to exit so swiftly though.*

EH Capital, wonder what's their background. I bet there's a Chinese connection there. How can there not be in this time and age? James texted, with a half-laughing, half-tearing emoji.

Sheldon sent an e-mail to all staff at 9 p.m.

To the Herald team:

Earlier this evening, Arcade has announced that it has entered an agreement for EH Capital to acquire the Han Herald Company. Further to the announcement, Arcade has assured this interim management team that under the agreement with EH, operations of the Herald, including staff headcount, will remain unchanged for the next six months till the time the deal is completed. If you have any questions, please feel free to approach your supervisor or me.

Best,
Sheldon

Sheldon purposely kept his e-mail brief. Unlike Theresa, he had no ambition to gun for the top job. Stability was his only desire. He had weathered different owners over the years. Whether it was Arcade or EH, it didn't matter. The background of EH, however, mattered for reporters, even though the *Herald* was expected to continue to be pro-China against the political landscape.

* * *

A week after the announcement and just days before the Lunar New Year, Sheldon held a town hall at the Hub. Before he started speaking, observant colleagues noticed him chatting with a tall Chinese man who was obviously an outsider.

'Good morning everyone. I hope everyone is well. I wanted to update you all on a few things this morning. The management has been working hard to repair the damage and it has been challenging. But we are very pleased today to share with you that we've persuaded most of our advertisers to stay with us. But we're not done yet, the road ahead remains tough. We have hired external forensic accountants for an internal audit and they will finish the review at the end of this month. The management has also met with Arcade and EH. EH has reiterated its commitment to keep our entire team unchanged and our editorial independence.' Sheldon paused before resuming.

'On that note, I would like to introduce this morning our new Editor-in-Chief Jack Hu. Given the unique circumstances we are in, Jack starts today. Please join me in welcoming him to the *Herald* family. Jack, would you like to say a few words?'

Sheldon's unexpected introduction of a new editor-in-chief stunned the newsroom, sparking a chorus of gasps. No one was more surprised than Theresa, James noted. *Well, there goes her ambition.* The unfamiliar looking tall man in a light-coloured shirt under a charcoal grey suit stepped forward.

'Thanks Sheldon. Morning everyone. It's a great honour to be here and to lead this newsroom, to continue leading the China conversation. The *Han Herald* exemplifies the highest standards in journalism and commitment to society as a media of accountability and trustworthiness. The coming months will be challenging as we reclaim some of our credibility and win back trust with balanced and insightful reporting.

'My door is always open, so feel free to come in for a chat, share your story ideas. I look forward to working with every one of you.'

In his last few weeks battling with the editors, James had come to the conclusion that anything was possible in this newsroom. He felt indifferent to the hurried appointment of Jack and thought it was part of a ploy that involved the Party. He was more curious as to which faction of the Party this new set-up served. Jack's entry into the picture could help in the task force reporters' pursuit to publish Edwin's story.

Since he's new he may have a fresh outlook on news story decisions, James thought. He was determined to bring that up to the new boss before Theresa had a chance to veto it. By then James was emboldened and felt he had nothing to lose, except his job—and he didn't care one bit. Two hours after the town hall ended, James walked into the new editor-in-chief's office with Mary, Victor and Daniel. They introduced themselves to Jack and gave him a brief download of their reporting work. Then they laid out the story to Jack and showed him their draft. The reporters had coordinated their presentation to Jack over coffee at Starbucks.

'The idea is to get Jack on board ASAP with publishing the story. The fewer details he has of what went outside the story the better,' James said to his colleagues.

'We'll brief him on the task force and what we found out, that Theresa and Pax were uncomfortable with unnamed sources in the story. But the good thing is we have gotten another source from the police, even though we can't name it, which backs up the doctor's report and gives the story credibility. Our pitch will be that this exclusive story will help rebuild the *Herald*'s credibility,' he said as the reporters nodded their heads in agreement.

Jack was now reading the draft before him. His eyes narrowed occasionally and his forehead creased. *The reporters are right, the story would help them regain lost ground,* he thought. After five minutes, he raised his head and looked at the four reporters from one to the other.

'This is a good story, backed by solid reporting. The copy has some rough edges and we need to edit down some of the language. We also have to run it by our lawyers before we publish it, just to be sure,' he told the reporters.

'As a courtesy, I'd let Theresa know we're publishing the story.' Then he added assuringly when he saw the reporters' worried looks, 'Don't worry, it's just a formality.'

'Thanks Jack,' James said. 'We really appreciate this.'

As the reporters walked out of the editor's room, they looked at one another, mixed with disbelief and elation. They felt a huge load had been lifted off their chests.

Jack was true to his words and at 6 p.m. that evening, the story hit the website. The explosiveness of the coverup by the authorities drew 100,000 clicks in the first hour, setting a new record of online traffic for the *Herald*. The story was picked up by nearly every international media outlet and put many government agencies in Hong Kong on a defensive stance. Ronny Yip, the Hong Kong deputy police commissioner who had tried to sway the narrative during the closed-door meeting at the *Herald* months earlier, called an urgent midnight press conference to deny the story.

'The *Herald*'s allegations are all hearsay by several unnamed sources. We strongly denounce the report, which has no truth in it.'

When he was grilled by the press to specify which part was untrue, Yip lost his cool and hollered at the reporters in the room. 'The force has been nothing but steadfast in upholding our integrity and duty to maintain law and order in this city. We have nothing to hide!'

At the regular Chinese foreign ministry press briefing the following day, the spokeswoman called the report 'fake news' and accused the *Herald*'s reporters of 'spreading rumours' to discredit the Hong Kong authorities.

'Interesting how Beijing doesn't mention China or the Party at all in its rebuttal. It's distancing itself and getting Hong Kong to take the fall,' Daniel said. James, Victor and Mary met again with Ben and Jessica, who invited the reporters for a coffee to express their thanks. Edwin's friends were thankful that the truth was finally out. Dr Leung, who provided the smoking gun to the case, sent a text message with thumbs-up and thank you emojis to James for keeping his end of the bargain in shielding his identity. James tried calling Vicky Law and found the number to no longer be in use.

While the story marked a triumphant first day for the new editor-in-chief, it dealt Theresa her biggest humiliation in the four years she was deputy editor. The day also came crashing down in one big swoop. She lost any chance to rise to the top at the *Herald* and the story she killed had become the story that everyone was talking about, its circulation poised to break all online traffic records. *Is it all over for me at the Herald?*

* * *

Jack's swift consent piqued James' curiosity more than ever of the new boss' background and that of EH. He began to scour the Internet and text his acquaintances. It took James a little while to trace the real owner of EH Capital. Under an intricate web of companies in between, the beneficiary owner was Eastern River Investments, a firm founded and controlled by Henry Zeng. Zeng wasn't your regular Chinese entrepreneur but he came from Chinese royalty, descendants of prominent senior communist officials. He was the son of a retired top Party official who continued to spawn influence in the Party commonly known as the Shanghai faction. The Shanghai faction was an opposing camp to the current regime. Zeng went to university in the US, majoring in international relations with a minor in journalism, based on an old report from a global business magazine James found online. The report about Chinese princelings studying in American Ivy League universities ran alongside a photograph of a younger-looking Zeng with his tennis club. Zeng was photographed putting his arm around the shoulder of a taller Chinese young man, which the caption described as Jack Hu.

'I'll be damned,' James muttered and fell back onto his sofa at home. He had been Googling for the last two hours. His mind returned to the last conversation with Sum Suk about factional infighting in the Party. *No wonder Jack was eager to run the story. The mouthpiece function never ceases*, James thought, *it's only a question of which faction of the Party you work for.*

James' biggest comfort in the New Year was that Edwin's wrongful death was now out for the world to know. *It's time to leave*, he concluded.

Ping, a text message popped up on his screen, from an unknown number.

Good story today. Can we meet tomorrow after work? SS

Sure.

Details later.

* * *

The Google navigation app brought James to a side lane on Centre Street in Sheung Wan district, on the western side of Hong Kong island. Sum Suk's choice of a venue was again an obscure tiny tea house, where passers-by would have to look hard to even notice that it existed and was open for business. James' source had again arrived earlier.

'Good story, you must be glad it saw the light of the day.'

'I guess we were lucky; the change in editorship helped,' James conceded and went on to tell him what he found out about the new owners and his interpretation of Jack Hu's connection to the Shanghai faction. He added, 'Thanks for the background context you provided the last time. It all came together.'

Sum Suk let out a voracious chuckle, with a twinkle in his eyes. The older man was unusually relaxed. 'The Party is always about whose interest you serve at any point in time. Officially, they needed to condemn the report as the ruler of Hong Kong. But in fact, they had already dumped it down on the Hong Kong Government and washed their hands of the matter. Of course, in the beginning, they would have pressured Jin to use the *Herald* to control the narrative, as they are so used to in the mainland. But your previous editors didn't deliver and it all ended in a mess, arrested for fraud and all.

'The current Chinese leadership isn't going to go down. That's the way it is with China. Your new owners will serve a different set of bosses, but they are still from the same Party. It's pretty much the same for the media in Hong Kong. You can never run away from the fact that this is Chinese territory. So the media is a pawn for Party infighting.' He stressed that the Party was only buying time with the 'one country, two systems' principle that 'supposedly upholds this city's freedom of speech and rule of law'.

'If I'm not wrong, the *Herald*'s narrative is about to change. Just watch,' Sum Suk said. Changing the subject, he asked James, 'Anyhow, what are your plans? Staying in journalism?'

'I'd like to but I don't think I can work in any Hong Kong media, knowing that I'd be a tool for Party propaganda,' James said with an underlying sense of helplessness. 'I'm considering taking a break from journalism, perhaps to work for non-profit organizations that advocate the need for a free press, or do a Master's degree abroad.'

'Not a bad idea to take a step back,' Sum Suk said. 'I'm also retiring in a couple of months and will move back to Guangdong. Come and visit me in a year's time. Hopefully, my orange orchard will be up and running by then and you can come to taste the fruit of my labour.'

* * *

James handed his resignation to Jack one month after his meeting with Sum Suk. The masthead editors were an entirely different team. Jack had brought in an executive editor that was his number two and a deputy executive editor as his third-in-command, effectively sidelining Theresa and Vijay. Vijay, finally admitting that he'd never rise in a Chinese-owned media company, resigned just days before James, with plans to move home. Theresa was busy meeting headhunters for her 'next big role' but the odds were against her, for lack of 'real world journalism experience' as one recruiter put it. Her army of deputies had quickly adjusted to the tune of the new editorial leadership. EH Capital also instituted a new chief executive officer while Sheldon remained as the COO, securing the stability that he wanted.

James hadn't found his next job but he had enough. He had never taken a break since he left university and he wanted to take this chance to do so. In the first month of Jack's editorship, the COVID-19 virus broke out in the central Chinese city of Wuhan, but the world and the World Health Organization officially learnt of this lethal new pathogen only a month later because the city's officials tried to cover it up. Beijing, later on, imposed strict controls on media reporting of the epidemic, which soon turned into a global pandemic.

The *Herald*, contrary to the previous editorship, was critical of Chinese leadership, writing stories and analyses that questioned the cover-up, Beijing's call to action and its ineffectiveness in battling the epidemic. The shift couldn't have been spelt out more clearly for James of the *Herald*'s role as a mouthpiece for the Party, albeit which faction it now served and to what end. Like Sum Suk alluded to, it would apply to all media companies in Hong Kong.

'It can get worse or better with change, if it comes in the form of another ownership. But the fundamental issue will not,' James told himself. As heart-wrenching as it would be to leave journalism, he was certain that it would be more painful to remain in the profession and watch those who controlled the newsroom throw out into the wind the values and principles he strongly believed in, to accommodate an increasingly oppressive political environment. The decision to leave brought some peace.

'James, you're a good reporter. It'll be sad to see you go. How can we interest you to stay?' Jack asked.

'Kind of you to ask. But I really need a break and maybe to do something else. Life is short and there's much of this world to see,' James answered.

'Well, if you ever want to come back again, the door is always open to you.'

'Thanks Jack and all the best to the *Herald*.'

Epilogue

Ground Zero

James was pondering about his next step when the coronavirus crisis escalated in Hong Kong in February and March 2020. The causes and the chain of events that led to the transmission to humans were unclear. What was certain was that the spread was rapid and it was lethal. In the three months after the mainland finally revealed to the world the outbreak, the coronavirus had claimed nearly 3,000 lives there alone. The crisis helped mute anti-government demonstrations in Hong Kong and held the media's attention.

'The Party seems to have all the luck,' one prominent student protester he befriended when he covered the demonstrations last summer told him. 'It's difficult to keep our movement going by staying home and social distancing, but we will strive. We almost think China purposely spread the virus to sabotage our movement!' The student winked and laughed. James chuckled along, comforted by the youth's persistence and determination. He knew from his own journalistic experience it took immense strength to stand by one's beliefs, especially when the authorities continued to rain condemnations and crackdown on them. Some of these protesters were just a third of his age.

'The government is waging a broad crackdown under a coronavirus cover,' a government prosecutor source revealed. James made a point to keep in contact with his most important sources. 'It has ordered the police to track down as many protesters as they can and to prosecute them in court. The force has more resources now that the number of large-scale demonstrations has dropped.'

The following month, police arrested fifteen prominent pro-democracy figureheads including media owner Jimmy Lai and former LegCo member Martin Lee. Weeks later, a 22-year-old protester was sentenced to four years in prison for rioting, the first demonstrator to be jailed. In the seventeen months since June 2019, 10,171 protesters were arrested, 2,389 cases were registered, with hundreds more—some as young as twelve years old—convicted, according to police figures.

The numbers saddened James. While he was able to leave the workplace that destroyed what he stood for, he still had to face the regression of free speech and civil liberties in his home city, under the cloud of escalating conflict with Beijing. The Hong Kong–Beijing friction reached a major defining moment in November 2019 when the Beijing-backed establishment camp was defeated in the city's district council elections as democracy advocates won 87 per cent of the seats, up from less than a third. Before the elections, the Beijing camp had always argued that there was a silent majority against violent anti-government demonstrations, a theory supported by Pax and Theresa, with extensive reporting by the *Herald*. That majority was also represented in Heather Hua's story of mainlanders living in Hong Kong, who feared reprisal for being Chinese citizens and speaking Mandarin. In the two decades after Beijing regained control of Hong Kong, 1.5 million mainland Chinese had relocated to the city. The landslide victory was a resounding public display of opposition against Beijing and that Hong Kong was slipping further away from its grip. Some state media outlets reprised the argument of foreign forces at play, aiding the democratic camp. The *Herald* followed suit.

Beijing's hard-handed tactic towards Hong Kong also played a large role in the January elections in Taiwan, which China considered a renegade province. President Tsai Ing-wen who refused to accept the One China principle as a basis for Cross-Straits engagement secured a sweeping win at the presidential elections. The slogan 'Today Hong Kong, Tomorrow Taiwan' sprang up afterwards to support Hong

Kong's protesters. As the epidemic-turned-pandemic sent the world teetering, China took advantage of that global distraction and launched its offensive on Hong Kong for the latter's defiance of Chinese rule. On the back of claims that it had the outbreak under control, Beijing and Hong Kong leaders spewed out rhetorics on a renewed push to implement Article 23 of the Basic Law, which stipulated that the local government shall enact laws to ban sedition, secession and subversion of the central government. The last attempt in 2003 met with a huge public backlash when half a million people marched on the street, forcing the government to shelve the plan. But China today was in a different position. Its global presence and influence was much greater, as was its grip on Hong Kong and the integration between the two economies.

Around mid-April of 2020, China's Liaison Office and the Hong Kong and Macau Affairs Office representatives for the first time publicly stuck their fingers into local LegCo affairs. They slammed pro-democracy legislators for delaying the selection of a chairperson for a LegCo internal committee, threatening the elected lawmakers with serious consequences for their 'dereliction of duties'. The interference contradicted Article 22 of the Basic Law, which stated that no department of the central government may interfere in the affairs of the special administrative region. The two offices argued that they weren't bound by Article 22, being 'agencies authorized by the central government' and not 'departments of the Central People's Government'. A Hong Kong Government document in 2007 stated that the liaison office was established under Article 22. After the Liaison Office's claim of this new position, the Hong Kong Government released three statements within hours that flip-flopped between contradicting the Chinese office's stance but eventually agreeing that the representative offices weren't entities established under Article 22.

An hour before the twenty-third anniversary of the city's return to Chinese rule, Beijing implemented the national security law for Hong Kong. The way the law was enacted—allowing the Chinese national security apparatus to pervade multiple layers of the society—sent a clear signal of the Party's sweeping controls to come, James interpreted.

It was introduced through a rarely-used constitutional method that bypassed Hong Kong's legislature and intended to counter acts of separatism, subversion, terrorism and collusion with foreign powers. Acts of inducing Hong Kong citizens to hate the government in Beijing or Hong Kong was also defined as a serious crime.

Just a few days after the law took effect, Beijing established the new security law office with mainland agents in a hotel that overlooked Victoria Park, a landmark where most rallies and demonstrations were held. Local authorities intensified their crackdown on protesters or anyone seen as opposing the government. It claimed that the protest slogan 'liberate Hong Kong, revolution of our times' constituted subversion and banned the protest anthem *Glory to Hong Kong*. Hundreds were arrested under the law. As 2021 was ushered in, police made a sweep of dozens more democrats and activists.

Sometime in the summer, just before the national security law was implemented, James began to record in writing what he saw, heard and interpreted of the events that unfolded, dating back to his experience and the developments at the *Herald*. Free of the burdening distractions from a toxic newsroom that tolerated one-sided coverage and distortions, he was able to write and tell his story with freedom and flair, as well as drive. As words turned into paragraphs, chapters into pages, he also felt the years of pent-up stress and frustrations escaping him. Before he knew it, an 80,000-word manuscript was completed. James titled it *Two Sides of a Lie*. A novel.